OVERCOMING
FEAR

The quest of a spiritual director or pastoral supervisor is to help those whom they companion to make connections between their experiences and the Mystery called God. Tim Lockwood, an educator and practitioner in spirituality, does this as he brings together the threads of personal experience, the Jesus Story, literature, the spirituality of the well known saints, film and more. He explores the stages of life and the key movements in the spiritual journey, particularly how the positive and negative phases we may encounter are potential spaces and places of grace where the Divine resides and is waiting for us. Tim whets our interest in the various dimensions of spirituality and explains them in such a way that they are invitations to growth and not something from which to shy. In this compendium, Tim weaves together a fabric of many spiritual themes in a readable and understandable manner. For any traveller on the spiritual road, whether you are just starting out or someone experienced over a longer period of time, Overcoming Fear: Trusting God in a Time of Change is an engaging book and a worthy acquisition to your spiritual library. I recommend this book highly.

Tim Moloney cfc,
National Chair, Conference of Spiritual Directors,
Australia

The author draws not only on Scripture but also on the personal encounters through film and literature which also reveal the struggles others have engaged in when undergoing the same God quest. But further to that, he also refers to his own personal concerns and realistic discernment issues about invitations received from his Congregation authorities. Each has something to say which encourages me as I pursue the quest through the various chapters. The sharing of their experiences gives me an understanding that I might never have considered and which enriches the journey of further discernment and contemplation, even hints on how I could change my way of thinking about various experiences of prayer itself.

Reading the signs of the times is also considered. How to deal with Covid-19, with the struggles surrounding corruption and fake news, with the cries of 'Black Lives Matter' are also issues that I as a person have to deal with. I am always confronted with issues of accountability and transparency in my dealings with my neighbour. The author indicates ways in which I can embrace these challenges and find the call within them that will change and enrich my life through these sometimes ordinary, but often extraordinary, events encountered.

I was very encouraged by the gradual realisation that the Spirit is still very active in our world, and even in my life today. I encourage you to take on the journey this book invites you into.

Br Tom Kearney CFC,
Interim Principal,
Tangaza University College, Nairobi.

Overcoming Fear: Trusting God in Times of Change provides us with a rich source for those interested in spirituality and spiritual direction.
The author shares his vast experience in spiritual discernment and offers us a wealth of material for personal and group reflection. The richness of the book is due to the author delving into the tradition of spiritualities and sharing his own personal experience.

David Gibson CFC
Formerly, Provincial of the Christian Brothers in Ireland.

One of the indicators of God's Spirit at work is that the work is both creative with new initiatives, and true to tradition. On that score, Tim Lockwood's book comes through with flying colours. In a practical, creative style, the book covers a wide range of human experience, supported by Tim's extensive reading of other religious and secular writers. Perennial spiritual values – desire for God, growth in relationship with God, prayer and discernment, attitudes to sin and suffering – are all treated fully, with practical everyday examples, often from the author's personal experience. Tim Lockwood's book encourages readers to delve into their own experience in these 'times of change' in church and society.

Brian Gallagher MSC,
Author of *Set me Free* and *The Eyes of God*.

In recent decades, Spiritual Direction has become significant for more and more people within the Catholic Church and beyond – more laity rather than seminarians, clergy, members of religious orders. Christian Brother Tim Lockwood has worked in Formation and is a Spiritual Director with experience in Australia and in Africa. This is evident in this book: scriptural explorations, spiritual authors both ancient and new, drawing on literature, cinema and – what makes powerful impression – personal stories. This is a book for those looking for spiritual direction, probing their search, issues of experience of God, fear, love, sinfulness, forgiveness. It is also a resource book for directors reflecting on their listening and their shared discernment.

Peter Malone MSC,
Heart of Life Centre,
Melbourne

Every Christian must be imbued with what Tim Lockwood presents to us and then must radiate that understanding to the whole world. God loves us passionately and has a loving plan to fill us with that love and so bring us to an unbelievable final destiny. God is present at the heart of all things and in the depths of our hearts. God is present even in the worst of times even though a nagging doubt assails us that this is not so. Nothing can ever separate us from this love because, in Christ, God has descended into all the hells and dark nights of our lives. In sharing these experiences, Christ has purified us of all that drags us away from God. We have been saved, for God is a saving God and not a punishing one.

Paul Castley MSC,
Author of *A Time to Hope*

Having taught in the Institute of Spirituality and Religious Formation, at Tangaza University College in Nairobi for well over ten years, Br Dr Tim Lockwood has been committed to sharing with his students, and many other people he had been journeying with in spiritual direction, a way of trusting and remaining in God's love.

In this book, he addresses the mystery of life as a journey undertaken in time, which requires having faith in God. The author invites and encourages the reader to especially trust in God in times of change as everything is in the hands of God. This is paramount for a human being, who is physical, spiritual and psychological.

Among many other things, the book recommends sharing our sinfulness with God, coming to terms with suffering, experiencing God's Kingdom now, overcoming doubt and despair, developing a contemplative attitude, walking humbly with God, exploring some life-giving ways of relating with God and discovering the truth about God from the Bible, as ways of dealing with fear in our lives, and therefore enabling us to rely on God's providence.

This book will be consoling and stimulating to readers as it is a reflection of the wide spectrum of the spiritual aspects of managing fear in life.

Rev. Dr Jude Mulenga Chisanga,
Tangaza University College,
Nairobi, Kenya

Most books on spirituality tend to be preachy; often showing off the writer's idealistic view of the world and himself. Not so with Tim Lockwood; he invites you to accompany him as he traces the foundations and impressions of our human experience of God. Drawing on years of life experience as a Brother, Lecturer and Spiritual Director, and different sources from the Scriptures, novels, poems, song and films, he weaves an intriguing tapestry from the light and dark threads of the spiritual journey. Throughout, you can hear Tim reflecting on his own struggles with ambiguity, dualistic thinking and the 'nagger' to mention a few of the hidden gems he holds up to the light. Tim touches the ordinariness of life with a lightness that leaves the reader space to ponder their own experience and even to interpret it with new understanding. As a Spiritual Director, I will be revisiting this text for some time to come.

Sr Loretta Brennan
Lecturer, Centre for Leadership and Management
Tangaza University College.

Timothy Lockwood's *Overcoming Fear* offers clearly articulated, down-to-earth insight and advice. The author, an experienced spiritual director, draws upon a wide range of experience and resources.

Above all, he draws upon the real human experience of himself and others, in different times and places, looking particularly at events in Australia, where he lived for most of his life, and Africa where he has worked for many years.

He integrates these with insights gained from novels and films, many of which deal with people in morally challenging situations His scriptural sources are illuminated by his knowledge of modern commentaries, along with references to masterpieces in the genre by such writers as John of the Cross, Theresa of Avila and Thérèse of Lisieux.

Chris Watson B.A. (Hons.) Ph.D, B.Theol,
Former Lecturer in English, LaTrobe University

OVERCOMING FEAR

TRUSTING GOD IN TIMES OF CHANGE

TIM LOCKWOOD CFC

Published in Australia by
Coventry Press
33 Scoresby Road
Bayswater VIC 3153

ISBN 9780648982241

Copyright © Tim Lockwood 2021

All rights reserved. Other than for the purposes and subject to the conditions prescribed under the *Copyright Act*, no part of this publication may be reproduced, stored in a retrieval system, or transmitted in any form or by any means, electronic, mechanical, photocopying, recording or otherwise, without the prior permission of the publisher.

Scripture quotations are from the *New Revised Standard Version Bible* © 1989, Division of Christian Education of the National Council of the Churches of Christ in the United States of America. Used by permission. All rights reserved.
And from *The Jerusalem Bible* © 1966 by Darton Longman & Todd Ltd and Doubleday and Company Ltd.
And from *The Psalms, A New Translation*, © 1963 The Grail England and Wm Collins Sons and Co. Ltd.

Catalogue-in-Publication entry is available from the
National Library of Australia http://catologue.nla.gov.au

Cover design by Ian James – www.jgd.com.au
Text design by Coventry Press
Set in Fontin 11 pt

Printed in Australia

Table of Contents

Foreword		viii
Introduction		xi
Section 1	Understanding and relating to God	1
Chapter One	Exploring More Life-giving Ways of Seeing and Relating to God	2
Chapter Two	Discovering the Truth about God in the Bible	22
Chapter Three	Our Ambiguous Relationship with the Mystery	50
Section 2	Stages in Spiritual & Psychological Growth	69
Chapter Four	Negative Aspects in the Stages of Life	70
Chapter Five	Positive Aspects in our Growth in Faith	87
Section 3	Discerning the Way	117
Chapter Six	Developing a Contemplative Attitude	118
Chapter Seven	Listening for God	145

Chapter Eight	Outwitting the Nagging Spirit	171
Chapter Nine	The Wind Blows Where It Will: Recognising the Spirit's Action Today	196
Chapter Ten	Walking Humbly with God	216
Section 4	**Spiritual Themes**	**241**
Chapter Eleven	Sharing Our Sinfulness with God	242
Chapter Twelve	Coming to Terms with Suffering	265
Chapter Thirteen	Experiencing the Kingdom Now	295
Chapter Fourteen	Overcoming Doubt and Despair	324
Index		345

Foreword

BR TIM LOCKWOOD's *Overcoming Fear: Trusting God in a Time of Change* establishes the importance of awakening in readers the desire to pursue their relationship with God. His extensive readings of other spiritual writings and his wealth of experiences display a profound insight into our need to search for God, especially in this modern time when spiritual awareness is most needed in the world.

He presents a spiritual understanding of the human person alongside a psychological consideration to show that the spiritual presupposes and builds on the psychological. Different chapters intermingle the writings of William Barry and Ignatian and Carmelite writers to inspire in others the desire to value more and more deeply their relationship with God.

As a life-long Catholic, sensitive to traditional of laws and doctrines, Br Tim nevertheless conveys clearly in this book that God is working in ways today that are different from the past. He recalls that, in his ministry, Jesus intended to revolutionise our view of God not slowly but dramatically; Jesus' imagination was possessed by God's aliveness. Br Tim reminds us that God in fact is not violent, but God is love. Jesus overcame violence with powerlessness and love. The disciples began to understand this idea of God only after the death of Jesus when they reflected on the resurrection. Br Tim indicates that there should be a revolution in our attitude to power in order to reflect God's power as Jesus presented it. Jesus knew the reality of heavy seas and of suffering and opposition but he saw these realities differently. Br Tim asks a very pertinent question: at what stage as priests, religious and people of God do we begin to understand these deep insights of Jesus to power, fear, uncertainty, faith and love?

For example, in some chapters, *Overcoming Fear* describes the nagging spirit that tries to wear us down with its cautions and unwarranted fears. We all struggle with the spirit of fear in our everyday encounter with the universe and we need to learn to overcome its wanton disturbances.

Capturing in the final chapter in this inspirational book that God works and speaks to us within the limitations and possibilities, within and outside us, the author demonstrates his capacity for psychological and spiritual penetration.

He speaks the truth when he says that, no matter how many books we read or how much creative thinking we do and how many revelations we have, we will never be certain of knowing what God wants. The Bible teaches us this if we approach the text with an open mind. We have to be constantly open to new understandings of God. If we understood God, we would lose the richness of the infinity of God.

Br Tim also explains in Section 2 of the book how our spiritual and psychological growth affects our relationship with God. This deals with the stages we go through in our life journey, starting from birth and moving through to old age and death. We notice that there is a pattern which moves from crisis to resolution of the crisis. He explains the spiritual dimension of this pattern, using mainly the writings of St John of the Cross who emphasises the final stages of union on this journey and of the great delight that this gives us.

Ambiguity is part of the reality of all human relationships which is expressed in the book of the prophet Jeremiah where the prophet pours out his sorrows to the Lord. Once we acknowledge the reality of this ambiguity, we can then talk to God about how we feel towards God. Though this may be difficult, it will help strengthen the relationship through the confidence in God that we are able to demonstrate. In addition, the author looks at how we can act against the resistance we discover in ourselves when God tries to get close to us.

This masterly book is for brothers, sisters, priests and the entire People of God; and anyone who sees their need of God's love and wishes to come close to God by deepening their spiritual search and psychological understanding of life. *Overcoming Fear* is interesting and easy to understand due to the simple and clear language used throughout. It is a book for our time, and I highly recommend it.

Sr Elizabeth Ngozi Okpalaenwe (MSHR, PhD).
Lecturer and coordinator of student affairs
and quality assurance
Psychospiritual Institute,
Marist International University College,
A Constituent College of the
Catholic University of Eastern Africa, Nairobi, Kenya

Introduction

THIS BOOK BEGAN as a number of articles I wrote while on a sabbatical year in Melbourne (2018-2019) after lecturing for ten years at the Institute of Spirituality and Religious Formation, Tangaza College, in Nairobi. I had a plan to do some writing during this sabbatical year since writing is somewhat different from preparing lectures.

Lectures require interesting material while writing requires also more accountability about sources. Writing also forces one to move away from the sources being used by simply quoting them and instead to develop one's own thoughts from these sources. Writing needs to be original while lectures do not have to be. Writing stretches one's creative capacities and is therefore more exciting and satisfying than preparing lectures.

My first two writing attempts were on how we can relate in more life-giving ways to God and on how the spiritual and psychological elements involved blend in the stages of human growth. Each of these pieces was eventually divided into two articles. With each of the remaining articles, I had in mind a certain length appropriate for a chapter in a book or a normal-sized journal article. Without having a clear idea of what would be the outcome, I kept writing because I had energy for it. When I had enough for what could be not just a number of discrete pieces but chapters of a book, I began to think of the idea of a book and contacted David Gibson, a fellow Christian Brother, who agreed to help me with the publication of a book.

Since I first presented some of these ideas in an academic setting, my first audience consisted of the students in my classes, almost all of whom were religious. There is therefore an academic component to the chapters of this book but my aim was to try to awaken in readers the desire to pursue their relationship with God. One of the sources I have found very appealing to myself is the books of William Barry. Barry encouraged me to try to inspire in others the desire to value more and more deeply their relationship with God. I was also very attracted to the writings of St Teresa of Avila and St John of the Cross. That means that in these chapters the reader will find a blend of Ignatian and Carmelite elements as well as other varied sources which see the spiritual life as the pursuit of an intense relationship with God.

I know that we are living in a time of great change in society and in the church. Today we hear bishops and others being mentioned with little respect whereas in the past this would have been unheard of. Attitudes to authority including in the church have changed. Catholics now make up their minds about what they believe and what church services they attend; and attendance has dropped off dramatically. These changes have happened gradually but inexorably to the extent that the language used to refer to God and to religious practices has changed enormously.

When I wrote the material in this book, I was going on

my experience of the church in Kenya where I was teaching. This book is now being offered to an audience which could come from any part of the globe and realise that the language and approach I use will not be attractive to everyone. I write from the point of view of someone who grew up when Catholics were taught to observe the laws of the church unquestionably. I am also a religious Brother. I hope that some of my own Brothers might read this book and find that it speaks to some of their own concerns and helps them in their spiritual search. Being a religious Brother means that I am not part of the hierarchy of the Church, but I am also aware that, as a Brother, I have a particular perspective that can be of help to others.

We have to say that God is working in ways today that are different from God's ways in the past. Even using the word God can be disconcerting to many people. There are Catholics who are excellent people and very faithful to the truth as they see it in the way they live their lives. I have great admiration for them and know that they are more concerned than I am with causes such as climate change, the payment of taxes, the preservation of the seas and of the earth, and just and compassionate working conditions especially for those working in dangerous occupations such as construction workers. They are concerned that the poor are properly provided for by government and are horrified at the treatment of refugees to Australian shores. I realise that all of these areas are of importance in the life of a Christian. Although this book has little to say about these important areas of life, my hope is that it may have something to say to these people about the area of their lives that I have already mentioned, namely, the passionate interest that all human beings have within them to what we have traditionally called God.

The first three chapters deal with ways of understanding and relating to God. My aim here is to help people trust God more and to believe in their hearts and not just their heads that God is loving as Jesus says he is. I use material from Walter Brueggemann and Richard Rohr to show how understandings of God gradually develop throughout the history of the Israelite people. I then use insights from James Alison to show how, in the gospels, Jesus' presentation of the God who comes from heaven is in stark contrast with the understanding of that of the Jewish leaders who believed in a God of violence and punishment. In the second section, I present a spiritual understanding of the human person alongside a psychological understanding to try to show that the spiritual presupposes and builds on the psychological.

The fourth section, the longest, looks at the theme of discernment in a number of ways, first, as simply having our feet on the ground and allowing ourselves to work within the boundaries of time and space and the unpredictability of happenings as they occur. The first chapter in this section on contemplative presence provides a framework for the following chapters. In one chapter, I describe the nagging spirit which tries to wear us down with its cautions and unwarranted fears. There is then a chapter on how the Holy Spirit, in contrast, opens up new possibilities for us. The final chapter in this section returns to the idea that God works and speaks to us within the limitations and possibilities within and outside us.

There is finally a chapter that deals with the perennial themes of suffering, sinfulness and doubt. I include in this last section a chapter on how we experience the kingdom of God through what we believe from Paul's letter to the Romans and through the healing and transformative presence of Jesus in our everyday lives.

I am very grateful to Hugh McGinlay of Coventry Press who has agreed to publish these fairly discrete pieces of writing as a book. I was delighted that he not only showed interest but gave me a positive answer immediately. Like every other creative activity, writing requires effort and faith and a willingness to put forward what one has, in the hope that it will be picked up and carried forward by others. The ideas in this book come from the ideas and efforts of others and my hope is that they will provide some others with help and inspiration.

Section 1
Understanding and relating to God

While all the chapters of this book intend to help us relate in more life-giving ways to God, this section deals directly with this theme. The first chapter gives suggestions about how we can delve more deeply into the image that Jesus in John's gospel has of God, something that turns out to be startlingly novel. The chapter gives ideas that may help the reader be more receptive to what Jesus is on about when they read the gospels in general. The second chapter goes to the Old Testament to show the journey that the biblical writers had in developing a more and more truthful and richer understanding of God's love for the people. The third chapter does not try to understand God but focuses on what happens when we try to depth more and more our relationships with God and the resistance that we encounter.

Chapter One

Exploring More Life-giving Ways of Seeing and Relating to God

IN THIS CHAPTER, we will look at how our view of God can grow from one of caution and even fear to conviction not just with our mind but our heart that God is loving and wants our good.[1] The New Testament, especially the gospel of John, insists on the need for belief. It is not just a matter of understanding that God loves us but of surrendering our whole selves to this love. We will look at themes such as the compassion of God and the abundance of God's giving in both Old and New Testaments. We will draw on James Alison's insights when we see how Jesus presents a new view of God in the gospel of John.[2]

Scripture scholars have told us that the Synoptic gospels present an ascending Christology while John's gospel presents a descending Christology. The Synoptics start with Jesus as a

---

[1] See books by William Barry especially *With an Everlasting Love: Developing an Intimate Relationship, with God.*

[2] James Alison, *Raising Abel: The Recovery of the Eschatological Imagination*, New York: Crossroad, 1996.

human being like us. Jesus lives in his own family as a boy and young man and then, at the age of thirty, becomes aware of his vocation to preach the good news of God's kingdom in ways that no one else before him had done. He brings God's healing and God's liberation; he preaches and tells us about God as he himself has discovered God. It is different with the gospel of John. In this gospel, Jesus is presented as one not starting like us but as the Word who has existed with God from the beginning. Jesus comes with divine knowledge. He shows us the world and life from God's point of view. He intends to revolutionise our view of God not slowly but dramatically.

Chapter 6 of the gospel of John shows Jesus miraculously feeding the people who have come to hear him in the desert. There is a boy with five loaves and two fish. Jesus tells the disciples to sit the people down and feed them with this food. Miraculously there is enough. This sign shows us the abundance of life and love, which God wants to show us through Jesus. This miracle is a preview of what Jesus is going to teach the people about himself as the living bread that has come down from heaven. Bread is one of the symbols used in this gospel to bring the truth about God to us. John's gospel has Jesus giving signs and wonders to reveal God: the miracle of the water turned into wine at Cana, the living water Jesus offers to the Samaritan woman, the light of the world Jesus speaks about when he cures the man blind from birth. John's gospel does not proceed in the form of a narrative of what Jesus does like the Synoptics but presents certain events as signs of God's direct presence in the world.

The signs and wonders that Jesus performs can expand

our imaginations to see that God's power is different from the power of force. The signs put us in touch with a God who is alive and magnanimous. They enable us to use not merely our understanding but our imaginations and our capacity to believe in something beyond the categories in which we usually think. This is a God who will answer our prayer because God really cares about us. We can move beyond the categories of tit for tat and of always receiving just rather than loving treatment for what we have done.

James Alison says that 'Jesus' imagination was possessed by God's aliveness'.[3] Jesus saw God as a God of life. In chapter one of John, Jesus finds Philip and invites him to follow him. Philip is enthralled by this invitation and tells his friend Nathanael that he has 'found him about whom Moses in the law and also the prophets wrote' (John 1:45). Nathanael is skeptical but follows Philip who leads him to Jesus. This is a scene coming from a descending Christology where Jesus has a special knowledge beyond that of the human. He says mysteriously, 'Here is an Israelite in whom there is no deceit'. In the conversation that follows, Jesus tells Nathanael that he will see greater things than what Jesus is saying and doing here. Jesus says to him, 'You will see greater things than these... Very truly I tell you, you will see heaven opened and the angels of God ascending and descending upon the Son of Man' (1:51).

In this early part of John's gospel, says Alison, there are two key images: the lamb of God who takes away the sins of the world and the wedding banquet. Jesus has told Nathanael

---

[3] *Raising Abel.*

that he will see the heavens opened, that is, he will see how God views the human condition. Jesus will show us who God really is. Another key idea that can help us is the idea of heaven. Heaven here signifies the absence of evil, total happiness and contentment. Jesus will tell us that God is unimaginably loving, in a way that we can barely dream of and yet in a way that we most deeply want. Here we move into what Alison calls the eschatological imagination. I will take here an example of this type of imagination from another gospel, that of Matthew.

After Jesus has told the parable of the weeds among the wheat, the disciples who are walking with Jesus ask him the meaning of the parable of the weeds (Matthew 13:36-43). Jesus explains that the Son of Man plants the wheat in the field but the evil one sows the weeds. Then Jesus explains:

> The Son of Man will send his angels and they will collect out of his kingdom all causes of sin and all evildoers, and they will throw them into the furnace of fire, where there will be weeping and gnashing of teeth.

Here Jesus is using both apocalyptic and eschatological language.[4] The angels symbolise heaven and the victory of good over evil. They will throw the evil ones into the fiery furnace. This is apocalyptic language. We must remember that Matthew (or Jesus) is not talking about God punishing the wicked but telling us that evil will not go unpunished. When we remember this, we will not be troubled by the

---

[4] This distinction between apocalyptic and eschatological language is made by Brendan Byrne, *Lifting the Burden: Reading Matthew's Gospel in the Church Today*, 115-116.

apocalyptic use of violence. But in the next sentence it is the eschatological imagination that takes over completely from the apocalyptic:

> Then the righteous will shine like the sun in the kingdom with their Father. Let anyone with ears, listen!

If we dwell on this line, we will get the real message of Jesus. Jesus' own image of God can become ours. The love that is at the heart of the world which we call God puts aside all the evil that habitually affects us. Our imagination now fills with the love and the goodness of God and the power of evil departs.

The Eschatological Imagination

The eschatological imagination is exemplified in Jesus' claim that Nathanael will see the heavens opened. In the changing of the water into wine at Cana we see what the reality of God is like. The eschatological imagination means to keep imagining what the world will be like when the kingdom of God finally does come. We have traditionally called this reality heaven. To develop this imagination, we focus our minds and hearts on the time when heaven becomes a reality for us. Jesus gives the parables of the treasure in the field and the pearl of great price. The man who finds the treasure in the field and the merchant who finds the pearl concentrate not on the difficulties in their present lives but rather on the goals of the treasure and the pearl for which they will give up everything. They stop focusing on present problems and miseries. Because they focus on what is in the future, they experience great joy in their lives now.

When the first martyr, Stephen, is about to be unjustly stoned by his accusers, something extraordinary happens to him:

> But filled with the Holy Spirit, he gazed into heaven and saw the glory of God and Jesus standing at the right hand of God. 'Look,' he said, 'I see the heavens opened and the Son of Man standing at the right hand of God'.

Stephen is filled with courage. His attitude is totally transformed and he is able to go through the terrible death by stoning. He is filled with joy just as he is about to be cruelly stoned to death. In the film by Robert Bresson, *The Trial of Joan of Arc*, Joan is fearless before her accusers during her trial and answers all their questions unhesitatingly. But then just before she is to be sentenced and burnt at the stake, her courage leaves her. She has been fearless because God has been speaking to her through the voices of two saints and of an angel. She relies on these heavenly voices. Now the certainty has left her. She returns to her cell and prays and the certainty and courage return. She now refuses to recant what she has said and done, is sentenced, and goes to her death with great courage, her eyes fixed on the cross which is raised in front of her eyes.

With this type of imagination, we see heaven in the midst of the sufferings and struggles we are presently experiencing. This is clear in the great book about heaven known as the Book of Revelation. This last book of the Bible describes the trials and sufferings of the saints. But it is also a book of great triumph and unimaginable joy. In the following passage from the Book of Revelation, we have the two images, which we have seen in the early chapters of John's gospel, of the heavens opening and the wedding at the end of the world:

> Then I heard what seemed to be the voice of a great multitude, like the sound of many waters and like the sound of mighty thunderpeals, crying out,
>
> 'Hallelujah!
> For the Lord our God
> the Almighty reigns.
> Let us rejoice and exult
> and give him the glory,
> for the marriage of the Lamb has come,
> and his bride has made herself ready;
> to her it has been granted to be clothed
> with fine linen, bright and pure'–
> for the fine linen is the righteous deeds of the saints.
> And the angel said to me, "Write this: Blessed are those who are invited to the marriage supper of the Lamb". And he said to me, "These are true words of God".'
> (Revelation 19:6-9).

Here we are celebrating the victory of God over all evil that confronts us here on earth. The passage is filled with joy which we can experience in reading it and putting ourselves into the place of these people who are already celebrating. We who read the passage and who do not yet possess the treasure can still participate in the joy of these people who stand before the throne of God. We too are filled with joy at the prospect of taking part in the marriage celebration of the Lamb.

Here is one further passage which gives a taste of the ecstatic joy we will experience when we finally gain our treasure:

> He said to him, 'Sir, you are the one that knows'. Then he said to me, 'These are they who have come out of the great ordeal; they have washed their robes and made them white in the blood of the Lamb. For this reason, they are before the throne of God, and worship him day and night within his temple and the one who is seated on the throne will shelter them. They will hunger no more, and thirst no more; the sun will not strike them, nor any scorching heat; or the Lamb at the centre of the throne will be their shepherd, and he will guide them to springs of the water of life, and God will wipe away every tear from their eyes' (Revelation 7:14-17).

Again in this passage, those who have followed Jesus in his sufferings are now before the throne of God, that is, heaven. All their sufferings have ended and they give praise to God continually, that is, they constantly express their joy in the presence of God. We know that we too will finally be in this great throng.

The Culture of Death

In chapter 8 of John's gospel, Jesus compares his Father with the father of the Jewish leaders. The Jews' father leads his children to lying and killing. Their god is the father of the first murderer, Cain (cf. John 8:44). This god is in fact the devil, someone who seems to be god but in fact is an obstacle to God. But Jesus claims that the God who has been revealing Godself to Israel is not the god they are putting forward. Their interpretation of God in fact turns him into Satan. This interpretation by Alison[5] of this dialogue is quite consistent with what we know traditionally of how Satan works, which is through deceit and counterfeit.

One major reason why the Jewish leaders are so wrong about God is because, until the time of Jesus, there is no other model for power than that of violence. It is only Jesus who does not know death who can begin to make accessible who God is, a God who has nothing to do with death. We, like the Jewish leaders, are caught up in notions of God as someone who uses power to overcome enemies. We see the human rules about justice and punishment, the only ones of which we are aware, and apply them to God. God in fact is not violent. And here we need to look briefly at how, in Jesus, God overcomes violence with powerlessness and love.

Before Jesus, no one was able to imagine God properly. Jesus presents a God who, as we have already seen, is utterly loving and wholeheartedly on our side. The disciples began to understand this idea of God only after the death of Jesus when they reflected on the resurrection. We can express their thinking as follows:

---

[5] This section on violence relies on James Alison, *Raising Abel*.

- Jesus died; he was innocent and was violently executed by those who thought they were right because of their false understanding of God.

- Jesus was the victim who accepted the situation and who did not fight back.

- Jesus' followers did not expect this. For them, for Jesus to die at the hands of his enemies, was a sure sign of defeat. This was what always happened.

- But when they reflected on the resurrection, they began to see God from a new perspective. At the resurrection, God raised Jesus, the slaughtered one, from the dead. This meant that God had a power greater than human violence.

We have seen how Alison sees the god of the Jewish leaders as Satan. St Ignatius Loyola also describes the evil one as a deceiver who puts forward to us ideas that seem to be truthful. We easily come under the spell of the temptations of Satan because they appear to us as logical and reasonable whereas they are anything but reasonable. In one of his books, William Barry gives the example of the hero in the film by Woody Allen, *Crimes and Misdemeanours*, who has a mistress and is also married. His relationship with his mistress becomes problematic and inconvenient. He wonders what he can do about this predicament and discusses the matter with his brother. His brother says that it is quite reasonable that he wants to stop altogether his relationship with the mistress: it is only right that he concentrates on the relationship with his wife and children. He then says that he can do something that will solve the situation. The solution is to hire someone to get the mistress off the scene. He does not say how immediately but his intention is to have the mistress murdered. He puts the idea forward to the man who dismisses it at first but then starts to see value in it. The episode shows how we can be persuaded to decide on plainly evil acts by the deceit of the evil force that is at work in the brother.

We hear and read stories that show how evil can deceive us practically every day in the papers. In *The Melbourne Age* of 31 July 2018, there is the story of a businessman of 76 who murdered his co-director, a woman of 49, with whom he had worked very closely and to whom he had been closely related. We do not know what his motives were. The woman had been very supportive of him and they had been close. Yet he murdered her probably out of anger and perhaps jealousy. We know how anger can distort our perception of things to the point where our mind is taken over with the desire to harm the other.

The harm we do others is not always physical. Our attitudes as well as our actions to others can be very destructive and hurtful as we all know. The cause is often jealousy, followed by rage. We have couples who have been very close, eventually ending by hating one another and wishing harm to the other. We become suspicious of the motivation of others. Men become afraid of women because they are ignored. The fear may be real or imagined.

Here is an example of a situation in which one person imagined ill intentions on the part of the other. The example shows the suspicions that develop in us because of previous experiences we have had. John, a spiritual director, waits for a lady, Anastasia, to come to him for a spiritual direction session. Anastasia sent a message to John to say she would be a little late. The time turned into more than forty-five minutes and John began to wonder if Anastasia was paying him back because he had missed their previous appointment. John tried to put this suspicion out of his mind but the thought stayed there. He remembered when he believed another woman had done this to him. Eventually, Anastasia arrived and it was obvious that she had not come late deliberately and John felt a load off his mind.

Overcoming the Culture of Death

The above are examples of the culture of death, which exists in our human nature. It is natural for us to believe that other people are hostile, that we are competing with them for scarce resources, and that it is either they or us who will win and not both of us. When, like John, we find that people act in a trustworthy way, we have the opportunity to steep ourselves in the positive imagination about the world and God that Jesus came to give us. John can dwell for a while on Anastasia's seriousness and honesty and as a result grow in his own trust in others and in life.

Jesus came to announce a whole revolution in our attitude to power. His death and subsequent resurrection show that love wins over violence in spite of what seems to be the case. Jesus himself had experiences that confirmed his faith in the power of love over violence. The Transfiguration, for example, occurs immediately after Jesus announces that he will suffer and die and rise from the dead. He goes up the mountain and sees the heavens open. This vision would have greatly deepened the positive imagination of Jesus. It moved him from focusing on his suffering and the apparent defeat involved in it to see that it was not a defeat at all. He comes down from the mountain filled with love and hope. He is filled with the life and goodness and love that come from the Father. He hears the voice say, 'This is my Son in whom I am well pleased. Listen to him'. We can imagine what an effect these words had on Jesus. It gave Jesus a tremendous love in his heart, which enabled him to go through with the suffering. Even though this story does not come from the ascending Christology of John, it is related because it builds the eschatological imagination which the Jesus in John's gospel constantly announces.

A conversion is needed in the way we see power and the way we see God. The truth about God is that God is not violent. We need to have our imaginations soaked in this new view of God as a God who does not punish, who does not become angry when we do not live up to certain expectations. We can gradually grow in confidence and love of God by letting ourselves be nourished by scripture. The gospel of the feeding of the multitudes in the desert fits this theme of the infinitely loving God who is much more loving than we can imagine and who can do more than we can ask or imagine. Surely this is the major theme of the whole gospel. This truth gradually becomes clearer to us as the conversion in our view of God takes place. There will be language in the scripture which gives the impression that God is demanding and that God is displeased when we sin and wants retribution. We can get this notion out of our head by deciding to look for the other side to any gospel story that gives this impression. Any language that speaks of God as demanding and vindictive comes from our human way of speaking and tells us about our own vindictiveness. We transfer our own desire for violence and desire for death on to God.

When we pray this gospel of the feeding in the desert, we can just stay with this lavish display of the love of God. This is the way God is. The wedding at Cana is another example of God's lavish love, which occurs not long before the feeding in the desert. In the image of the wedding, all is restored and sin forgiven and an abundance of goodness and plenty overflows into our lives.

Let us take another gospel passage – that of Jesus coming to the disciples on the water and of Peter walking towards Jesus (Matthew 14:22-33). First, the disciples are struggling on the sea. The sea has become rough and they are finding it hard to make any headway. In fact, soon they begin fearing for their lives. Jesus comes towards the disciples walking on the lake and they are terrified. This figure of Jesus is foreign to them and they are afraid and think of their safety immediately since they are in a culture of danger and death and of self-preservation. But Jesus is not in that culture. Jesus knows the reality of heavy seas and of suffering and opposition but he sees these realities differently. In the midst of the struggle, Jesus knows that the Father, who loves them infinitely, is also there with them and constantly supports them. The Father not only supports them but fills them with delight. Fear is taken away. Peter has a sense of this at first and asks Jesus to bid him cross over the waters. At first, he succeeds but then his conditioning sets in and he begins to be afraid. Being afraid is part of the culture of death. He calls out to Jesus and Jesus 'put out his hand at once and held him'.

Experiences Showing God's Love

We have just seen how reflecting on Scripture can help build our eschatological imagination, that is, an imagination filled with the strong sense that God loves us with a love that is difficult for us to grasp. It is very helpful for us to record these experiences at the end of a day or by writing them in a journal to recall later. Here are some examples of such experiences:

- A sister comes for spiritual direction and speaks about how God loves her. I too, the director, feel God's goodness as I hear that someone else experiences this love. I think at these times that I am the instrument of God for this person and therefore God loves me too.

- A student unobtrusively gives me a gift of a calendar and I see that she is enjoying the course I am teaching her.

- The affection that others show me in small ways.

- Someone gives a vote of thanks and I feel that he means what he says.

The following are two experiences of people experiencing God's love, which appear in John Horn's book[6] on his experiences of giving spiritual direction to others. The first person, Alenah, was thrilled when she had the experience of Jesus as her friend. This sense of his friendship made her feel very close to Jesus. She was filled with the sense of how good and loving Jesus was. Sometimes she thought of Jesus as her lover rather than friend and these experiences were even more important to her.

The other example is that of Melissa. Melissa had a sense of being taken care of in her ministry. She felt that it was not her who was doing the work but Jesus. In fact, she felt that while ministering to others, Jesus was actually giving her an experience not of work but of vacation. She also had a sense that she was being washed in mercy. She was being naked with God and being loved in this experience.

Certain thoughts can also help us to deepen and stabilise this sense of the love that God has for us. I will list some here in the hope that some may be helpful to the reader and that they will encourage the reader to list their own helpful thoughts and return to them when necessary. Here are some of the thoughts:

- 'Give and gifts will be given to you, full measure, pressed down, shaken together and flowing over will be poured into your lap' (Luke 6:38).

- It does not help to feel stressed. God does not want it.

---

[6] The two examples of Alenah and Melissa come from John Horn, *Healing Prayer*, 62ff.

(Instead we can recall times when we feel confident and assured).

- God is always doing new things. (We can choose to remember times in the past when we were sure that God was there rather than times when we were doubting God's love under the power of desolation).

- It is when we are struggling and in difficulties that we can show we are true followers of Jesus.
  (We can say to ourselves, 'You have won God's favour' as the Father told Jesus at the Transfiguration. Difficulties and struggle are not signs that God is absent but the opposite.)

- I cannot be perfect, but I can keep talking to God in my prayer asking him to help me to be better.

The following are some similar thoughts from Richard Rohr:[7]

- Let it go! Let go of the fears.
  Do not hoard. Do not cling – not even to life itself. Let it go, let it be – 'Not my will but yours be done. 'Father, into your hands I commend my spirit' (Luke 22:42; 23:46).

- Cling to nothing.
  There is nothing to be renounced or resisted. Everything can be embraced, but the catch is to cling to nothing.

---

[7] These thoughts are from Richard Rohr, *The Naked Now: Learning to See as the Mystics See*, New York: Crossroad, 2009

Life and God ask us to let go of our false self, the passing egoic identity we've manufactured in order to cope and survive.

- Be satisfied in the Naked Now.
  Non-dual thinking is learning how to be satisfied in the naked now, 'The sacrament of the present moment' as Jean Pierre de Caussade called it.

- Pray until you have driven out all the negative thoughts.
  We can decide to get rid of these destructive thoughts and feelings.

- Every day, we must choose to live in love. It is mostly a decision, not a feeling.

- Our task is simply to embody heaven now.
  (Heaven is love of God and neighbour, union with God and with neighbour.)

- Prayer is sitting in the silence until it silences us, choosing gratitude until we are grateful, and praising God until we ourselves are an act of praise.

- Being anxious is like being alert.
  When he says, 'Be awake, be alert!' (Mark 13:33-35), Jesus is not threatening. He is talking about the forever, eternal coming of Christ now... and now... now, now. God's judgment is always redemption. Christ is always coming. God is always present.

In this chapter, we have focused on ways we can see God from God's point of view. This is how John in his gospel tries to raise our awareness of God's incredible love for us. We looked at the culture of life that is presented to us especially in John's gospel and how this contrasts with the culture of death from which, from our human point of view, we see the world and God. We took some examples from various gospels to notice this culture of life which Jesus constantly teaches and shares with others through his cures and healings. We have just looked at how we can cultivate a culture of life through reflecting on how God is constantly interacting with us in our daily experiences. We followed this with some thoughts that keep before us a culture of life rather than death.

References

Alison, James, *Raising Abel: The Recovery of the Eschatological Imagination*, New York: Crossroad, 1996

Barry, W. & Connolly, W. J., (1982) *The Practice of Spiritual Direction*, New York: Harper and Row, 1982.

Barry, William, *With An Everlasting Love: Developing an Intimate Relationship with God*, New York: Paulist Press, 1999.

Byrne, Brendan, *Lifting the Burden: Reading Matthew's Gospel in the Church Today*, London: St Pauls, 2004.

Horn, John, *Healing Prayer: Practical Mysticism and St Ignatius' Spiritual Exercises*, Omaha: IPF Publications, 2013.

La Mott, Anne, *Help, Thanks, Wow: The Three Essential Prayers*, Riverhead Books, 2012.

Rohr, Richard, *The Naked Now: Learning to See As the Mystics See*, New York: Crossroad, 2009.

Toner, J., S.J., *A Commentary on Saint Ignatius' Rules for the Discernment of Spirits*, St. Louis: Institute of Jesuit Sources, 1981.

Chapter Two

Discovering the Truth about God in the Bible

IN THIS CHAPTER, we will see how the notion of God developed in the Old Testament and came to a climax in the teaching and life of Jesus in the gospels of the New Testament.

Walter Brueggemann[8] shows how there is a development of the understanding of God in the Old Testament. We can see this most clearly by distinguishing between the sections called the Law and the Prophets. The books of the Law, that is especially the first five books of the Old Testament, are concerned with putting down a good foundation for what developed into the nation of Israel. The Law deals with tradition and custom and order as well as awe at the presence of Yahweh. We find the importance of respecting and obeying the commandments particularly in the Book of Deuteronomy. Deuteronomy keeps telling us that if we obey the commandments and the ordinances of Yahweh, we will

---

[8] Walter Brueggemann, *Theology of the Old Testament*. Almost the whole book is devoted to this development. See specially pp. 117-407.

prosper. Above everything else we must be obedient. We must not deviate from what is written in the law. The writers of this book knew that the first thing that had to be put down was a good structure in which to operate. This solid structure was absolutely essential for the development of a strong community. Until this structure was established, the community was in constant danger of collapsing. The message of obedience is a constant refrain in the book. Here is just one example of the message:

> Now, Israel, hear the decrees and laws I am about to teach you. Follow them so that you may live and may go in and take possession of the land the Lord, the God of your ancestors, is giving you. Do not add to what I command you and do not subtract from it, but keep the commands of the Lord your God that I give you. You saw with your own eyes what the Lord did at Baal-Peor. The Lord your God destroyed from among you everyone who followed the Baal of Peor, but all of you who held fast to the Lord your God are still alive today (Deuteronomy 4:1-4).

The writer tells the people to add nothing to laws and to subtract nothing. They are to follow the Law literally. When we start as children, this is the way we obey the things that our parents tell us. This sort of exact obedience is necessary at this initial stage. The writer also offers the promise of a reward: if they obey, they will enter the promised land which is their goal. Thirdly, the writer tells them that if they do not obey the laws, they will be punished as their ancestors were when they followed not Yahweh but Baal.

Let us look now at the section that follows this:

> See, I have taught you decrees and laws as the Lord my God commanded me, so that you may follow them in the land you are entering to take possession of it. Observe them carefully, for this will show your wisdom and understanding to the nations, who will hear about all these decrees and say, 'Surely this great nation is a wise and understanding people'. What other nation is so great as to have their gods near them the way the Lord our God is near us whenever we pray to him? And what other nation is so great as to have such righteous decrees and laws as this body of laws I am setting before you today (Deuteronomy 4:5-8).

By obeying all the decrees of the Lord (Yahweh), the people will show their wisdom to the other nations, and they will be well thought of. It is not just a matter of obeying a powerful God. This God, Yahweh, is different from the gods of the other nations. Yahweh is not far away from his people but is near them. The writer implies that their Lord loves them and cares about them. This is the reason why they are to obey him faithfully. Their faithfulness to the law will also show not only their obedience but their love for this wonderful God that they have.

The above passage continues:

> Only be careful, and watch yourselves closely so that you do not forget the things your eyes have seen or let them fade from your heart as long as you live. Teach them to your children and to their children after them. Remember the day you stood before the Lord your God at Horeb, when he said to me, 'Assemble the people before me to hear my words so that they may learn to revere me as long as they live in the land and may teach them

to their children'. You came near and stood at the foot of the mountain while it blazed with fire to the very heavens, with black clouds and deep darkness. Then the Lord spoke to you out of the fire. You heard the sound of words but saw no form; there was only a voice. He declared to you his covenant, the Ten Commandments, which he commanded you to follow and then wrote them on two stone tablets. And the Lord directed me at that time to teach you the decrees and laws you are to follow in the land that you are crossing the Jordan to possess. (Deuteronomy 4:9-14)

This passage too speaks of the goodness of this God who gives them these commandments. It is a loving relationship that exists between God and the people. They are to be proud of Yahweh and to pass down this love and honour to their children so that the nation will never forget the source of their good fortune. Yahweh is the God who has given them these great blessings.

There is another important element in this teaching of the school of Deuteronomy, namely, that Yahweh will not hesitate to punish them if they do not obey the commandments. Again, we must try to see this element according to the stage of development of the nation. They are still a young nation and thus the sanctions that will be imposed if they do not obey the decrees must be strongly emphasised. Here is an example of what will happen if they do not follow the commandments:

> After you have had children and grandchildren and have lived in the land a long time – if you then become corrupt and make any kind of idol, doing evil in the eyes of the

Lord your God and arousing his anger, I call the heavens and the earth as witnesses against you this day that you will quickly perish from the land that you are crossing the Jordan to possess. You will not live there long but will certainly be destroyed. The Lord will scatter you among the peoples, and only a few of you will survive among the nations to which the Lord will drive you. There you will worship gods of wood and stone, made by human hands, which cannot see or hear or eat or smell. (Deuteronomy 4:25-28)

The writer seems to expect that the people will eventually grow tired of keeping the commandments since it is such a great temptation! He tells them that the Lord's anger will blaze out and they will be utterly destroyed. We note the fierceness of the threat intended to instil fear into the people. If love is not enough then it must be supplemented by fear. However, to be fair to the Deuteronomic writer, we must mention (though not quote) what follows in the passage. The passage continues that if the people do turn away to other gods, Yahweh will still pursue them and eventually bring them back to him.

In the above long passage (quoted in segments) we have seen how the Deuteronomic school emphasises the following pattern: there is a great relationship between Yahweh and the people which begins with Yahweh revealing himself to this poor and insignificant people. Yahweh will continue to send them blessings as he/she did in the past especially through delivering them out of Egypt and leading them to the promised land. Yahweh will do his part but only if the people also fulfil their side of the relationship (called covenant) by obeying the law and by worshipping only Yahweh. If the people obey the law they will prosper; if they do not obey the commandments and abandon Yahweh, Yahweh will not hesitate to punish them.

This insistence on the exact following of the law at this stage of the history of Israel was necessary to establish a strong foundation for the continuing existence of this people whom Yahweh had chosen. The message is simple: obey the law and Yahweh will bless you. When we get to the historical period of the Prophets much later in the history of the people, there emerges a different awareness. The prophets see that the reliance on keeping the law has become mechanical and hypocritical. The leaders and many false prophets and the people in general continue to offer sacrifices and follow the commandments externally but they ignore the spirit of the law which is to love their neighbour and to give special attention to the 'widow and the stranger', that is all those who are in some way marginalised. The prophets speak on behalf of Yahweh: 'These people honour me with their lips but their hearts are far from me' (quoted in Matthew). By the time of the prophets beginning with Amos and moving to Isaiah and Jeremiah and the other prophets, a critical consciousness has developed. There is an interior struggle going on in the people to be faithful to Yahweh interiorly rather than simply in the exterior. The prophets sow within the leaders and the people in general a sense of self-doubt. Richard Rohr says, 'They have to leave their false innocence and naïve superiority behind them and admit that they don't always live according to the law'.⁹ He continues, 'They move into self-reflective and self-critical thinking'.

The teaching of the Prophets represents a new stage of consciousness of the people. It is a move similar to that of childhood and adolescence into adulthood. It is a move from external adherence of the law to the struggle to follow the dictates coming not from external authority but from their own internal authority.¹⁰ There is a struggle going on in them also about how they view Yahweh. Their view of Yahweh becomes more complex and varied. This emergence of critical consciousness continues with the Wisdom literature, a third stage of development which we must add to the stages of the Law and the Prophets. The Wisdom literature includes the Psalms, Qoheleth, Ecclesiasticus, Wisdom, Sirach and Job. There is a definitive move away in these books from the sense that Yahweh has given Israel all the answers and that the other peoples, whom they called the pagans, are totally ignorant. Instead, it becomes clear to the people of Israel that they had something to learn from the accumulated wisdom that these other people possessed. They could no longer see things in black and white: we are right and they are wrong; Yahweh loves us but does not love them. This development is painful for the people. Again, it means an overhaul in their understanding of Yahweh as we see most starkly in such books as Qoheleth and Job.

---

[9] Richard Rohr, *Things Hidden*.
[10] Cf. Stages 3 and 4 of James Fowler's *Stages of Faith*.

Testimony and Counter Testimony about God

Walter Brueggemann calls the Deuteronomic view of God and the people the official testimony to Yahweh of the people. Yahweh is loving and faithful and will shower blessings on the people if they obey his commandments. Underlying this testimony is the belief that good people will find blessings showered upon them and wicked people will have misfortunes coming upon them. Another aspect of this official testimony is that the people of Israel are loved by Yahweh far beyond any other people.

But as well as this official testimony, there are other types of testimony to Yahweh. Brueggemann calls these types of testimony counter-testimony. Even in the patriarchal writings we find Abraham interceding with Yahweh on behalf of the wicked city of Sodom (Genesis 18:16-32). Abraham hears that Yahweh plans to destroy the city because of the wickedness of the people. Abraham approaches Yahweh saying, 'Are you really going to destroy the just man with the sinner? Perhaps there are fifty just men in the town. Will you really overwhelm them, will you not spare the place for the fifty just men in it? Do not think of it! Will the judge of the whole earth not administer justice?' In response, Yahweh says that he/she will not destroy the city if he finds fifty just men in it. Abraham does not stop there but bargains with Yahweh for forty-five and then forty and then thirty just men. Yahweh finally says that he will not destroy Sodom if he finds only ten just men.

The relationship between Yahweh and Abraham is much more flexible here than the Deuteronomic writer would have us believe. In fact, Abraham almost blames Yahweh for planning to destroy the city. The least we can say is that he speaks in a very familiar way to the majestic Yahweh who is Lord of all the earth. Here we have a different tradition which allows human beings to bargain with Yahweh and, even more important, which believes that Yahweh will listen to these prayers and yield to what is asked. Brueggemann says that these are signs of a counter-testimony to the major testimony we have seen in Deuteronomy. In this counter-testimony the people are much more free and familiar with Yahweh.

Again, when Yahweh says that he will destroy the whole world with a flood because people have become so wicked, we are told, 'But God had Noah in mind, and all the wild beasts and all the cattle that were with him in the ark' (Genesis 8:1), meaning that Yahweh cared too much for Noah and his sons and the animals to destroy them. Instead of destroying them he had ordered Noah and his sons to build an ark. God in effect changes his mind and does not destroy the earth. After the waters subside Yahweh tells Noah, 'Never again will I curse the earth because of humankind, because the inclination of the human heart is evil from infancy. Never again will I strike down every living thing as I have done' (Genesis 8:21).

We have perhaps a more vivid example of humans freely discussing whether Yahweh should destroy the people of Israel after the people worship the golden calf which Aaron has allowed them to make (Exodus 32:7-14). Moses speaks to Yahweh almost as an equal. He puts forward reasons why Yahweh should not let his 'wrath blaze out against (the people) and devour them' (32:9-10). Moses' arguments are that the Egyptians will claim that Yahweh led his people out of Egypt and then let them die in the desert. Secondly, he tells Yahweh to remember his promises to the patriarchs, Abraham, Isaac and Moses. The exchange ends in Yahweh relenting and not destroying the people. In another exchange between the two, Moses refers to the people as Yahweh's people while Yahweh refers to them as Moses' people. In these passages, we see a God who does not stand on his dignity, as it were, as we might expect from Israel's major testimony about Yahweh where the majesty and splendour of Yahweh are exclusively emphasised.

We see counter-testimony strongly also in Qoheleth, Jeremiah, Job and the Psalms. Qoheleth, the Preacher, does not subscribe to the mainstream belief that the good prosper and experience happiness because of their faithfulness to Yahweh. He goes further and says that happiness itself is an empty reality and not worth pursuing. He says that life is no more than a succession of events ending in death for both the wise and foolish alike (cf. Qoheleth 3:1-11). Such discourse would be unheard of in the Deuteronomic literature.

In the prophecy of Jeremiah, we hear Jeremiah cursing the day of his birth and wishing that his mother had never delivered him (cf. Jeremiah 20:14). In one of his 'confessions' Jeremiah complains to Yahweh, 'Why is my suffering continual, my wound incurable, refusing to be healed? Do you mean to be for me a deceptive stream with inconstant waters' (Jeremiah 15:18)? There are few places in the Old Testament where someone speaks to Yahweh in such an intimate, accusatory, way.

The book of Job is equally 'shocking' to those who think of the presentation of Yahweh in the Old Testament as being constantly harmonious and respectful. In the book of Job, the three 'friends' of Yahweh tell Job that he must have committed some sin that has caused his loss of property, wealth, health and family. They insist that Yahweh is punishing him for these sins. It is just a matter of confessing his sins and being restored to the friendship of Yahweh and then his good fortunes will be restored. Job will not accept that he has sinned. In doing this, he is denying that Yahweh always blesses those who live good lives and obey Yahweh strictly. In the book, there is also a constant dialogue going on between Job and Yahweh. In these exchanges, Job, like Jeremiah, does not hesitate to tell God exactly how he feels. He complains to Yahweh and even expresses angry words to Yahweh. Here is one example of the way Job speaks to Yahweh:

> Will you never take your eyes off me
> Long enough for me to swallow my spittle?
> Suppose I have sinned, what have I done to you,
> You tireless watcher of humankind?
> Why do you choose me as your target?
> Why should I be a burden to you?
> Can you not tolerate my sin,
> Nor overlook my fault?
> It will not be long before I lie on earth;
> Then you will look for me, but I shall be no more
> (Job 7:19-21).

Job here tells God exactly how he feels. He puts aside good manners and speaks aggressively and angrily to Yahweh. Furthermore, he challenges the accepted beliefs that Yahweh should be concerned about our sins since we all sin. Why should Yahweh worry about our sins? This would be an unheard-of statement among faithful Israelites of a few generations earlier.

A Central Passage: Exodus 34:5-9

Moses has asked Yahweh to show his glory, that is to show himself. Moses is saying, 'Show us what you are really like. We know a lot about you but what is the central thing about you'. What follows happens on the mountain where Yahweh has given the ten commandments to Moses. Yahweh comes down from the skies in a cloud. Yahweh comes out of the cloud and says about himself: 'The Lord, the Lord, a merciful and gracious God, slow to anger and rich in kindness and fidelity' (v. 6). Moses at once bows to the ground in worship and says, 'If I find favour with you. O Lord, do come along in our company; yet pardon our wickedness and sins, and receive us as your own' (v. 8).

This passage is generally thought to be a key one for the people and a normative one against which other descriptions are to be seen. It is a 'stylised and self-conscious characterisation of Yahweh,'[11] a classic statement of what the people believed about Yahweh. It was probably 'a creedal statement used in ceremonies to give glory to Yahweh'. The people would have often returned to this statement. They knew that this is what Yahweh was like because they had experienced his love for them.

---
[11] Brueggemann, *Theology of the Old Testament*.

Notice that in the passage Moses falls to the ground. He does this because of the holiness of Yahweh. As well as the intimate closeness, they nevertheless knew that Yahweh was totally different from them and that the Israelites were to approach him not just as some other reality but as the reality that stands behind every other.

Yahweh is 'a gracious God full of tenderness and compassion, slow to anger and rich in mercy and fidelity'. This is what we all want to believe and what we need to believe to be happy in our lives. God is rich in tenderness and faithfully loves us in all the happenings of our lives. I used this passage in speaking to a group of Australians visiting Kenya for a week and spending time with people from the slum district of Kibera. I said to the group that maybe they saw some of this belief in the poor people they had met. They saw these people with nothing but still radiating happiness, love and hospitality in spite of everything. If we are to see God as a God of tenderness and compassion, we may need a change of perspective. People in the Kibera slums can bring about this change for us. Interaction with them can break down our hardness and cynicism.

The day I spoke to this group was the feast of the Trinity and the gospel for that day begins with the famous words, 'God so loved the world...' (John 3:16). This statement is also an amazing statement about the truth of God and one that finds us off guard because we often think that we have to put ourselves on the defensive and think we have to justify ourselves before this God who is the God who has been revealed in the whole of the history of the people of Israel and now in the whole world since the time of Jesus.

We can ask ourselves: Do we believe that the world is good enough to be loved by God so much? Is this how we see the world? If we do, we can see that we also, as part of this world are loved. We usually focus on how weak we are and how much we and others fail. We look at the world in what amounts to despair. But the message of the readings of John 3:16 and Exodus 34:5-9 invite us to see the world and ourselves as God's beloved world and full of possibility.

Why does God have to say that he is slow to anger? And why does Moses have to say that they are a stiff-necked people? It is because of what had just happened in the passage. The people waited for Moses to come down from the mountain where he was talking to God. They became impatient and started speaking in complaint and in rebellion against Yahweh who had led them out of Egypt. Aaron, the brother-in-law of Moses, was left in charge of them but he listened to them and they made a molten calf of their jewelry and precious objects and worshipped the calf.

This was a terrible rejection of Yahweh who had been so good to them and who had rescued them from slavery.

Moses has a good relationship with God and he intercedes on behalf of the people. He and Yahweh are very familiar and Moses can speak to God as a man speaks face-to-face with another. That is why Moses asks God to come with them on their journey through the wilderness. And that is why he calls the people stiff-necked. Yahweh is slow to anger. He does not vent his anger on the people but agrees to Moses' plea to go with the people and to accept that they are rebellious and stubborn and ungrateful and forgetful and impatient. This is the way we too are. The story is telling us that Yahweh is faithful and reliable and loving and will not give us up when we fail or when we cannot live up to what we would like.

Adjectives to Describe God[12]

This statement of Exodus 34:5-7 features a variety of adjectives.[13] For each of these adjectives Israel had examples of how God had shown these qualities since the time they had been chosen and made his people:

Yahweh is merciful (*rhm*). There are many times and events when the people experienced that Yahweh was concretely merciful to them. This adjective is closely connected to the word 'womb' which has the same root. The term suggests that Yahweh acts like a mother and with a mother's love, gratuitously, without need of compensation or hope of benefit. Yahweh will get nothing in return from this merciful activity. God acts freely and generously.

Yahweh is 'slow to anger'. The adjective translates as God having 'long nostrils' and perhaps indicates that God's long nose allows divine rage to cool before it threatens Israel.

Yahweh has 'steadfast love' (*hsd*). This term is related to tenacious fidelity in a relationship, readiness to continue to be loyal to the one to whom one is bound.

Yahweh abounds in faithfulness (*'emeth*). The word evokes complete trustworthiness and reliability which then becomes the term *'true/truth'*. The words *hesed* and *'emeth* become a

---

[12] I owe the basis of this to Brueggemann, *Theology of the Old Testament*.
[13] Brueggemann, *Theology of the Old Testament*.

much-used word pair in the Old Testament, together marking Yahweh as utterly reliable and trustworthy (cf. John 1:14).

In this passage, the only word used more than once is *hsd (faithful love)* suggesting that this word is of special significance. The paragraph culminates in the surprising and rarely used word 'forgive' (*ns*) This final statement uses Israel's full vocabulary for sin ('forgiving fault, crime and sin, yet letting nothing go unchecked, and punishing the parent's fault in the children and the grandchildren to the third and fourth generation!'). Moses then falls to the ground and says boldly, 'If indeed I do enjoy your favour, please, my Lord, come with us, although they are an obstinate people; and forgive our faults and sins, and adopt us as your heritage.'

In this second half of verse 7, the emphasis is on the other side of God's relations with us: that Yahweh takes sin seriously and punishes it to the fourth generation. What does this indicate? It indicates that besides Yahweh's faithfulness, there is also Yahweh's hatred of sin. It indicates that Yahweh cannot be pinned down and made into something we can manipulate. It also refers indirectly to the holiness of Yahweh emphasised in the way Yahweh came on to the mountain and how the people could not go up the mountain. This second half also indicates that being loyal to Yahweh is demanding. It will cost the people (and us) everything.

Does this other side of Yahweh as one who 'lets nothing go unchecked' and 'punishes the parents' faults in the children and grandchildren' fit with the God who is so utterly merciful and compassionate? It is a fact that when we read a passage like Exodus 34:5-9) we can get stuck on the negative side. All the warmth and love we feel in response to God's love for us can get hijacked. How can we account for this? I think we have to say that it is not God who is directing our attention in this negative way but a force of evil which is constantly working against God's intentions for us. Here is a simple way of distinguishing between the work of God and the work of this force of evil. God encourages us when we are moving towards him, that is towards love, but discourages us when we are going in the opposite direction.[14] God's action in this latter case can be strong and off-putting. But we must realise that we are being deceived and moving towards death and God has to be strong with us to get us moving in the right direction. We have to ask ourselves when we feel discouraged: Is this the evil spirit who wants to discourage me from moving towards greater life? Or is it God who wants to warn me that I am going in the wrong direction?

In the case of the discouragement we feel when we think of God punishing the children for the crimes of the parents, we must suspect the work of the evil spirit. The truth is that God does not punish us. The passage means, rather, that when we do wrong, our actions have consequences. Ronald Rolheiser quotes the following verse from the Book of Revelation: 'So the angel swung his sickle over the earth and cut the earth's vintage. He threw in into the great winepress of God's fury' (Revelation). This is indeed a frightening scenario. Does it mean that God gets very angry with us and wreaks violence on us? Rolheiser's answer is no. What he says the passage does mean is 'that the chickens always come home to roost, that our actions have consequences, that sin

---

[14] See Ignatian Rules of discernment, rules 1 & 2 of Set One in Jules Toner.

wreaks havoc on the planet and our own souls drive us to anger, self-hatred, and lack of forgiveness, and that this feels as if God is angry and is punishing us'.[15] God is doing nothing of the sort!

God's Overflowing Abundance

Richard Rohr speaks of three major symbols that run through the Bible, namely, water, blood and bread.[16] It is through water that Yahweh leads his people out of Egypt. Water flows from the rock in the desert (cf. Numbers 20); the stream flowing out of the Temple in Ezekiel becomes a mighty river that sweeps all before it (Ezekiel 47); the people cross the Jordan to enter the Promised Land (Joshua 3); Jesus offers the Samaritan woman living water that will satisfy her thirst eternally (John 4); water flows from the side of the dead Christ; Jesus himself is the living water (John 7). Water symbolises God's overflowing love. The medieval mystic, Mechthild of Magdeburg, imagines the love of the Trinity as water flowing out to all. The predominant image here is flow and water symbolises this best. God's love flows out to the whole of creation.

The second symbol Rohr finds is blood. Blood symbolises transformation; letting go of unneeded baggage. Again, the image of flow is important. The flowing of blood symbolised death to the false self. Jesus says of the wine at the Last Supper, 'This is the blood of the New Covenant which will

---

[15] Ronald Rolheiser, *Internet Archives*.
[16] Rohr, *Things Hidden*.

be poured out for you for the forgiveness of sins'. The symbol here is complex. The wine is the love of Jesus poured out; it is also the symbol of Jesus' death. In Jesus, God loves us without the spilling of blood. Rohr says, 'The crucifixion is not tit for tat but the eternal nature of God flowing towards us as water and blood (cf. John 19:34)'.[17]

Finally, we have the symbol of bread which symbolises nurturing. There are innumerable references to bread in both Old and New Testaments. In the Old Testament, we have:

- The manna, the miraculous food provided during the journey in the desert
- The feeding of the widow by Elijah
- The bread which David and his troops take from the sanctuary when they are hungry
- The banquet that God provides for us in Isaiah.

In the New Testament, we have:

- The feedings in the desert
- The Last Supper
- The bread of life in John
- The breakfast which Jesus prepares by the seashore for his disciples.

One of the verses of the psalm in the readings of the 17th Sunday of ordinary time (Year B) is the following:

> The Lord is gracious and merciful
> Slow to anger and abounding in steadfast love.

---

[17] Richard Rohr, *Things Hidden*.

> The Lord is good to all,
> and his compassion is over all that he has made
> (Psalm 145).

As I thought of this theme of God's abundant love and mercy coming from these lines from Psalm 145, I saw how they are closely related to the theme of abundance. This theme of abundance comes out strongly in the readings of this Sunday from 2 Kings where one of the prophets orders someone to feed 100 people with some loaves of bread and the gospel where Jesus goes up a mountain and finds himself with many people and with a boy who has five barley loaves and two fishes. The theme is the abundance of God's love and mercy to us in the midst of our poverty.

I had felt God's graciousness to me in the few weeks before this Sunday. God is certainly abounding in love. This love is being shown in the world today, which speaks a different language from that of Exodus. But this abounding compassion of God is still flowing to us and to all who are trying to do their best. I noticed how so many films show people expressing in imperfect but rich ways this abounding love that is everywhere in the world. A young married woman in the film *Take This Waltz* is attracted to a man whom she meets on a plane. She makes a great effort to nurture the relationship she has for her husband, but in the end, she goes with the other man. We may judge that she has failed in her commitment to her husband. Her behaviour is shot through with ambiguity, but there is no denying that she does her best to love her husband and the man she finally goes with. Another movie, *Red Satin*, is about a Tunisian woman in her forties who is bored in the house and is doing her best to keep her daughter from going astray. She has a great interest in dancing and almost by accident she goes to a cabaret where she meets one of the dancers who is good to her. She goes again and gradually becomes involved until she herself begins dancing. She feels some guilt about this dancing but she also knows that it gives her life. How are we to judge this woman? In fact, her involvement in the cabaret makes her more compassionate to her daughter. How are we to judge also the young woman who goes with the man who is not her husband?

As I reflected on these two movies, I became aware that all human behaviour is ambiguous to some degree. We love God and we love other things. I had no doubt that these two women in the two movies were loving people and were doing their best to love and to make decisions to lead them to greater love and life for others and for themselves.

Let us return to the idea of bread. We will begin with the scene in Exodus when God sends manna to the people when they are wandering through the desert. The passage from Exodus announces one of the major sins of the people: their grumbling that God does not provide for them. The Israelites say to Moses and Aaron:

> Would that we had died at the Lord's hand in the land of Egypt, as we sat by our fleshpots and ate our fill of bread! But you had to lead us into this desert to make the whole community die of famine! (Exodus 16:3).

They have forgotten how grateful they were when they came victoriously through the waters of the sea. They have forgotten the miracles that God had worked for them to get them out of the clutches of Pharaoh. Now in the desert when things are difficult, not only do they not appreciate how God has been with them but they bitterly and rudely complain. They make fun of God and say they liked being slaves in Egypt because they had their 'fleshpots' and 'ate their fill of bread'. They are saying that they prefer slavery to being looked after by God.

God, instead of rejecting them, sends them food in the form of manna in the morning and quail in the evening. But God still wants to know if they will accept his authority. God acts in a moderate, patient way. His behaviour is like a patient father with a petulant, wilful teenager. God gives them what they need in this difficult time of their journey through the desert.

We should note in this passage how God and the people are relating. We do not find here the God of majesty who gives the tablets of stone to Moses on the mountain. Here, we do not have God laying down the law that if the people deviate, their children will be punished to the fourth or the thousandth generation! Instead, we have a God who puts up with ingratitude and insolence from his people.

This reading from Exodus is linked with Psalm 78 and part of Jesus' discourse on the bread of life in John. The response to Psalm 78 is: 'The Lord gave them bread from heaven'. The psalm speaks about the manna not in terms of just keeping the people alive. Instead it says:

> He commanded the doors of heaven opened;
> He rained manna upon them for food
> And gave them heavenly bread.

We are speaking here again of God seen from the point of view of heaven. We can relate this verse to Jesus saying to Nicodemus, 'You will see the heavens opened and, above the Son of Man, the angels of God ascending and descending' (John 1:51).

In the discourse of Jesus on the bread of life (cf. John 6:24-35), Jesus contrasts his attitude to the bread with that of the crowd who are thinking only of bread which will fill their stomachs. Jesus, by contrast, is speaking of bread which will satisfy them eternally. Jesus is speaking about the bread from God's point of view while the crowd is speaking from the point of view of earth; God's point of view is the view of love and abundance, the crowd's the scarcity and of getting what they can.

The following reflection tries to give an example of how we can experience this sense of God's abundance of which I think these readings about bread are speaking. The first reflection illustrates times when we are tuned into the way God is constantly providing for us with great abundance.

As well as a certain tiredness as I looked back in the evening, I also felt that the blessings of the day had overflowed. My cup was overflowing and I said to myself: 'all this throbbing' (see the poem by Rumi below) is a wonderful gift to me from God. In my prayer, the passage of the loaves and fishes also came to me. That gospel passage of the miraculous feeding in the desert and the passage of the miracle at Cana are great stories that capture the feeling I had after that day and after many other days after I had taught and given spiritual direction. This was a helpful insight for me. It put flesh onto the stories themselves and showed me concretely how God does lavish us with his/her gifts and blessings so that they overflow. I used the gift I had as best I could and abundant blessings came to me 'pressed down, shaken together and flowing' were poured into my lap (Luke 6:38).

When we agree to take on something which involves new material for us and it turns out well, we gain new confidence. We may recall the words of Isaiah 60 which is one of the readings for the feast of the Epiphany:

> Your eyes will be radiant at what you see
> And your heart will throb and vibrate (Isaiah 60:5).

That word 'throb' may be helpful to describe our mood sometimes. Throbbing indicates an intense joy and satisfaction, which come from the efforts we make to do what God wants. The throbbing we feel is a response of God to us. It is God communicating very directly with us. St Ignatius' Basic Prayer reads,

> Every time I have responded to your love, I have experienced your life filling my heart to overflowing.

The experience fills us with a new confidence and the confirmation that we are doing the Lord's work and in tune with God's plan for us and for the world. It is God telling us to go on with whatever ministry we are involved in. When we feel this throbbing, we remember not the doubts but the courageous, positive and delightful thoughts, not fearing the struggle when things get difficult.

Those lines of Isaiah on the feast of the Epiphany about our hearts throbbing can move us deeply when we hear them.

This is perhaps central to the feast of the Epiphany. On this feast we celebrate what is actually going on in our lives.

When thinking of the passage from Isaiah, I remembered when being in Tamale, Northern Ghana, as novice director, I had agreed to change from teaching 'hour classes' to classes that extended over the whole morning, that is, three hours. I often did not know exactly how much content I would need for each morning. All I knew was that a considerable amount would be needed. I enjoyed teaching the classes. I think that it was because I had a sense that something new was happening to me. I had been involved for several years with novitiate classes and never before had I taken classes for the whole morning on a regular basis. It was during this time that I first came across the Sufi poet, Rumi and these lines of his:

> Congratulations dear heart!
> You have joined the circle of lovers,
> Tell me in your own words when did all this throbbing begin?
>
> 'I was absorbed in my work in this world
> but I never lost my longing for home.
> One day, exhausted with no strength left,
> I was lifted suddenly by the grace of Love.
> To describe this mystery there are no words'.[18]

My mood of being really alive, my pulse and my heart throbbing, continued. While finding the classes tiring, I was also really enjoying them.

---

[18] rumi-poem.blogspot.com/2013/02/congratulations-my-dear-heart.html

When such an experience happens, we move from relying on ourselves to joining Rumi's 'circle of lovers' and those who see the heavens opened. We are motivated by love in quite an intense way. What we experience is now exciting as would be the case when lovers are in each other's company. Our hearts throb in just that way.

God gives us great happiness. We see this in Psalm 23: 'You have prepared a banquet for me in the sight of my foes/My head you have anointed with oil, my cup is overflowing'. When we do what God wants as far as we know, that is, if we respond to God, God fills us full to overflowing. This is the experience of many. This longing for God keeps pushing us throughout our lives. It is never fulfilled but in the process we get great happiness.

We Will Never Understand God

We have seen how the understanding of God developed in the Old Testament. Rohr call the Old Testament a 'text in travail'. There is a constant and never-ending struggle to articulate how God had intervened in the history of the people of Israel. There is testimony and counter testimony. We have to hold many views of God in balance while throwing out old understandings which we now know to be not true. It is dangerous when we come to assume that one understanding of God is the true one. We will then feel free to commit atrocities on others as has happened with Muslim extremists such as Al Shabaab terrorists who kill 149 students and staff at a university in Garissa, Kenya, because they were not Muslim. We can think that God cares for others but not for homosexuals or criminals or murderers or even people who belong to a different faith from our own.

The truth is that no matter how many books we read or how much creative thinking we do and how many revelations we have, we will never be certain of knowing what God wants. The Bible teaches us this if we approach the Bible with an open mind. We have to be constantly open to new understandings of God. If we understood God, we would lose the richness of the infinity of God. We have to be content that we will never know why God allows evil to flourish, or why there have been persecutions of minorities throughout history, or why there is much lack of openness among leaders of the church.

We might think there is little compassion in the world and that God should do something about it. Instead we are called constantly in scripture to trust God without knowing why certain things happen or why things are the way they are. Our access to God is not so much through understanding as through faith. When we really believe, we will see compassion and love and care everywhere, that is, we will see God's action everywhere, and we will not be cowed by the seeming pervasiveness of evil.

References

Brueggemann, Walter, *Theology of the Old Testament: Testimony, Dispute, Advocacy*, Minneapolis: Fortress Press, 1997.

Fowler, James W., *Stages of Faith*, San Francisco: Harper and Row 1981.

Hansen, Michael, *The First Spiritual Exercises*, Notre Dame, Indiana: Ave Maria Press, 2013.

_____, *The First Spiritual Exercises: A Manual for Those Who Give the Exercises*, Notre Dame, Indiana: Ave Maria Press, 2013.

La Mott, Anne, *Help, Thanks, Wow: The Three Essential Prayers*, Riverhead Books, 2012.

Rohr, Richard, *Things Hidden: Scripture as Spirituality*, Cincinnati: St Anthony Messenger, 2007.

Rolheiser, Ronald, *Internet Archive: 'Angels with Sickles and God's Fury'*, July 2016.

_____, *Internet Archive: 'On Reading Difficult Passages of Scripture'*, June 2016.

rumi-poem.blogspot.com/2013/02/congratulations-my-dear-heart.html

Toner, J., S.J., *A Commentary on Saint Ignatius' Rules for the Discernment of Spirits*, St. Louis: Institute of Jesuit Sources, 1981.

Chapter Three

Our Ambiguous Relationship with the Mystery

IN THE FILM, *Take This Waltz*, mentioned in the previous chapter, we see a young woman, Margot, on a plane, beginning conversation with a young man, Daniel, who initiates the conversation. It is obvious at this early stage that there is a strong attraction between them. We are told in conversation that Margot is married and it turns out that Daniel lives across the road from her and her husband. Margot is in love with him but she does not say no to Daniel who is very interested in a relationship with her. The movie continues in this way for some time with Margot having some very spontaneous interchanges with her husband showing that she really cares about him and that they get on well in the marriage. But there are also one or two occasions where we see friction.

Margot starts to spend more time with Daniel until she really believes that she is being called to leave the marriage to be with him. The movie now focuses on Margot and Daniel and unobtrusively we see the marriage breaking up. We do not know how the husband and his family feel until, after some time, she courageously returns to face them. The husband and his relations are uncomfortable when she returns in the middle of a social gathering. Margot spends time there but it is clear that her life is now going to be with Daniel. Michelle Williams who plays Margot plays the part in such a way that we, the viewers, see things mainly from her point of view. We tend to excuse her behaviour since she is so charming, not realising that she is being unfaithful to her husband. Nevertheless, it is clear that she is a good person and believes that she will be happier with Daniel in spite of her marriage commitment.

The movie brings up sharply the ambiguity we human beings show in our behaviour. I have titled this chapter our ambiguous relationship with the Mystery in the sense that Margot has some sense of the mystery of life and that in her relationship with the two men with whom she is involved, she has a sense that this mystery is moving her in one direction rather than the other. The movie takes the side of her going with Daniel. What is the truth? Or can we ask that? Is it not more that Margot has to go in the direction that she feels is true to who she most deeply is while at the same time being aware of her obligations to others?

I wish to take two more films to support what we already see: that human behaviour towards life or the mystery is ambiguous. The first of these further films is *Red Satin* (also quoted in the previous chapter), a Tunisian film about a widow Lilia who suspects her teenage daughter, Salma, of having an affair with a musician, Chokri. She tracks Chokri to his workplace and enters the exotic world of the Red Satin cabaret. Though initially repulsed by the sexy, sordid and smoky atmosphere, Lilia keeps returning. She at first strongly disapproves of the happenings at the Red Satin. But her experience of going there is at the same time exhilarating for her. She finds kindness and affection from one of the dancers who invites her to do some alterations to her clothes. She finds companionship and she also wants to learn more about herself. She finds a huge contrast between what she has learned from her Tunisian Muslim tradition with the values she finds at the cabaret. In spite of her reservations about being there, she finds that the visits give her life. Though the atmosphere is 'sexy' she feels respected by those who see her dance. She finds now she can better understand her daughter and as a result the daughter's attitude to her changes from distance to warmth and love.

Life Is Ambiguous

What are we to make of Lilia's experience and the decision she makes to continue to go to the Red Satin Cabaret? It is good for her to hold on to her traditional beliefs but it is also true that her experience of this new life has values which she desperately needs. Neither the tradition nor the cabaret is totally good. More importantly, Lilia's decision to continue to go to the cabaret is determined by values that are partly good but also potentially dangerous. We certainly do not condemn her for the decision she makes. Ronald Rolheiser, in speaking about how our adult lives develop, says:

> Work, interrelations, love, sex, friendship, aging, all of these are complex, messy businesses, partially full of pain, pettiness, limit, compromise and death... No one goes

through life without having his or her dignity, freedom and dreams, frustrated and stepped on. We are not angels, free soaring spirits, unencumbered by the limits of time and flesh. Our souls are born enfleshed in soil, pain, blood and smell.[19]

There is a saying that says: to act is to sin. If we imagine ourselves never doing anything wrong or never breaking a rule, we will never do anything because fear will dominate our lives. Like Margot and Lilia, we will all be faced with decisions where we have to choose between two options both of which seem good. The criteria that should guide us are not whether we are breaking rules or staying strictly to our religious beliefs, but what is most compassionate for the other and for our own lives, what will lead to life for both our traditional beliefs and what will give us life. Put another way, we have to break the false gods which tell us that we have to act in a certain way no matter what.

The third film is *Suite Française*. In a Nazi-occupied village during the Second World War, the lives of the local inhabitants are turned upside down by the arrival of French soldiers who are to be billeted with the families. Lucile is a young woman living with her mother while her husband is away fighting in the war. The German officer who is chosen to stay with them, Bruno, is a sensitive and attractive young man who plays the piano and who does not fit their image at all of the cruel occupier. At first, the two women refuse to talk to the officer. But the daughter, Lucile, is desperately lonely and is attracted

---

[19] Ronald Rolheiser, *Forgotten among the Lilies: Learning to Love Beyond Our Fears*, New York: Doubleday, 2005.

to the young man living with them who constantly seeks her friendship. The relations between the two gradually thaw and they eventually fall in love. In the end, both Lucile and Bruno separately make acts of heroism which save the lives of many local people. We see here the messiness, complexity, pain and pettiness involved in the big themes of life such as love, sex and friendship of which Rolheiser spoke.

The ambiguity in ourselves we are speaking of can cause us to become despairing at times because of our failure to be faithful to the Mystery guiding our lives and at other times to be filled with consolation and encouragement. The ambiguity is often caused by the unjust and cruel behaviour we hear of others. We can even find ourselves behaving in this same way. Recently, I received a blog from a friend who is gradually deteriorating from motor neuron disease. He said that in the previous month he felt discouraged and noticed himself going into his shell. The atrocities he was hearing in the world were causing this discouragement, not his own physical deterioration or worries about his approaching death. I put the news I got from this friend alongside this statement from the Buddhist writer, Thich Nhat Hanh, which I had used to lead community prayer at about the same time:

> Waking up this morning, I smile.
> Twenty-four brand new hours are before me.
> I vow to live fully in each moment[20]

My reaction to this statement in the light of my friend's

---

[20] Thich Nhat Hanh, *The Heart of the Buddha's Teaching*, New York: Broadway Books, 1998.

blog was that external events do not have to lead us to discouragement and despair. This does not mean that we do not care what happens in the world but it simply means that we cannot do anything immediately to change the situation. Dorothy Day's advice in this situation is to do what we can and leave the things we cannot do in God's hands. I formed the intention of writing to my friend to tell him this. Others in the prayer I led shared their responses to the statement by Thich Nhat Hanh and they were similar. All said that they agreed that they too would wake up and smile at the twenty-four hours ahead of them in spite of their misgivings.

The poet, Gerard Manley Hopkins addresses this same theme in his poem, *God's Grandeur*.[21] Here is the first stanza of the poem:

> The world is charged with the grandeur of God.
> It will flame out, like shining from shook foil;
> It gathers to a greatness, like the ooze of oil
> Crushed. Why do men then now not reck his rod?
> Generations have trod, have trod, have trod;
> And all is seared with trade; bleared, smeared with toil;
> And wears man's smudge and shares man's smell: the soil
> Is bare now, nor can foot feel, being shod.

The poet is thrilled at the grandeur that he sees in the world which constantly manifests itself in the things we see. But very quickly his imagination becomes weighed down by the stubbornness of humanity who work against this

---

[21] Gerard Manley Hopkins, *God's Grandeur and Other Poems*, New York: Dover Publications, 1995.

goodness and beauty. The poet at this stage is like my friend with motor neuron disease and the rest of us who so quickly feel burdened by the faults and inconsistencies we see in ourselves and in the world. The life energy in Hopkins fights against this negativity until he is able to cry out triumphantly:

> And for all this, nature is never spent;
> There lives the dearest freshness deep down things;
> And though the last lights off the black West went
> Oh, morning, at the brown brink eastward, springs –
> Because the Holy Ghost over the bent
> World broods with warm breast and with ah! bright wings.

Ambiguity in our conscious relationship with the Mystery

This poem introduces a new element into our topic. So far, we have been saying that we humans act ambiguously to the mystery that we see consciously or unconsciously in our lives. In the poem, the mystery is named the Holy Ghost. We can move now to looking at how we relate consciously to this mystery in prayer. An important theme in prayer is that of total devotion and commitment of ourselves to the Mystery. (We call this Mystery God and I will use these terms interchangeably.) In Matthew's gospel, for example, there is a very strong theme of giving ourselves totally to God, not to pray so as to be seen by others or give alms to be admired. Our motivation is to be solely that of love of God. We are to give up everything, to lose our lives without thinking anything of it.

This theme is also very evident in the psalms, in liturgy and in popular spirituality. Psalm 1, for example says that the one who loves the Law of Yahweh and follows it day and night will be always happy. The psalm seems to be saying that to be happy, we must be totally unambiguous; we must be whole hearted. This psalm begins:

> Ah, how happy those of blameless life
> Who walk in the Law of Yahweh.
> How happy are those who respect his decrees,
> And seek him with all their heart.

Again, the message seems to be the same. We are to have our eyes fixed always on God and not to deviate. I remember that as a teenager I used to be discouraged by the prayer at Mass when the priest washes his hands. He prays that he will of blameless heart. I wondered: how can I be blameless and how can I do what is good all the time? I now realise that it is the desire to be blameless that is important. The feast of the Immaculate Conception celebrates the fact that Mary was conceived without sin and committed no sin in her life. The prayer for the feast asks that we be like Mary in being sinless even though we know this is impossible.

Let us take the hymn *Be Thou My Vision* as an example of popular piety which has this same theme of having our hearts set totally on God. The hymn asks that we have the Lord in our vision continually and that this be a great source of joy for us. We want to be with no one else. The Lord is our 'heart's great love'. With the Lord we do not need riches or praise since the Lord is our inheritance and we do not want praise from anyone as long as the Lord is first in our heart.

It is my belief that we receive great consolation from this theme which comes so often into the prayer resources that we use. Why is it so popular? I believe it is because it taps into something truthful about us, namely, our desire for God. We have no doubt that we want to desire God above everything else. We want to desire nothing else except God even though we know we desire other things. We do desire other things besides God. But when we sing the hymn *Be Thou My Vision*, we put aside our desire for other things and desire only God. The reality of our desire for God blocks out the other reality and rightly so. From one point of view, we do desire only God. But at the level of our actions we desire other realities which compete, often successfully, for our attention.

Let us look at some striking declarations of love for God above everything else. One is the prayer of St Ignatius of Antioch before being thrown to the lions in the coliseum:

> There is no advantage for me in the attractions of the world nor in the kingdoms of this age. It is better for me to die into Christ Jesus than to rule over the ends of the earth. It is Christ whom I seek who died for my sake. While I am still alive, I write to you, but my passionate desire is to die. For my passionate desire has been crucified and there is in me no fiery love of material thing.

What of us who did not have this special grace that Ignatius of Antioch had at his death? We wholeheartedly say this prayer with him because it is what we most deeply want though, unlike him, we may not be able to carry out the act of martyrdom.

Paul also declares that everything else is rubbish if he 'can only have Christ and be given a place in him'. (Philippians 3:7-11). All he cares about is to know Christ 'and the power of his resurrection and to share his sufferings'. He says this with such tremendous enthusiasm that we who read his declaration want to follow him. It is like being in a procession where the leader says, 'We are here only because we are followers of Jesus Christ and for no other reason!'

Here is one final statement of a person who feels totally identified with God:

> She (the soul) tastes there a splendid spiritual sweetness and gratification, discovers true quiet and divine light, and tastes sublimely the wisdom of God reflected in the harmony of his creatures and works. She has the feeling of being filled with blessings and being empty of evils and far removed from them.[22]

The writer, St John of the Cross, is describing the state of a person who has advanced far along the path of union with God. We who read this description know that we are far from this state but are delighted with it and would with all our heart wish that it was describing us.

In *The Interior Castle*, St Teresa of Avila speaks of the time in the journey when the person feels that anything it can do for God seems little. The weakness she used to have is no longer there and everything except God wearies her.[23]

Dealing with ambiguity in prayer

These passages show how strong within human beings is the desire for God. As well as this desire, there is also resistance

---

[22] The *Spiritual Canticle*, 14:4.
[23] Cf. *The Interior Castle*, 5:2:8.

to God. Barry and Connolly give suggestions to directors in dealing with resistance in their directees.[24] In this direction situation, the person is serious about their relationship with the mystery. The person may have a very powerful experience of God and be encouraged by the director to spend time with God talking about this experience. To his surprise, the director finds that she does not get time to reflect on the experience giving the excuse that she has not had time.

A personal experience of such an experience came to me recently. It was on the anniversary of the death of a Brother, Paul. The anniversary was announced with little response from me. Then, as the prayer time went on, the details of Paul's death came to me with great intensity. I remembered how miserable I was at Paul's death and how I recalled that his death could have been avoided had another person, Bob, and myself acted differently. I could hardly face it when the hospital phoned me to tell me that Paul had died. We were in Tamale in northern Ghana and I had to phone Australia and Rome to tell those involved of the death. At first, I experienced a superficial sense that it was inevitable that Paul had died at this time. Then the reality hit me that a mistake had been made in how we had dealt with Paul's illness and that it could have been prevented. I went to bed without much more happening.

The next day was taken up with visits to the police to report the death and to the morgue where the body was. I came back at lunch time and it was decided that I would

---

[24] Barry, W. & Connolly, W. J., *The Practice of Spiritual Direction*, New York: Harper and Row, 1982.

accompany the body back to Melbourne. In the late afternoon, Bob and I collected the body from the morgue and began the first part of the journey which was to Accra, a drive of about nine hours. Bob and I were in great desolation on this journey though some things happened to assist us. The vicar general in Tamale purchased for us a very fine coffin; and on the way when we were stopped by police asking what we were carrying, we were immediately allowed to continue when the police heard that we were taking a body to Accra for burial. We arrived in Accra at about 5.00 a.m. and put the body in the morgue and proceeded to the hostel of the SVD Fathers. I remember getting out a little booklet of extracts of Julian of Norwich. At this time, I was at my lowest ebb. It seemed that we would never be able to get over this terrible thing that had happened for which we were responsible. I opened the booklet and read that God ordains everything to happen the way they do and that God does this with enormous love and compassion. When I read this my attitude changed immediately. I felt better.

We had breakfast and we went to do the things that were needed to arrange for the body to be transported. We returned to the guest house and spoke outside to a priest who happened to be there. I started to try to explain. He got me to sit down and said to me, 'In Ghana, we have a belief that a person dies where and when God wants them to die'. He said this in a calm, affirming way that again brought me great peace. The remainder of that day was spent arranging with public servants to give us the necessary permissions to transport the body. We met many seemingly impossible barriers but all these obstacles disappeared one by one. Bob left me eventually and I was left on my own to do some remaining things and to board the plane. By this stage my desolation had left me. I had no fears about what I was to tell people about the death nor did I experience any guilt that I was responsible for it. What I remembered in the prayer which sparked these memories was a conversation I had with one of the Brothers at the cemetery in Melbourne where he said that Paul had been like his namesake Paul, the apostle, taking the message of the good news of the gospel to Africa and other parts of the world.

I have narrated this personal experience in detail to show how vivid can be our experiences of mystery which assure us that this mystery which we call God certainly loves us and clearly shows us this love. Now what happened to me after the funeral and after I had returned to Tamale? I quickly forgot the certainty that I felt of the Mystery giving me unmistakable signs that I was loved in the midst of all the mistakes and sadness. Life went back to normal. Did I spend time with the Mystery, giving thanks for the love that I had received? I probably did but it soon faded from my memory. And what about my vivid remembering of this experience which brought it back to me as though it were happening again? I did thank the Mystery but it has gone from my mind in the midst of the other things that have happened.

Barry and Connolly say that it is not just that other concerns block out these vivid experiences of God's love, but that movements that they call counter movements work against the love we feel. These counter movements happen because we remember other times when God did not seem to be looking after us. Unconsciously, we also expect God to be helping us with every single thing we do and if God does not, then we think that the vivid experience of love of God that we experienced may not have been as real as we thought. We see here the ambiguity that occurs in our relationship with the Mystery.

Facing our resistance to the Mystery in our prayer

When the directee in spiritual direction experiences resistance to God, Barry and Connolly advise that she recall that all our relationships with Mystery are ambiguous because of our human weakness. They advise the director to help her see that she is caught between love of and confidence in the Mystery and love of other conflicting desires. She may also reflect on how there is ambiguity in other areas of her life. For example, she may be in conflict with friends, discouraged in some area of her work, angry at something that has happened. Ambiguity is part of the reality of all human relationships. Once the directee has done that, she can then talk to God about how she feels towards God. Though this may be difficult, it will help strengthen the relationship through the confidence in God she is showing.

We have an excellent example of our ambiguity to the Mystery in the book of the prophet Jeremiah. In chapter eight, Jeremiah pours out his sorrows to the Lord. In doing this, he tells Yahweh that he doubts Yahweh's faithfulness to him. The people are stricken with a terrible wound and Jeremiah himself shares this wound. Was not following Yahweh to be a cause of joy and happiness? Instead he has been afflicted with a wound that is incurable. No matter what he does, he can find no balm for the wound. (In fact there is no cure!) We can say here that Jeremiah is truly in touch with his negative feelings to the Mystery and is not afraid to share these doubts with that Mystery.

In chapter 15 starting at verse 15, Jeremiah continues his remarkable conversation with Yahweh. At first, he pleads with Yahweh to remember him and to bring punishment to those persecuting him. But then Jeremiah remembers the painful things that have happened to him. Where was Yahweh when these misfortunes were happening? Yahweh was nowhere to be seen. Jeremiah emphasises that he did nothing to deserve these misfortunes but had continually done his best to avoid the company of those who spoke against Yahweh. Jeremiah then says these defiant words, words that most of us would never dream of saying to Yahweh:

> Why is my suffering continual,
> My wound incurable, refusing to be healed?
> Do you mean to be for me a deceptive stream
> With inconstant waters? (Jeremiah 15:18)

Jeremiah has returned to his image of an incurable wound. He again accuses Yahweh of providing no cure even though Yahweh had promised to look after those who were faithful to him. But we are not prepared for the next question which asks if Yahweh is going to be like a stream that cannot be relied on. Is this ambiguity on the part of Jeremiah in relation to Yahweh or is it ambiguity on Yahweh's part? It does not matter because we know that in this dialogue, light will come. In fact, we know that Yahweh is not ambiguous and will not be an inconstant stream for Jeremiah; and Yahweh is not even fazed by this outburst by Jeremiah. Yahweh replies:

> If you come back,
> I will take you back into my service;
> And if you utter noble, not despicable thoughts,
> You shall be as my own mouth.
> They will come back to you,
> But you must not go back to them.
> I will make you a bronze wall fortified against
> the people...
>
> I mean to deliver you from the hands of the wicked and redeem you from the clutches of the violent (15:19-21).

This reply of Yahweh reassures us that he will continue to be with Jeremiah and that this sort of honest talk is accepted, even if it questions Yahweh's faithfulness.

A similar pattern of dialogue happens in chapter 20 when Jeremiah tells Yahweh that Yahweh has seduced him. He complains that he has such an unpopular message to give to the people that he receives only ridicule and derision. But eventually Jeremiah realises that in all this struggle Yahweh is there supporting him and will not let his enemies defeat him.

The relationship between Jeremiah and Yahweh, I believe, does have the element of ambiguity on Jeremiah's side. The exchanges we have looked at show that it is part of the normal relationship between a person who speaks honestly with God. We can also conclude that God not only accepts honesty in the way we speak to him but encourages it since it allows the relationship to deepen.

Finally, we have in Matthew's Gospel, the parable of the weeds among the wheat (Matthew 15:24-30). In this parable, we hear that an enemy mixes weeds along with the wheat which the farmer sows. It tells us that there is good and bad in the world and also that there is good and bad in each of us. God has made us good but there are evil forces at work that work against God's good work. God knows this and is patient with our ambiguous responses in our relationship with God as well as in our life in general. God accepts that we will have mixed motives in our behaviour and that we will not be able to do always what we promise God that we will do. Another way of saying this is that we desire to do good and to love God but we sometimes or often fail to act on this deep desire. God is patient with our half-heartedness and failures. If God is patient with us, we are to be patient with ourselves and with others. If we want our relationship with God to be strong, then we must be like Jeremiah and pour out our negative feelings to God, our doubts and even our suspicions that God is deceiving us.

Conclusion

In this chapter, we began with some examples from films of people who are genuinely good in their intentions but are ambiguous in the decisions they make and in their relations with others and their commitments to these others. We said that this ambiguity covers practically the whole of human attitudes and behaviour. We then went on to see how this ambiguity occurs in our relationship with the Mystery or God when we genuinely try to grow in our relationship with God. We are sometimes depressed by the ambiguity in ourselves and especially in the world at large, especially when this ambiguity takes the form of genuine injustice, cruelty and oppression of others.

At these times, it is good for us to remember that the deepest desire of the human heart is to love and be loved and that this desire will eventually prevail. We looked at how we can act against the resistance we discover in ourselves when God tries to get close to us. Finally, we took the example of Jeremiah to show that when our ambiguity takes the form of criticism of God and the sense that God is not being faithful to us, the best thing to do is to tell God honestly every suspicion and doubt we have of God. In this way, we can use the ambiguity in the relationship in order to grow in loving intimacy with this Mystery whom we also call God.

References

Barry, W. & Connolly, W. J., *The Practice of Spiritual Direction*, New York: Harper and Row, 1982.

Hopkins, Gerard Manley, *God's Grandeur and Other Poems*, New York: Dover Publications, 1995.

Rolheiser, Ronald, *Forgotten Among the Lilies: Learning to Love Beyond Our Fears*, New York: Doubleday, 2005.

St John of the Cross, *The Collected Works of St John of the Cross*, Trans. Kieran Kavanaugh, O.C.D. and Otilio Rodriguez, O.C.D., Washington, D.C.: ICS Publications 1991.

St. Teresa of Avila, *Life*, in *The Collected Works of Teresa of Avila*, trans. Kieran Kavanaugh and Otilio Rodriguez, Vol.1, Washington, D.C.: Institute of Carmelite Studies, 1976.

May, G. (1991) *The Awakened Heart: Living Beyond Addiction*, New York: Harper Collins.

Thich Nhat Hanh, *The Heart of the Buddha's Teaching*, New York: Broadway Books, 1998.

Section 2
Stages in Spiritual & Psychological Growth

This section consists of two chapters that deal with the stages we go through in our life journey starting from birth and moving through to old age and death. We notice that there is a pattern of balance, moving to crisis and then to resolution of the crisis. In the crisis period, we do not know if we will ever get back to an even positive keel and whether can this be seen as a negative phase. But we find that we do get through the crisis and we feel not only a sense of balance but of elation and joy. We can call this the positive phase. Then the pattern starts again. The first chapter deals more with the psychological dimension of this personal growth while the second chapter deals with the spiritual dimension. The treatment of the spiritual dimension is derived mainly from the writings of St John of the Cross who emphasises the final stages of union on this journey and of the great delight that this gives us.

Chapter Four

Negative Aspects in the Stages of Life

ST AUGUSTINE TELLS US that our hearts are restless until they rest in God. St John of the Cross, in *The Ascent of Mount Carmel*, speaks constantly of the things we have to surrender in order to reach the top of the mountain. At the top of the mountain, however, we will still not have attained God because God is beyond everything we can understand, imagine or even experience. He says we can attain God only by faith; which means never attaining God fully in this life.

In this chapter, we will emphasise this sense of never arriving, of being satisfied with experiencing 'nothing' which is the way John saw our life journey of human beings. The 'nothing' of which John speaks expresses itself in various ways in our lives. Some of these ways are the letdown and the disturbance we feel when we are plunged into another challenge in life, and the disenchantment that comes when people and things are not the way we expect. We move through states of stability into transitions that throw us off balance where we wonder if we will ever get back to 'normal'. Another similar dynamic related to disenchantment is the way we idealise people and things, and then suffer the letdown of seeing that they cannot measure up to the unrealistic expectations we have of them.

In the next chapter, we will move to what John of the Cross says about these realities as they relate to our growth towards God as this growth happens in prayer since it is this aspect that he deals with. We see how, for John, the journey ends in union with God. We will study the nature of this union to see that it is still not the end.

The Movement from Satisfaction to Dissatisfaction

We move from satisfaction to dissatisfaction and from stability to instability. The baby is comfortable in the womb and then the baby goes through the crisis of birth. Eriksen details the stages of trust versus distrust in the first year of life followed by the crisis of autonomy versus shame and doubt of the first five years of life, and so on with his remaining stages. At each stage, the growing person reaches some degree of stability only to be destabilised by a new very critical challenge. The infant has been described as 'one big blooming buzzing confusion', completely secure and identified with the parent figure. Here the child has no responsibilities and is able to pay attention and be fascinated by the outside world. But then from the ages of 2 to 5 years, there is a crisis of stubbornness where the child strives to separate itself from this surrounding world. The dimension which Freud called the ego comes to the fore and the child is able to manage his/her life appropriate to her age.

In these stages, we can say that it is the spiritual dimension latent in the child which is striving to be released. This emergence of the spirit in the person goes on throughout the whole of the person's life. In childhood, it is the vital or bodily dimension which is dominant. But then in pre-adolescence at about 13 years, it is the functional dimension that becomes dominant.[25] The state of pre-adolescence is an abstractive way of being in the world.[26] The child withdraws from lived involvements and participation in the surrounding world. The child at this age shows a great ability for abstract thinking and for logical reasoning. The child now loves to debate and to find causes and explanations for why things are the way they are.

At the negative stage of adolescence, the movement through the stages of life takes a turn away from stability to often acute instability. In fact, the adolescent may not know if he can keep going. The pre-adolescent was bursting with vitality; she was enthusiastic, adventurous and a loyal member of her group. Now all this comes to a sudden end. She withdraws from her group; becomes bored, indifferent and lonely. She moves around the house in an aimless fashion with nothing to look forward to. The adolescent may say, 'I don't want to be by myself, and sure as hell don't want to be with anyone else'. The language of the adolescent is negative: 'Nothing ever happens around here'; 'Nobody loves me'; 'Shut

---

[25] In many of his books, Adrian van Kaam speaks of the three dimensions of the person: vital, functional and spiritual. See *Human Formation*, New York: Crossroad 1985.

[26] I am using here material from Bernard Boelen, *Personal Maturity: The Existential Dimension*, New York: The Seabury Press, 1978.

up'; 'Drop dead'; 'I don't care'. The adolescent suspects others of being 'phoney', is ruthlessly critical of older people, enjoys criticising and breaking the rules.[27]

After a period of stability in our twenties, we move into the age 30 transition.[28] For the first time we realise there are limits to what we can do. We thought we could stay up all night to finish an essay or enjoy ourselves at a party. We thought that we were going to rise through the ranks of our profession to the very top. Now it begins to dawn on us that these expectations were not realistic. In our thirties, we come up against the limits of our physical energy. We thought we could keep going at the same rate we did in our twenties, but now we find we get tired. We think that we are being taken for granted. At this point, the challenge is to move to a deeper, more spiritual part of ourselves and to accept that our physical energy is limited. Questions may arise: what am I doing all this for? For how long will I be able to do it?

At mid-life, usually put at about forty-five, we really start to feel our limits. Commitments that were exciting now seem a drag. The commitments may be not just to work but to family and other relationships. Men may wonder what has happened that women no longer seem as attracted to them as they used to be. In the novel, *So Long a Letter*, by the Senegalese writer, Mariama Ba, the father of the female narrator starts giving his attention and lavishing his gifts on his daughter's girlfriend. This satisfies him for a time but he quickly finds

---

[27] Some of these adolescent expressions come from J. D. Salinger, *The Catcher in the Rye*, and are used by Boelen.

[28] Levinson, Daniel, *Seasons of a Man's Life*, New York: Random House 1986

that he cannot satisfy her. He cannot fit into the trousers he had; he does not have the energy to go out with her. His advances to the young woman naturally alienates his wife and his daughter until eventually the marriage breaks up, causing great suffering to the wife and daughter as well as to himself.

Even if we do not have any major breakdown in our relationships at this time of midlife, and even if we have been successful in our profession, we still feel unsatisfied. We wonder whether the fulfillment of our dreams is just a myth. We may begin to realise that we are not meant to be fulfilled. We ask: has our life really mattered to anyone? In our professional lives, we see others 'in favour'; they are now chosen ahead of us to hold the positions of importance that we thought we were entitled to. We seem to have been 'passed over'. Writers, for example, quickly go out of favour. Our success now doesn't seem like success. We think to ourselves: so what? What have we been 'busting' ourselves for? This sense of dissatisfaction often comes long before midlife. At 19, Boris Becker won Wimbledon. He was initially thrilled but then questions began coming to him: What else is there for me to achieve? Fame, holding positions of authority, writing books, amassing money, none of this satisfies us.

Unfinished business now has to be dealt with. Our lack of commitment in relationships becomes more apparent to us. Men recognise that they have difficulties in self-disclosure in relationships. They realise how shallow most of their relationships are.[29] Now it becomes more obvious that we

---

[29] McClone, Kevin, P., *'Male Intimacy'*, *Human Development*, 23.1, 2002, 5-11.

have avoided responsibility all our life. We can't avoid facing up to this problem because it starts to prevent us from coping and functioning. This 'unfinished business' may be much more obvious to others. Sometimes, we manage to continue to function effectively even into our sixties and seventies but it may be at great personal cost. We may be afraid that we are not on the right course.

If we're not on the right course, there seems little time to find out. People at midlife question the career they are in, the relationships they are committed to. Is teaching what I am I really called to do? Is this man the one I should be married to?

At physical level, this is the time where a person may discover he/she has high blood pressure. He may have a heart attack or a stroke. Our moral faults are more apparent (what John Shea call our 'moral bankruptcy'): our greed, lack of discipline, lack of social responsibility, unresolved anger and resentment. Any or all of these faults may come to the fore and we start to realise we'll never really be free of them. The person at this stage may panic: What can I do? What am I good at? Do I have the energy to keep going in the job I am in? What will get me through the rest of my life?

Triggers to awakening of faith in adult life

Sue Delaney examined what happens to women's faith at this midlife point.[30] She studied women who found that they had

---

[30] Delaney, Sue, 'Women Beginning a Spiritual Quest', *The Way*, Vol. 44, 1 (2005), 33-44, and 'Women in Search of a Way', *The Way*, Vol. 49, 4 (2010), 41-54.

reached a crisis such as those we have described. The person may be disillusioned by society's values. The atmosphere or surroundings were often not encouraging them to ask deeper questions about their lives but they still wanted to move into this unknown area. Many had inherited religious traditions that did not speak to them. churches they belonged to did not encourage questions but they still asked them. Events that triggered these responses were the following:

1. Death of husband. The wife wondered what happened to her husband when he died. Where did he go?

2. Ill health.

3. A young French woman, Liselle, became interested in Indian religion and in the teaching of a certain monk; she became his follower.

4. An unexpected spiritual experience: a dream or 'abnormal' experience such as hearing a 'voice'.

5. Disillusionment at mid-life. One woman, Rosemary Hamilton at 48 years felt at the peak of her career. She had fulfilled all her goals of marriage, professional life, success. Now she felt a yearning for something more.

Rohr mentions the four stages of life referred to in Hinduism: the student, the householder, the forest dweller and the beggar.[31] The student corresponds to adolescence and young adulthood, the second to the stage where the person

---

[31] Richard Rohr, *Internet Daily Meditations*, 15 August 2018.

makes his mark in the world. In the final two stages, the person moves away from frantic busy-ness and spends time alone in the forest. Being a forest dweller takes time and there will probably be not many fruits for some time. Western culture shrinks away from this task. Westerners feel decidedly uncomfortable to move into this more passive attitude. Finally, the forest dweller becomes the beggar, someone who seems foolish to those in earlier stages of life. It is necessary to go into this form of asceticism in order to become more enlightened and less dependent on success, popularity, our own efforts and abilities.

In this sketch of the stages of life, we see the pattern of engagement followed by a time of withdrawal, emptiness, incompleteness and even nothingness. The negative phase, however, is one of great possibility in spite of the pain. It is a special time when we can be responsive to the Mystery. By accepting what is happening, love can break out in new ways that weren't possible beforehand. We can become generative for others. We may start realising that our love is needed and precious. Now we can minister to others in a new way by being with and accepting them rather than doing something for them.

Our motivations can mature. We can give up power, prestige and relevance a little more. There can be a great purification of our motives if we accept the negative phase. We might continue doing the same things but we now do them for different motives and in a different way. We are more able to look, at least a little, at the possibility of death and accept that there is a positive side to getting older. Our society doesn't see this positive side. We can come to a new self-acceptance and peace.

Until now, in this chapter, we have not tried to look at how the Mystery has been operating in these stages. But we know it is God who has been working and we can say that if it is God, then the result is going to be one of constant surprise and even pain. We know that we would not have planned these painful experiences of nothingness for ourselves. If it had been up to us, we would have gone from strength to strength and from fulfilment to fulfilment. But we have come up against Mystery, the Mystery which directs our lives and takes us along paths that we cannot understand.

At these greater depths, comfort and sensuality can become more integrated into the rest of our lives. Our pleasure can be transformed into joy and become more something shared with others. The way we move out of 'nothingness' is by letting be, that is, letting ourselves and all others to be the way the Mystery allows us to be. We start loving this Mystery which is guiding us. Above all, we know that the Mystery is in charge and demands surrender on our part.

We will look now at one more dynamic that fits this pattern, namely, experiences of fascination and enchantment followed by disenchantment.

The Experience of Disenchantment

In Patrick White's novel, *The Eye of the Storm*, Sister Flora Manhood, who is one of the three nurses of the chief character Elizabeth Hunter, and a young woman with a sensuality that attracts men, decides to go to Basil Hunter, the son of Elizabeth, to try to persuade him not to put his mother into a nursing home. She waits at the reception of the hotel where he is staying and when she meets him, finds herself immediately the object of his attentions. He is beside her on the same couch after giving her a drink and soon she is responding to his sexual advances. At first, she is absorbed in the sexual passion involved. But after waking during the night beside him, she discovers that the excitement has gone and all she wants is to get out of the room.

As she leaves, she wonders if she will be pregnant with his child. She returns home, eats a big breakfast and sleeps late. As a result, she finds she has to rush to get to her shift of nursing Elizabeth Hunter. She is worried that Mrs Hunter, with her sixth sense, will guess or discover what has happened. By the end of the day she is sure that she has conceived, and the delights of the sexual encounter have so evaporated that she finds herself disillusioned and miserable. She speaks to one of the other nurses, Mary de Santis, when the latter comes to relieve her. She believes Mary to be a good woman but, as a result of Basil Hunter's advances to her, Flora is now finding herself questioning even Mary's virtue. As she leaves the house, she wonders whether there is any goodness left in the world:

> When there was nobody left to respect, neither Sister de Santis, nor Mrs Hunter... certainly not Sir Basil Hunter, the Great Actor, she must concentrate on this child who had, perhaps, been planted in her and whom she would love with all the love and strength she could raise. But who was there for her boy to love and respect?[32]

---

[32] Patrick White, *The Eye of the Storm*, Melbourne: Penguin, 321.

Flora has been profoundly shocked by Basil Hunter's behaviour towards her. She believed that someone of his social standing would not take advantage of her in this way. As a result, her whole trust in life has been threatened. As the novel proceeds, we realise just how profoundly disenchanted she is. Flora has discovered weakness and even evil in another person whom she somehow thought was above such evil. Basil Hunter has failed to live up her expectations of him.

This sort of disenchantment always surprises us. Another person, on whom we were relying in some way, fails to live up to our opinion of him or her. In being disenchanted we discover not only the weakness of another but also their otherness. They are not what we thought they were. In many cases, others do have a responsibility not to scandalise us, especially if they are older than we are, or if we are in some way in a vulnerable position. But it is also an enlightening thing to be confronted with the otherness of the other even when they have no particular responsibility towards us.

As children, we are challenged to see others as different from ourselves. We wish to hold on to the sense of fusion with the other. It is a wrench to discover that we are different from them and they from us. It brings us up with a start and we discover that we have to leave the comfortable place of being one with others. Our initial experience of life is of being united with our mother. We enjoy this union and later on in life we have a hankering to return to this almost paradisal oneness with all others represented as they are by our mother. When people act differently from what we expect, we feel ourselves being torn away from that paradisal bliss.

Men put women on pedestals and expect from them behaviour that is not compatible with the real limitations of human beings who happen to be women. Consider the following example. A man sees a woman as being a wonderful person. She has the gentle qualities he seldom sees in others. When he asks her, however, in what he considers a reasonable way, why she was unable to be present at a meeting, she looks at him in an aggressive way and tells him that she is not going to wait around all morning when the time of the meeting is changed. Her reaction, when he reflects on it, is disproportionate to the request he has made of her. He is taken aback and for a while finds himself alienated from young women who seem to him to be human beings so different from himself that it is impossible to relate with them. He cannot reconcile this behaviour with what he has internalised as appropriate feminine behaviour.

This tendency to idealism occurs also in the realm of the family. Some families are obviously dysfunctional, causing problems for children that are well-nigh insuperable. Other families appear from the outside to be places where everything goes well, where parents never quarrel and where children grow up well-adjusted and free of scarring. I am beginning to believe now, however, that such families do not exist. One may be at first dismayed by the apparent bitterness of Alice Miller's portrayal of families in *The Drama of the Gifted Child*.[33] Miller says that enormous cruelty and malformation took place in the families of the children she studied. But the more one learns about what actually happens

---

[33] Alice Miller, *The Drama of the Gifted Child*, Basic Books, 1996.

in families, the more one comes around to thinking that she is not exaggerating. An apparently ideal Catholic family of eleven children turns out to have been a place where the father made life hell for his long-suffering wife and his many children through his use of physical violence. Such knowledge came out when one of the boys in the family displayed erratic behaviour in his teen years. We know now that the incidence of sexual abuse of children in families is far greater than anyone imagined.

A man in his early sixties comes to church each Sunday. He is a 'pillar' of the church and, to an onlooker, someone who has brought up a family without great difficulty. He is often seen with his teenage daughter. An onlooker would think that here is a man whose life has unfolded without great stress. The only slight discrepancy to this picture is the man's chin, which juts out a little too defiantly. The truth of the matter is that he is a lonely and needy man, possessive of his daughter, and never really accepting of his wife's death several years earlier. A young mother or father appears self-assured and sophisticated. I may feel at first overawed by the apparent balance of this person, until I realise I am seeing them through the eyes of a young boy looking at his own mother as a young woman. To a boy, one's mother seems powerful and peaceful because he sees through the eyes of his own dependency. Then I switch to seeing that young man or woman through the eyes of the mature age male adult that I am and I see that their situation is not what I imagine. I realise that this apparently well-integrated and poised person has endured a childhood full of faults and difficulties. I am pulled up with a jolt and wrenched out of my idealistic attitudes towards women when I remember that one in four or five women have been sexually abused as children.

There is a film by the Spanish director, Carlos Saura, where the main character, a middle-aged balding man suddenly, almost in mid-scene, is transposed into himself as a boy. Through this device the director is able to show how much the man's perceptions are influenced by the boy who remains in him. It is the boy in the man who idealises young women and who wants to see all families as havens of security and belonging because of his own needs for these realities. In David Malouf's epic, *Harland's Half Acre*,[34] we gradually realise that Malouf's aim is to dethrone the father gradually in the eyes of his readers. As the sons get older their father becomes a very imperfect man whose relationship with them becomes more self-interested rather than nurturing and protecting.

Perhaps it is impossible for sons to move away fully from idealising their mothers.[35] For a son, a mother is more than simply another human being. She symbolises in herself the very goodness of life. Children do not question the goodness of their mothers. Hence when the boy grows to adulthood, he may never shake off completely this image of his mother as somehow embodying life. Certainly, he may find himself looking after his mother as she looked after him as a child. Yet, it will take a great deal for him ever to see her as merely another human being.

This view of what is real and good seems to be what Robert Bly has of his father in his poem, 'My Father at Eighty-

---

[34] David Malouf, *Harland's Half Acre*.
[35] Besides idealising, we can also demonise our mothers.

Five'. It is evident from the poem that Bly has demonised rather than idolised his father up to this point. Now that his father is dying, his prejudices and dislikes fade and he sees his father as an eccentric, impatient, annoying, but lovable man:

> My arm on the bedrail
> Rests there, relaxed,
> With new love. All
> I know of the troubadours
> I bring to this bed.
> I do not want
> Or need to be shamed
> By him any longer.
> The general of shame
> Has discharged
> Him, and left him
> In this small provincial
> Egyptian town.
> If I do not wish
> To shame him, then
> Why not love him?[36]

At his bedside, Bly regrets that he has never really appreciated his father during his life and hence has never expressed the love that his father would surely have appreciated. Now he finds himself wanting to speak on behalf of his father who wasn't himself trained or able to articulate the pain and love inside him.

---

[36] Robert Bly, *Common Ground*.

This meeting with the real rather than the ideal can happen every time we negotiate a transition in our lives. In transitions, we move from what is no longer a realistic view of some aspect of our lives to one that is at least more realistic. We are constantly moving, unless we are going backwards, from an unconscious or taken-for-granted attitude towards a conscious one. In this way, we can say that we are constantly moving out of the unconsciousness of childhood with its sense of vital communion with others. This move makes us feel uncomfortable but it is the only way to keep growing in our own individuality. Perhaps we are in danger of falling back into the comfortable infantile unconscious and will do so unless we are courageous enough to keep accepting and moving towards what is real.

The experience of disenchantment, that is, the moving from an ideal image of others to a real one, is necessary in our spiritual unfolding. It moves us from a pre-personal, unconscious stance to one where we can personally choose to love others for who they are. Our love for others then becomes real although we may think at first that we are losing the very capacity to love. Our love for others deepens because we see them now in their struggle.

To this point, we have discussed the need for reversals or what we can call experiences of nothingness, during the stages of life, from the point of view of philosophy and the social sciences. In the next chapter, we will look at the same reality from the point of view of our progress in faith.

References

Barry, William, *With An Everlasting love: Developing an Intimate Relationship with God*, New York: Paulist Press, 1999.

Bly, Robert, *Common Ground*, Dacotah Territory Press.

Boelen, Bernard, *Existential Thinking*. New York: Herder and Herder. 1971.

_____, *Personal Maturity: The Existential Dimension*. New York: The Seabury Press, 1978.

Delaney, Sue, 'Women Beginning a Spiritual Quest', *The Way*, Vol. 44, 1 (2005), 33-44, and 'Women in Search of a Way', *The Way*, Vol. 49, 4 (2010), 41-54.

Malouf, David, *Harland's Half Acre*, Melbourne: Penguin, 1985.

May, Gerald G., *Addiction and Grace*. San Francisco: Harper and Row, 1988.

Miller, Alice, *The Drama of the Gifted Child*, Basic Books, 1996.

Rohr, Richard, *Internet Daily Meditations*, 15 August 2018.

White, Patrick, *The Eye of the Storm*, Melbourne: Penguin, 321.

Chapter Five

Positive Aspects in our Growth in Faith

ST JOHN OF THE CROSS speaks of the importance of the dark night in our spiritual journey. Iain Matthew in *The Impact of God* comments on St John's dark night not so much from the point of view of prayer but from that of our experiences. He translates what John says about changes in our prayer as we go into the night into what happens in our experience outside of prayer.[37]

Night is the time when consolation goes. It contains the sense of disenchantment, disillusion, emptiness and helplessness that we have already examined. But John does not see the night as unattractive. In fact, he is very attracted to it. It is the place where we encounter God. It is true that night indicates struggle. It is a state of tension between struggle and encounter with the Beloved. What enthuses John is the purpose of the night but also the journey itself through the night. The paradox is that in the struggle, we

---

[37] In this next section, I am borrowing from *The Impact of God*, chapters 9 to 14. See also, Matthew, *John of the Cross: Seasons of Prayer*.

experience the urgent desire to go further. The night leads us into contemplation, which is a deeper form of union with God.

Difficulties and struggles which often seem meaningless actually lead us on our journey to God. They are a part of that journey. The darkness is a necessary part of the healing process we are going through. We have the feeling of being out of our depth but God is actually flowing into us. This idea of the inflow of God in night is a key one in our growth in prayer. We are 'being widened or expanded'[38] and this is painful. It is taking us beyond the comfortable and familiar. An example of this would be going into a new culture where we are ignored or where we think things are being done wrongly. We leave one place where we have authority and find ourselves somewhere else where all our power and control is taken from us.

We are actually being changed because God is giving himself to us. John's teaching on the dark night incorporates all our feelings of inadequacy and failure and inferiority. It is addressed to those who are treated unjustly and have power taken from them. This night takes us into the suffering of others and of the world.

Let us look at experiences of the night as they happen to us before we take them to prayer. These experiences are the action of God leading us further on the journey to our final goal, but on the surface they may look very mundane and down to earth. Here are a few:

---

[38] Matthew, *The Impact of God*, chapter 9.

- Working with someone or dealing with someone whom you think or know is not being truthful in what they say (e.g. a wife falsely claims her husband has been cruel to her because she is in love with someone else).

- When we think someone is being unfair in a relationship.

- When someone is holding a grudge against us and is being very cool to us and won't admit it.

- When we face some limitation in ourselves which we have been denying for a long time but now the truth comes home to us e.g. we have been hypocritical or self-righteous; we have been blaming others but now we realise that the fault was ours e.g. impatience which puts others off and isolates us.

- When we believe or know we are right on a particular matter but others deny the truth and disregard us.

- We discover we have a sexual addiction or some other form of addiction.

- We discover that others are isolating us or do not like us.

These experiences are negative and painful but John tells us we can be encouraged by the thought that God is doing something in us and that we are growing. They are happenings which we mostly do not choose. They may even involve situations which are morally wrong. This does not matter as long as we do our best to work against them. One thing they have in common is that we have little or no control over them. John sees these negative experiences as a great adventure. When our confidence or something else we rely on is taken from us, we can then see our need for God. God then becomes significant.

Here are some further experiences of night:

- Others seem to be able to do things much more easily than us and their efforts are appreciated but our efforts don't seem to be appreciated.

- a younger person comes along and everyone starts talking about him while we are ignored.

- a young woman/man to whom I am attracted takes no interest in me.

When these things happen, God can come to us. God can start having an important place in our life. Before this we did not have any place for God.

This experience of night can be a romantic, enchanting, thrilling experience; like going to a secret rendezvous with a lover. In the text of John's poem, 'The Dark Night of the Soul' which follows, we see this romantic, thrilling dimension:

> 1. One dark night,
> fired with love's urgent longings
> – ah, the sheer grace! –
> I went out unseen,
> my house being now all stilled.
>
> 2. In darkness, and secure,
> by the secret ladder, disguised,

– ah, the sheer grace! –
in darkness and concealment,
my house being now all stilled.

3. On that glad night,
in secret, for no one saw me,
nor did I look at anything,
with no other light or guide
than the one that burned in my heart.

4. This guided me
more surely than the light of noon
to where he was awaiting me
– him I knew so well –
there in a place where no one appeared.

5. O guiding night!
O night more lovely than the dawn!
O night that has united
the Lover with his beloved,
transforming the beloved in her Lover.

6. Upon my flowering breast
which I kept wholly for him alone,
there he lay sleeping,
and I caressing him
there in a breeze from the fanning cedars.

7. When the breeze blew from the turret,
as I parted his hair,
it wounded my neck
with its gentle hand,
suspending all my senses.

8. I abandoned and forgot myself,
laying my face on my Beloved;
all things ceased; I went out from myself,
leaving my cares
forgotten among the lilies.

We see here the intensity of John's feelings about this journey to God through the night. There is no mention of pain and suffering but of the deep union of two lovers. The words of the poem invite us into deep and loving prayer with our Lover who is God who has led us without our knowledge. The soul, as John calls the person, places herself totally into her lover's care and follows unquestioningly. There is no mention of suffering and pain, no self-pity.

When we read the poem and know that it is the basis of John's thinking, we can read the commentary on it in the spirit of joy that John intends. The poem and the commentary fill us with a deep love of God. Rather than feeling weighed down by our sufferings, we now see the reason for these sufferings. John's treatment of the dark night is a deeply encouraging vision of the joys and pains we all experience in life. It puts a new meaning on our failings, our disappointments, our failures and other negative experiences which normally lead us into desolation, that is the sense of being separated from God.

In *The Ascent of Mount Carmel*,[39] John says that 'the mortification of the appetites' is necessary. We must rid ourselves of all possessions as we have been taught by Jesus

---

[39] *Ascent of Mount Carmel*, Book 1:5.

(Luke 14:33). We must 'raise our attitudes above childish things'. John insists we have to make the effort. We need 'an habitual effort'. John speaks of three tasks that must be accomplished:[40] we 'must cast out strange gods, all alien affections and attachments; we must purify ourselves of the residue; and finally, our garments must be changed, that is, we must be clothed in a new understanding of God. This last task is what God will do for us'.

We see from the previous paragraph that John's language and presentation can sound technical; it needs to be applied to our own experiences. John's context is prayer but the same tasks apply also in our lives. We may not often talk about how we grow in prayer, but we often try to formulate how we grow psychologically and spiritually in the daily interactions of our lives. John becomes somewhat more concrete in a later chapter of *The Ascent*. He says we must be inclined not to the easiest but to the most difficult; not to the most delightful but to the most distasteful.[41]

Recently, I had some time at breakfast with a female visitor who was visiting our community. She spoke about a Polish woman who was a teacher. The Polish lady was completing a Ph.D., hoping that she would get a higher position as a secondary school teacher. Our visitor said that the work for the Ph.D. was of no practical use and did not help the Polish lady be a more effective teacher. Secondly, there was no hope that she would get a better position in the school where she taught because those filling senior positions would

---

[40] *Ascent*, Book 1:7.
[41] *The Ascent of Mount Carmel*, 1:13:6.

not leave any for her. What struck me was how our visitor had already decided that the studies of her friend were of no use and that the school staff would not help her improve her position. The conversation told me that our visitor was closed to any new possibilities because her opinions had become so solidified that she could see no new possibilities. She was not inclining to 'the most difficult' or 'the most distasteful' options. In fact, she was totally closed to these harder options.

Iain Matthew helps us to apply these teachings of St John of the Cross in our struggles to leave behind negative and unhelpful behaviours. In commenting on *The Ascent*, Matthew speaks of going beyond sympathy for ourselves. The first area we can look at is personal weakness. We have to stop taking the easy way out by ascribing blame for our difficulties onto others. If we let our anger burst out, for example, we are the ones who are responsible; if we experience shyness, it is not enough to look back at our childhood and lament the fact that we were given little opportunity to perform in public; if we are lustful, it is important to take the blame ourselves; if we are very dependent on a relationship, we have to admit this to ourselves and take small steps to become less dependent.

The second area is that of negative happenings. These negative happenings may be people insulting us, disregarding us, being better than us, or experiences of failure or rejection. Instead of feeling sorry for ourselves, we can try to accept these negative realities. We can work at being calmer, more outgoing, more chaste, less dependent. In fact, we have to do as much as we possibly can to overcome these limitations. We can take our negative feelings to the Lord and wrestle with them, telling God exactly how we feel about them. What we are not to do is to wallow in our feelings and pity ourselves that life has been so harsh to us. Instead we need to let go of the feelings and move on courageously.

John sees all these difficulties as the stuff of the dark night which God invites us into. These difficulties are the very materials which can strengthen us spiritually. Iain Matthew gives the following suggestions for the night which he thinks is in the spirit of John:[42]

- Decide to trust God. Trust that God knows where we are going though we do not.

- Look upon all the details of our lives, especially suffering, as the will of God for us. God knows and allows every little thing that happens to us.

- See everything as part of the providence of God. St John says that people who treat us badly are 'God's special workmen' because it is from these negative experiences that we grow. We do not grow much, if at all, when things go smoothly.

- Stay with the suffering since it is healing and brings great blessings for us.

- When we are burdened, remember that we are joined with God.[43] When we feel that we God is close to us, sufferings seem easy.

---

[42] *The Impact of God*, chapter 9.
[43] *The Impact of God*, chapter 9.

- Go through difficulties that test our patience since virtue and strength of soul will develop in us from these difficulties.

Going through the night greatly strengthens the relationship between God and us. Attachments to comfort, dependence on others, success, status, money, fall away. That is, if we keep at it. One quality that John emphasises is the ability to endure boredom and lack of sensible consolation. If we just stay in the presence of God in prayer without the assurance of any positive feelings or any other satisfactions, John says that God will take us eventually into deeper places of our selves. In John's time, people longed to have visions in their prayer and voices speaking to them. They wanted something tangible which would prove to them that God really was there. They were like the rich man in the parable who, when he died, asked Abraham to let him appear to his brother who was still alive to tell him to change his life. (Jesus' reply was that the brother already has enough signs.) In our day, we avoid more than anything else being alone and being bored. According to one philosopher, people today cannot endure silence. They demand to be continually entertained. Our culture demands that we be in a 'permanent ecstasy'.[44] For today's readers John's message is to stay in the silence and the boredom and, if you stay there, you will eventually experience God and you will be delighted.

---

[44] I am unable to locate the source of this expression.

John describes it in this way:

> It remains to be said, then, that even though this happy night... darkens the spirit, it does so only to impart light concerning all things, and even though it humbles a person and reveals his miseries, it does so only to exalt him; and even though it impoverishes and empties him of all possessions and natural affection, it does so only that he may reach out divinely to the enjoyment of all earthly and heavenly things, with a general freedom of spirit in all.[45]

Only One Thing

This quotation from *The Dark Night* tells us that the purpose of all our asceticism is to enable us to enjoy all the wonderful gifts that God has for us in the natural world and in all the people we meet. John tells us here that once our hearts are ready, we can enjoy everything. Going through the night enables us to open to God. Having been thus opened to the love of God, John, in *The Spiritual Canticle*, frequently refers to the longing we have in our heart to go beyond all God's gifts and to want only God who is our Beloved. This is a constant theme in *The Spiritual Canticle*. In Stanza Two of the Canticle, it is clear that the searcher wants only one thing, namely, to find her Beloved. The sheepfolds of the hills represent all the creatures of God, in this case, the angels. The soul asks of everything she meets news of God. This is a journey with just one thing in mind, namely, union with the Beloved. John

---

[45] *The Dark Night*, Book 2, Chapter 9:1

emphasises that at this stage we have to search for God. If we do not search for the Beloved, we will not find him. We have to go looking and follow up every lead we find. It is like when we want something. We want it but we then think of the effort it will take to get it. We will have to move out of our comfort zone and ask people for help who might not be very forthcoming with it. We have to swallow our pride and do the unpleasant thing and ask. John also says that, at this stage, 'we are sick, we suffer and we die'. That is, we are barely able to function because we are consumed with love for the one we are seeking.

In Stanza 2 John advises us to head for the mountains (virtues) and for watersides (mortifications). We will practise the virtues and we will do any mortification that is necessary. Here what is being emphasised is the longing for God that is driving us. It is a compelling force that gives us the energy to do everything that is necessary. We will make any sacrifice and think nothing of it. We put aside anything that may attract us for the sake of this big prize which is more important than anything else. All the other attractions are mere trinkets and 'rubbish'[46] that now mean nothing to us in comparison to being one with the Beloved. Think of this stanza of one of the hymns of the Hours:

> Alone with none but Thee, my God,
> I journey on my way.
> What need I fear when Thou art near,
> O King of night and day.

---

[46] Cf. Philippians 3:13-14.

Or the song of the St Louis Jesuits, based on one of the psalms:

> For you are my God,
> You alone are my joy,
> Defend me, O God.

Stanza Four of the Canticle continues with enquiries which the soul makes of 'woods and thickets', that is, of the natural elements, earth, water, air and fire. All of these elements are reminders of the Beloved since they have been left by him who made them. She even asks the heavens (the green meadow) of news of God. Even the heavens and heavenly things are not the Beloved and are not worth anything if we cannot be with the Beloved. We do not want the rewards of God or any other gifts of God but only God himself. We do not even want people who act as the messengers of God. We are at the stage where we leave people and the created world behind in the sense that we know that they in themselves are not what we ultimately want.

The soul knows that the Beloved has left all these traces of himself in the world. The image John uses is of the Beloved strewing all these things here and there as reminders of himself. If all these traces of the Beloved are so beautiful, what must the Beloved himself be like! The soul by this stage is distraught. She can hardly keep herself grounded on the earth. She does not know how she can keep living. Only one thing will satisfy her and that is the Beloved in the flesh.

The soul by this time wants no more messengers (Stanza Six). She asks the Beloved not to send her any more reminders of himself since they are only tormenting her. Earlier, she was happy to be with the reminders of the Beloved but no more. Stanza Seven says that all the reminders the Beloved is sending are wounding the soul more. They represent only 'stammering' compared with the reality of the presence of the Beloved himself. The soul complains that the Beloved is playing with her. He knows that she is in a terrible state and still will not come. The Beloved has stolen her heart but refuses to carry it off. The pace and urgency continues to build. John is trying to describe what is happening to the soul in this pursuit of God. It is a hectic, passionate experience. By Stanza 12 John has in his commentary:

> At this period, the soul feels that she is rushing toward God as rapidly as a falling stone when nearing its center. She also feels that she is like wax in which an impression, though being made, is not yet complete. She knows, too, that she is like a sketch of the first draft of a drawing and calls out to the one who did this sketch to finish the painting and image.[47]

These stanzas reach a climax in Stanza 13. The soul tells the Beloved to withdraw his eyes from her since she can bear it no longer. She tells him that she is 'taking flight', that is, that her soul is leaving her body. At first she thinks that her journey is ending and that she will possess her Beloved. The Beloved, however, replies, telling her that the journey is not over and that she is to return to her normal state. There is more territory to be crossed before the soul will be at rest.

Then we make quite a remarkable disclosure. We find that the Beloved too, is wounded in this love relationship. He is a

---

[47] *The Spiritual Canticle*, Stanza 12:1

'wounded stag'. I say the disclosure is remarkable because now the reader knows what this journey means not just to the soul but to the Beloved of the soul. There is just as much at stake for God as for the soul. This mutuality is something very precious. It tells us in clear terms that God really is very close and that God does love us and will not hold back in the relationship.

Psalm 62: An Example of Wanting Only One Thing

The heading for Psalm 62 in the *Jerusalem Bible* is 'Hope in God Alone'. This theme and the entire psalm fits very well with the theme of John which we have just treated of putting everything else aside and relying only on God. The psalm begins:

> In God alone there is rest for my soul,
> From him comes my safety;
> With him alone for my rock, my safety,
> My fortress I can never fail.

We, like the psalmist, can enjoy being alone because we remember that God is with us. We need nothing else. God is our rest. With God, our rock, our safety, our fortress, we are impregnable. This is the type of peace we feel when we believe God is with us and that God is looking after us. There is no power that can match the power of God. This gives us great confidence. He can face any danger, any challenge.

We are not talking to anyone. Instead, we are taking time to listen to the Spirit about what to do next. At this point, God is more attractive to us than anyone or anything else. We want to be alone to experience God's attractiveness and to fall under God's spell. We feel that in the silence God embraces us. We may be able to feel God's arms around us.

Kierkegaard speaks about being 'that individual'. He is attracted to the adventure of being alone with no one else. He claims that, in this way, we discover who we truly are. We are social creatures and experience God in our relationships and interactions with people. But before this, we are individuals and need to develop an interiority where we can be comfortably by ourselves and be aware of God in our depths. Kierkegaard lamented the loss of this interiority in his time and we can lament it even more in ours. We are not encouraged to spend time alone. We are afraid to turn off our earphones. It may feel unnatural for us today to be alone without music bursting into our ears or without looking up someone on our phones.

Kierkegaard's insight fits well with Psalm 62 which demands that we be alone. Like the writer of the book of Wisdom, he knew that we come into the world alone and depart from it alone.[48] If we want to accomplish anything with our lives, we have to make our own choices. Kierkegaard himself built a deep inner life when he realised that he was not being called to marry the woman he loved, Regine, and who loved him. After that came a very productive time of his life when he wrote books which would influence the direction of philosophy after him.

We need to stop distracting ourselves with merely everyday concerns, business, work, things that cause us to

---

[48] Cf. Wisdom 7:1-6.

lose focus and the sense of ourselves. At these times, we lose ourselves in our work. We need to withdraw and ask ourselves what we want to do with our lives and what is important for us.

Verse 5 of Psalm 62 says:

> Rest in God alone, my soul!
> He is the source of my hope.

Ultimately, we cannot rely on anyone else but God; not on our friends, not on experts and authorities. No one else except God can fulfil the longing in our hearts. There are many things that delight us. One is the enjoyment of relationships between men and women. A man can be enchanted by the beauty and charm of a woman, but that woman, like every woman or man, is only a weak human being. The attraction a man feels for the woman will weaken and leave him with the realisation that the woman cannot fulfil his hopes as he thought she could when he was under her spell. We cannot rely on our own abilities or our capacity for hard work or the prospects that work situations offer us.

The psalm continues:

> Ordinary men are only a puff of wind,
> Important men delusion;
> Put both on the scales and up they go,
> Lighter than a puff of wind (Psalm 62:9).

When we get some perspective on what is important, we find that the President of the United States or the Prime Minister of Australia are not as important as we thought. As the years go by, what seemed crucial proves to be of little importance. People's opinions, what they say, criticisms and grumbling, even opinions people give which may disturb are really nothing to be concerned about. In the play *Julius Caesar*, Mark Anthony is aware of this reality when he looks at the dead body of Caesar:

> O mighty Caesar! dost thou lie so low?
> Are all thy conquests, glories, triumphs, spoils,
> shrunk to such little measure?[49]

In contrast to when we are young, we realise, as we get older, that things do change but we are still constantly surprised when things are taken away from us. Mark Anthony had the insight to see that with his violent death Caesar's victories and glories suddenly meant nothing. Verse 3 of Psalm 62 speaks of deceit as the sole intention of the wicked. The tactic of the devil and of our own inner negative voices is to feed us lies and fears intent on harming us. But we realise when God is with us that what the devil tells us is trickery with no basis in reality. We can reject this voice and send the devil packing. Verse 7 says,

> Rest in God, my safety, my glory,
> The rock of my strength.

When everything else goes such as consolation and other good feelings, there is still abundant hope because God, to change the image, is our love, our Beloved. We can keep saying this, 'You are with me and you love me and I love you'.

---

[49] *Julius Caesar*, Act 3, Scene 1.

Union with the Beloved

We have looked at reversals in the stages of life, in our experiences of disenchantment, and have seen that in our journey to God we experience incompleteness. What does John say about what happens when we actually come to union with God? This is what authors of his time and earlier called the spiritual marriage. Up till this stage of union, it is the time of betrothal and preparation but now the soul is united to the Beloved. This represents a new stage in John's poem.

First, we have two stanzas (14 and 15) where the soul thinks lovingly of the beloved. The urgency and frenzy of the previous stanzas has gone. Now there is peace:

> My beloved, the mountains,
> And lonely wooded valleys,
> Strange islands,
> And resounding rivers,
> The whistling of love-stirring breezes.

> The tranquil night
> At the time of the rising dawn,
> Silent music,
> Sounding solitude,
> The supper that refreshes, and deepens love.

We sense that the soul is near or with the Beloved. She speaks lovingly of him and we can tell that she is at peace. But even now the Beloved is elusive. He is the mountains, that is, he is high and exalted. He is associated with strange islands. Why strange? It is because the soul has entered a new form of prayer. This new prayer is very satisfying but it is also mysterious. It is without words and cannot be turned on and off but is a gift from the Beloved. This is what happens when we enter more deeply into our relationship with God in prayer. We find that God becomes very wonderful and attractive but not someone we can understand.

Stanza 14 describes the new prayer. The night is now tranquil. The intensity has diminished and the light of dawn is appearing. John calls the prayer 'silent music' and 'sounding solitude'. It is music, something soothing and beautiful, but it is also silent! It is sounding with many resonances but it is also solitude. Again, we see that God is not to be fully owned by us. God is the beloved who loves us in the same passionate way that we love him, but God is also beyond us and other than us.

After the tranquility of Stanzas 14 and 15, the bride returns to being concerned with the distractions and temptations that can possibly disturb the tranquility. In other words, it is a fragile tranquility. The bride wants the foxes (the sensory appetites) caught since they can wreak havoc in the vineyard; the north wind (spiritual dryness and the affective absence of the Beloved) must also be stilled. The bride wants the south wind (the Holy Spirit) to come. The stanzas continue in this manner. The bride is experiencing the beloved but the experience can easily be upset by disturbances within ourselves from unruly appetites and desires.

In Stanzas 24 and 25 the bride is very hopeful and expectant of being totally united with the beloved. Finally, in Stanza 26 the bride experiences this union:

> In the inner wine cellar
> I drank of my Beloved, and when I went abroad
> Through all this valley
> I no longer knew anything,
> And lost the herd that I was following.

This experience of union is what the bride has been searching for earnestly. Now she experiences it. Now all the distractions, vices, appetites, allurements have no influence over her. She is safely free of them and can enjoy her Beloved. The bride now spends her time in acts of service for her Beloved. Her will and the will of the Beloved are one. Nothing else interests her. She savours this experience for as long as it lasts. In these stanzas, John is describing the peace that comes from the experience of union. But the intense ecstasy involved in the experience does not last. Life goes on but without the turmoil and frenzy of the period before union.

The Time After Union

After the experience of union, we might expect that we would experience unclouded joy. This is not the case. If we look at Mansion 7 of *The Interior Castle* of St Teresa, we find that all the ecstatic and extraordinary experiences she had in Mansions 5 and 6 subside. At first glance, we might think that these experiences leading to union, as we have seen them in *The Spiritual Canticle*, are what is really important in this journey to God. The reality, however, is that it is our fidelity in the normal experiences of our lives that is important more than the extraordinary experiences. Both John and Teresa warn against putting too much emphasis on extraordinary experiences. We will look now, with the help of the work of Thomas Keating[50] at the trials that continue even after union.

Keating believes that the dark night of the soul acts as a therapy for us. We let go of wanting to control our prayer and surrender to what God is doing in leading us to prayer beyond words and in letting God flow into us. In this new prayer of contemplation, we experience 'the redemption of Christ'. Keating explains that this does not mean going over our sins and making reparation for them, but letting God heal the wounds of our past so that we can open ourselves more fully to God's presence. We go into our depths and there we experience God. In these depths, the healing takes place often without our knowing it. A memory from the past comes into our minds. We let it be there and then let it go and, in the process, healing takes place. It is God who is doing the work and not us.

Distressing thoughts come in this way but they eventually pass and the frequency of their appearing begins to lessen. The healing can include our attitude to sin. Whereas before we were burdened by guilt, we now let the guilt go and begin to see ourselves as God sees us. Gradually, we move into the state of union. There are no great experiences but there is a quiet peace: 'The change manifests itself in the feeling that everything is okay even though we may feel awful'. This is the reality: at the surface we may be experiencing turmoil but more deeply within us we are at peace. St Thérèse of

---

[50] I am using here material from Thomas Keating, DVDs, Contemplative Outreach Ltd.

Lisieux tells us that this is what she experienced during the last months of her life.[51] At one level, she was experiencing darkness but more deeply she felt peace which she said was at the level of faith.

Keating, as well as John and Teresa of Avila, describes union as a state rather than as a one-off experience. After union we are different in spite of the continuing trials and sufferings. Keating says that the Holy Spirit grasps our will. We experience in our depths an attraction to God that is like perfume. We are attracted and our desire for God becomes stronger.

Another element of the journey remains after we reach the state of union, namely, the dark night, not of the body, but of the spirit. God is now working not through consolation but through faith. The grace of God is flowing into the person and the person knows it in some way. At another level there may be doubts about whether God even exists at all or whether God loves us or cares about us. We may have doubts about whether we love God or have done any good in our lives. The 'exuberant' mysticism which is so much of *The Spiritual Canticle* and of which St Theresa speaks in her fifth and sixth mansions, has disappeared.

This is the night of the spirit and this night purifies us of any reliance on people or on good feelings. We become freed of any delusions of ourselves as saints or heroes. Our concepts about God and how God is working in our lives and the lives of others is shattered. We now know that we know nothing about God. We accept God on God's own terms.

---

[51] St Thérèse, *The Last Conversations*.

To surrender to God on God's own terms means to stop idolising our images of God as we idolise our heroes. Every idea we have of God including our understanding of what it means to be loving and compassionate, has to be overthrown. It is not God who is being overthrown. Rather it is our false understandings of God that are falling.

This union with God is transformative. Keating gives the following effects of this transforming union:

- Our false self dies. Nothing now can turn us away from God's love.

- We feel empathy and concern for others but without emotional involvement. We are now free to be present to people at the deepest level.

- We have energy to serve God and the needs of others.

- New dimensions of reality are now revealed to us. We see God, others and the world at more profound depths.

- We go beyond the world without leaving it. That is, the concerns that we thought so important are now revealed for the actual importance they actually have rather than what we thought they had.

- We are able to recognise God's presence in every experience.

- We now serve without expecting a reward.

- We live in the present moment.

I will elaborate on just one of these effects of union with the Beloved, namely, that of being able to recognise God's presence in every experience. Before we reach this union, we have moments of grace where we are aware of God's presence. We practice living in the present moment and through this practice are struck by actually experiencing God's presence in some of these moments. Recently, I visited two aunts, one ninety-six and the other ninety-three after being away for more than two years. I had spoken to one of them a few times and sent letters. The aunts were anxious to see me and me them. In the visit, I had a very satisfying chat with the two of them together. There have been some negative feelings between one of these aunts and some of the members of my family. But in our conversation, there was no negativity. I had a sense that God was guiding our conversation. I then took one of the aunts out for coffee and again the meeting was a very happy experience for both of us. When I returned home, it struck me that something special can happen when people visit each other. It can be like the visit of Mary to Elizabeth where the two were aware of the child in the womb of Elizabeth and what was happening to both Mary and Elizabeth. The visits are different from the encounters we have with people with whom we live. They are special visitations of God.

I saw much similarity in this visit and one I later had when I visited my grand-nephew who was with his wife and their new born baby in hospital. The delivery of the baby had been without problems but after twenty-four hours, the baby suddenly lost consciousness. Several seizures followed which did some damage to the brain of the baby. I contacted my nephew, Nicholas, and arranged to visit them in the hospital. I knew that this meeting was important because it gave me an opportunity to be with my nephew (who was also my godchild) at this crucial time. I went to the hospital, talked first with Nicholas on his own and then with the wife and baby. Without going further, I knew that this visit was a time of grace for me and possibly for my nephew and his wife and child. If, after transforming experience, we perceive God's presence in every experience, then every experience is like these two I have described.

If we think further about where we might find the presence of God in ordinary experiences, we may find them even in encounters with people we meet momentarily such as someone who helps us choose glasses or who mends our shoes or helps us fasten our watch band. We can extend these examples to imagine how we might reach the stage which happens in union when we are aware of God's presence at every moment.

There is one further point that Keating makes to show that, even when we reach the summit of the Mount Carmel, we still find nothing. Keating says that divine union is not an experience but a permanent sense of God's presence. Then he says that union is 'the land of divine no-thing-ness where we do not hold on even to a sense of our own identity. Our identity at this point is to be what God wants us to be'. John of the Cross says that on the mountain we find nothing. Keating says that we lose the sense of our own identity. Either way, in the experience of union with God it is clear that God remains a mystery for us.

It is in this sense I think that John says that when we reach the top of Mt Carmel we will find nothing. He is emphasising the apophatic nature of God. When we have said, and experienced, everything we can about God, we still must say that God is as big a mystery as when we started on the journey towards union.

Conclusion

In this chapter, we have used the image of the dark night of St John of the Cross to show we have constantly to go through darkness to arrive at union with God. We have given examples of the dark night and seen how Psalm 62 insists that nothing except God will satisfy us. Thomas Keating's treatment of the night confirms that we never, in this present life, shrug off the dark night completely. Even when we reach the top of the mountain, still there is nothing, that is, our union with God remains incomplete.

References

Barry, William, *With An Everlasting love: Developing an Intimate Relationship with God*, New York: Paulist Press, 1999.

De Caussade, Jean-Pierre. *Abandonment to Divine Providence*, trans. John Beavers. Garden City, New York: Doubleday, 1975.

Keating, Thomas, *Invitation to Love: The Way of Christian Contemplation*, London: Bloomsbury, 2011.

———, *Divine Therapy and Addiction: Centering Prayer and the Twelve Steps*, 2008.

Kraft, William. *The Search for the Holy*. Philadelphia: Westminster Press, 1971. Direction, San Francisco: Harper and Row, 1982.

Malouf, David, *Harland's Half Acre*, Melbourne: Penguin, 1985.

Matthew, Iain, *The Impact of God*, London: Hodder and Stoughton, 1995.

———, *John of the Cross: Seasons of Prayer*, Oxford: Teresian Press, 2014.

May, Gerald G.,, *Will and Spirit: A Contemplative Psychology*. San Francisco: Harper and Row, 1982., *The Awakened Heart: Living Beyond Addiction*, New York: Harper Collins, 1991.

———, *Addiction and Grace*. San Francisco: Harper and Row, 1988. Otto, Rudolph. *The Idea of the Holy*, trans. John W. Harvey. London: Oxford University Press, 1950.

Rahner, Karl. *Foundations of Christian Faith*, trans. W. V. Dych. New York: The Seabury Press, 1978.

Rohr, Richard, *Internet Daily Meditations*, 15 August 2018.

van Kaam, Adrian, *Personality Fulfillment in the Spiritual Life*. Denville: Dimension Books, 1964.

———, *Fundamental Formation*, Volume One, New York: Crossroad Publishing 1983.

_____, *Religion and Personality*. Denville, N.J.: Dimension Books.

Welch, John, O.Carm., *When Gods Die: An Introduction to St. John of the Cross*, New Jersey: Paulist Press, 1990.

White, Patrick, *The Eye of the Storm*, Melbourne: Penguin.

St. Teresa of Avila, *Life*, in *The Collected Works of Teresa of Avila*, trans. Kieran Kavanaugh and Otilio Rodriguez, Vol.1, Washington, D.C.: Institute of Carmelite Studies, 1976.

St John of the Cross, *The Collected Works of St John of the Cross*, Trans. Kieran Kavanaugh, O.C.D. and Otilio Rodriguez, O.C.D., Washington, D.C.: ICS Publications 1991.

Section 3
Discerning the Way

This section opens with a chapter on developing what I call a contemplative attitude. This attitude is also called mindfulness or non-dualism and is the basis of discernment since it teaches us to put aside our assumptions at what we see before us and to see simply what is there. Such an attitude is the basis of discernment since it enables us to hear the Lord's voice speaking to us in everyday events. In this chapter on discernment and on others in this section, I give some lists and suggestions which invite the reader to consider the topic from many diverse angles and to see how the material relates to his/her own experiences. One of the chapters, 'The Wind Blows Where It Wills', shows how the Holy Spirit is working in the church today in ways that are leaving church leaders behind. Another chapter examines how a negative or 'nagging' spirit seeks to sow confusion and discouragement in our minds to prevent us from moving forward into new areas of life and growth.

Chapter Six

Developing a Contemplative Attitude

IN THE TALK which was part of a cardiac rehabilitation program I attended, the speaker, an occupational therapist, answered my question on mindfulness. The talk was on sleep and she said that mindfulness was a good way of relaxing and therefore of preparing for sleep and a good activity to help ourselves go back to sleep when we passed through one of the ninety-minute sleep cycles that happens each night as we sleep. She described mindfulness as forgetting about the future and also of putting aside the past and being present to just what is happening in this present moment. She gave an example of how our minds tend to go into automatic when we are doing something such as driving. We intend to take a turn to the butcher's shop to pick up meat for the evening meal on our way to work but when we get to the turn off for the butcher's, we find ourselves driving straight ahead. We do this out of habit. It seems that it would be easy to focus on what is happening in this moment but it is anything but.

As I listened to this explanation of mindfulness, it struck me that it is very similar to a type of thinking which people are rediscovering at the present time, namely, non-dual or contemplative thinking.[52] In contemplative thinking, as in mindfulness, we are simply in the present moment just noticing what is going on without making any judgments about what is right or wrong or what is better or worse. Things that happen come into our mind and we do not try to sort out who was right in what happened. We do not judge our own or others' thoughts; we do not judge whether we have done better than someone else or whether we or they are right. As in mindfulness, we try to be totally present to what is happening now. If our mind is distracted, we simply come back to what is happening at this present moment. In this chapter, I will use the terms non-dual thinking, contemplative thinking and the contemplative attitude almost interchangeably.

Non-dualistic Thinking and Dualist thinking

We need to distinguish non-dual thinking from dualist thinking. In dualist thinking, we make distinctions between ourselves and others. We see ourselves over against them and this leads to comparing ourselves with them. One of the characteristics of dualist thinking is distinction or separation. I am separate from this other person. I think differently from her. This is the normal way we think because we see ourselves as little selves different from other little selves.

---

[52] Two authors who deal with non-dual or contemplative thinking are Bede Griffiths, *The River of Compassion*, and Richard Rohr in his daily meditations on internet and in *The Naked Now*.

In non-dual thinking, we see both ourselves and others not as separate but as part of something bigger. We are both part of a greater whole. We go beyond the differences to what is underneath. This practice empties us of our pre-conceived notions of what is good and what is bad. We just accept what is there. Everything is part of us and we are part of everything. We stop resisting and we simply accept ourselves and others. When we stop resisting the differences, much of our restlessness disappears.

Hindus use the term *advaita* to describe our relationship with God.[53] *Advaita* means not two but not one either. Romano Guardini describes it this way:

> Although I am not God, I am not other than God either. The direct intuitive realisation that although I am not God, I am not other than God either, fans out in all directions. Although I am not you, I am not other than you either. Although I am not the earth, I am not other than the earth either. As this soaks into me, what are the implications of this in the way I act in the world, in relationships with other people?[54]

We can speak of the large self and the small self. The large self is the deep self where we are all united with one another and with God. When we engage in non-dualist thinking, we are operating out of the large self. When we focus on how we are different from others, we are operating out of the small self. We can also call our small self the ego, or our sense of identity. In our ordinary activities, we do need to see ourselves

---

[53] Cf. Bede Griffiths, *The River of Compassion*.
[54] Romano Guardini quoted in Richard Rohr, *Internet*.

as different. We need to be able to manage our own lives. We need to have a strong sense of our small self; we need to have reasonably defined barriers between ourselves and others. If we do not establish these barriers, other people, who do not know their own barriers, can make unrealistic demands on us and confuse our sense of our own independence. We need a degree of independence from others as well as a reasonable degree of porosity between us and them. We need to think our own thoughts and notice how they are different from the thoughts of others. We have the desire to achieve and so we see ourselves in competition with others. We try to be better than them. Competition is necessary but it can quickly take over from our sense of mutuality between us and others.

From what I have said about the need for a strong sense of our small self or ego, it becomes clear that the development of the large self and of the ability not to compete and to allow many different positions to be present at the one time is not easy. It is something which the major religions encourage in us. We can call the capacity to act out of the large self the contemplative attitude (also called contemplative thinking and non-dual thinking). The following passage from Bede Griffiths shows that non-dual thinking requires much discipline and application:

> Get beyond the dualities – good and evil, right and wrong, pleasure and pain, gain and loss, and discover the Absolute, the Eternal, the One beyond everything, that Spirit that is in you, in everyone and in everything. That is the main theme of the Gita. In the older theory, the *sannyasi* gradually withdrew from action. He began by withdrawing from mundane activity and discovered the

Spirit within and then further withdrew until he became completely detached from everyone and everything and he withdrew finally from all action. The teaching of the Gita is to detach oneself... and then, in that freedom of the Spirit, we must be ready to do whatever is required of us.[55]

The whole of the *Bagavad Gita* on which Griffiths is drawing is on deals with developing this non-dual thinking. As Griffiths says, the goal is to discover the Absolute or what Christians call the Mystery of God. When we discover this Absolute, we become free from the attachments to being right or being comfortable or being the winner. We are evidently working now out of our larger self where we are at one with all. Ignatian spirituality in the Christian tradition in the same way emphasises how important it is for us to be detached from our own preferences in the context of making a decision. Both approaches speak of the attachments we have to the elements of the small self.

Experiences of the Contemplative Attitude

Certain experiences that we do not plan can bring take us into a contemplative attitude. Rohr says,

> Moments of great love and great suffering are often the first experiences of non-dual thinking. Practices of prayer largely maintain that many people first experience non-dual thinking in deep love and suffering.[56]

---

[55] The River of Compassion, 30.
[56] Richard Rohr, *Internet Daily Meditations*, 30 January 2017.

When we experience the loss of a loved one or have a heart attack we suddenly see things very differently. Our opinions no longer matter so much to us or the lecture we have to give or the plans we have for the future. What is important in that moment is, to take the first example, the loss of this beloved person or the fact that we ourselves have narrowly escaped death. When we have had an experience where our heart, for example, is involved, we can also become more patient and accepting of others as they are. (We can also say that most people as they get older become more accepting and patient.) I began this chapter by speaking of a talk on sleep given by an occupational therapist. The young woman who gave the talk was very wide around the hips. When she wrote on the board we had a good view of her from the back and I could not help think that in a classroom of adolescent boys there would have been titters of laughter. But in this class of people who had recently suffered heart attacks, it seemed that it was only myself who noticed that our presenter was overweight. All the group were interested in was what she was presenting and whether that material could help them sleep better. The fact that they were getting over heart attacks enabled them to overcome the dualities of a person being overweight or not.

Similarly, experiences of being loved, as Rohr says in the above quotation, can move us into a contemplative attitude. To give one example, I was participating at a workshop where the presenter asked us to think of a person whom we felt loved us and of the time when we particularly felt that love. I thought of a sister who had recently died of motor neuron disease. I had visited her just before she died and when I thought of her, I remembered how supportive she had been to me when she was my spiritual director for many years. I was overwhelmed by the sense of love that she had for me. Other things such as my responsibilities, my plans for the future, my failures in the past became very unimportant. When we read familiar poems which we love, when memories come to us where we were secure or cared for or appreciated and where we felt we belonged, we similarly experience a sense of being part of a larger whole and differences fade.[57]

The following quotation from Frederick Buechner indicates what happens when we move into a contemplative attitude. He writes:

> Stop trying to protect, to rescue, to judge, to manage the lives around you... remember that the lives of others are not your business. They are their business. They are God's business... even your own life is not just your business. It also is God's business. Leave it to God. It is an astonishing thought. It can become a life-transforming thought... unclench the fists of your spirit and take it easy... What deadens us most to God's presence within us, I think, is the inner dialogue that we are continuously engaged in with ourselves, the endless chatter of human thought. I suspect that there is nothing more crucial to true spiritual comfort... than being able from time to time to stop that chatter...[58]

---

[57] Recently I led a prayer which I titled 'All Things are Passing' which helped those present move to the deeper levels of themselves. I used two poems, one 'Sonnet to the Man Who Invented the Plastic Rose' and the other Walt Whitman's 'Out of the Cradle Endless Rocking'.

[58] Frederick Buechner, https://wwwgoodreads.com/author/quotes/19982.Frederick_Buechner

When we sit by the sea and let ourselves be soothed by the waves, we can find ourselves moving into a contemplative mood where all the conditionings of our brains to focus on what we have to do and what others think of us and how we have to reach excellence, fade.[59] We are just there judging nothing. We let go control and let ourselves be there in that present moment without having to do anything. This experience can just happen but we can also develop strategies that facilitate our moving into this contemplative mood. Gerald May advises us to practise the prayer of presence which he discovered through reading Brother Lawrence of the Resurrection.[60] The first thing to do is to stop trying to bring on this mood. Instead of doing something, we can form an intention of wanting to be in this mood. We can also remember times when we felt ourselves in love with a person or a thing. In these times our brain is not in control and our heart takes over. May quotes the line from *The Song of Songs* to illustrate this:

I sleep but my heart is awake (5:2).

This line sums up May's thought: that underlying all our activities, anxieties and endeavours is the desire to be loved. This desire comes to the surface in experiences such as the ones I have given. No matter how much we become addicted to activity, performance and other preoccupations of the small self, the desire to love and be loved remains and needs only to be reawakened.

---

[59] May, G. (1991) *The Awakened Heart: Living Beyond Addiction*, New York: Harper Collins.

[60] Br Lawrence of the Resurrection, *The Practice of the Presence of God.*

Another example of dualist thinking where we see ourselves over against others is described in this second quotation from Frederick Buechner:

> Of the Seven Deadly Sins, anger is possibly the most fun. To lick your wounds, to smack your lips over grievances long past, to roll over your tongue the prospect of bitter confrontations still to come, to savour to the last toothsome morsel both the pain you are given and the pain you are giving back – in many ways it is a feast fit for a king. The chief drawback is that what you are wolfing down is yourself. The skeleton at the feast is you.[61]

Buechner here highlights the destructive pleasure we gain from holding on to things that others have said or did at some time to us. We do get a smug pleasure from them by holding on to them and even nurturing them. But at a great expense. At these times, we are more or less consciously denying that we are part of the larger loving whole which is the hallmark of the contemplative attitude. We are going against the Holy Spirit and in the process our worldview shrivels and we isolate ourselves more and more from others. We commonly call this state hell. Instead, let us be magnanimous. We need to be aware of what is going on, that is, recognise the falseness and malice that is involved and then reject them in favour of life. The perverse pleasure will otherwise lead to our own spiritual death.

On the other hand, when we forgive people who have hurt us, consciously or unconsciously, we opt for life and for the

---

[61] Frederick Buechner, https://wwwgoodreads.com/author/quotes/19982.Frederick_Buechner

contemplative mode of thinking. Jesus realises that this act of forgiving is not easy for us and as a result, in the prayer he taught us, he links our forgiving others with God forgiving us: 'Forgive us our sins as we forgive those who sin against us' (Matthew 6:12). It is helpful for us to look back on our lives for times when we felt hurt. We can allow the hurt feelings to come back to us and talk about them to God. Then we can ask God to help us forgive that person or persons. Recently, an incident came to my mind from many years ago. It was when I submitted a manuscript to a publisher. An attractive young woman came to visit me and said that she was sure that my manuscript would be very interesting not just at an academic but at a popular level. This was when I had written only a couple of chapters for a small magazine on the topic. On the strength of the young woman's words I wrote the full manuscript of some 180 pages in the next seven or eight weeks. I submitted the manuscript and suggested a couple of people who might critique the manuscript for the publisher. A few weeks later I received a short note, not a visit, from the same young woman saying that she regretted that her firm would not publish the manuscript. This memory does not come to mind often but each time it does I find that there is a small residue of hurt that is still present that I need to acknowledge and then let go of, with God's help.

Moving to Non-dualist Thinking

Let us now look at several examples of dualistic thinking. The first couple are very fresh in my mind and may be very common to many of us. I went to have breakfast in the community dining room early. Someone was there having his breakfast. I noticed that he had not attempted to unload the part of the dishwasher that had gone through the cycle. I had my breakfast and later came back to find the same person there with a lot of uncleaned material on the counter where the clean dishes from the dishwasher had to be put. I decided to begin to empty the dishes anyway and another community member came in who helped me. Luckily in this instance the two of us did not say anything to the one who had made things inconvenient for us, but I had heard many sotto voce comments from others criticising those who offended in this way. Here is an example where non-dual thinking would help. We would not judge the person offending but at the same time remind him what he was doing in his own time.

The second very fresh example was when I was watching women's golf and then the final of a men's PGA Major. I found myself feeling very negatively to the women who were playing, thinking that they were very elitist and selfish. Later, I heard the winner of the Women's British Open being interviewed. She was asked how young girls could be introduced into playing golf. She said that the best way would be to make it fun for girls even when they were very young, help them see it as play rather than something serious, make the holes easy and limit the number of holes. As a result of the interview, I had to change my view of women golfers. My dualist thinking had been thoroughly exposed. With men golfer also, I thought to myself that these golfers were very privileged and also very egoistic. Then I heard the winner of one of the PGA Majors interviewed, and again I had to review my judgment. The winner, Brooks Koepke, was very modest and humble. It was clear that he was grateful that he had won and did not consider himself superior to others who did not have his golfing skills. Once again my dualist, separatist thinking had been unmasked!

Here are a few further scenarios inviting us to non-dualist thinking:

- We read a biography of a woman comedian which someone gives to us. In reading of her struggles and noticing her honesty and goodness in what she writes, our opinion of her changes.

- We are invited to a meal by our married friends. We have an enjoyable meal and conversation. Later, we are sad that these friends of ours will not enjoy this time of their retirement forever and that it could be taken away from them at any time.

- The priest celebrating the Mass is evidently dying. We are shocked to see his struggles to go through the actions and to get through the celebration. I think: why do we have to struggle like this and why does illness and death have to be part of life?

The first scenario is of misjudging someone. But the second and third scenarios are about our lack of acceptance of the passing of time. These may seem less reprehensible than those previously but nonetheless, they indicate thinking where we are making judgments about the way reality is rather than accepting reality as happens in non-dual or contemplative thinking. The following statement from

Bede Griffiths further explains the notion of non-dualistic as opposed to dual thinking:

> The aim (in non-dual thinking) is to see the one reality in every manifestation. One has to see God in everyone and everything and to recognise that the good is present in the midst of evil. That understanding, it is true, can be dangerous. Gold and stones are the same in one way. But one should also be able to discern the difference. God is speaking to us through everything and we have to discern the presence of God in every situation.[62]

The emphasis here is the importance of focusing on the larger reality of which we are a part. It is from this premise that the need arises to let go of the dualities of comfort and suffering, right and wrong, good and evil, success and failure. The focus on the one reality takes our attention away from the difficulties in trying to understand that we are first to refrain from making any judgments or distinctions.

We will look now at some examples of dualistic thinking which are described in more detail; and the false conclusions we can make from this thinking. The first concerns a retreat where the sister leading the retreat discovered a deeper reality beneath what appeared on the surface. The sister asked the participants, 'What colour is God for you?' No one offered a reply until eventually a middle-aged woman, who was a prostitute, responded. She said that, for her, God was green. This was because, after being out all night working, she would come home sometimes battered, sometimes treated badly, and would lie in the bed and look at the wall and remember

---

[62] *The River of Compassion*, 30.

the words of Psalm 23: 'He leads me by green pastures; he revives my soul; when I walk in the shadow of death he is with me'. When she remembered these words, she knew that God listened to her, loved her and cared for her.

When we hear this story, we may be moved to the point of tears. If so, well and good. But a more important point is whether we really think that God loves this woman who is a prostitute as much as this. Does God not care that she has been acting in an immoral way? When we can hear this story and not wonder how God can love her so much, we will know that it is the contemplative attitude that is motivating us.

Here is the second example and a personal one with some similarities to the previous example. It involves my conversation in the staff room with a fellow lecturer, Ojore, and two priests who were also lecturers. Ojore had been telling us of his research into the cultural practice of women who were dispossessed when their husband died. Her house would be taken from her by the family of the husband with little regard for her or for the children that she might still be responsible for. The late husband's brother may be prepared to enter into a marital relationship with her and care for her children and, as a result, the woman would re-take possession of the family's house and possessions. Ojore asked how we can know if the woman really loves the man or whether she is doing it for financial reasons. He said that some women are not sincere in these situations. In response, I said that prostitutes can be sincere and then go out on to the street to seek clients straight after praying to God. There was silence and then the three broke out into laughter. Then I explained that I had heard prostitutes pray sincerely like this but still act as prostitutes. They stopped laughing. The story shows that we judge others and consider ourselves superior. What about the attitude of Jesus to prostitutes? Do we really see this situation without creating dualities of who is right and who is wrong? This is the challenge.

In dualist thinking, we see each person only as an individual self, each separate from the other. As a result, we compare ourselves with the other selves. We become envious with what they can do that we cannot. We become jealous that someone we like likes another more than us. We think of ourselves as right and the other as wrong. For example, someone picked me up on referring to a book as a 'silly little book'. When I thought about this later, I realised that I was dismissing the views of the author of the book as of no worth. I thought I was superior in thinking of the matters discussed in the book than the thinking of the author, even though he had written a whole book to develop his points.

We may not say it but we think: my tribe is superior; my country is better. Alternatively, we may develop an inferiority complex, thinking that we are always inferior in our views and opinions and actions that the other.

Letting Go Control

In dualist thinking, we need to be in control while in non-dual thinking we do not have to be in control, and as a result, we shake off the burden that control puts upon us. We need to work at this issue of letting go control. An example comes readily to mind where I found myself being burdened by the need to prepare a prayer for the community which would be very creative and which would have an impact on those present. I played around with ideas for the new prayer and then tried to give definite shape to them. At this point, the thought came to me that I had to ensure that it really hit home to the participants. As a result, I began to feel burdened. I detected myself doing this and realised that I had to let go control of the prayer. I just had to do as much as I could in the preparation and leave the rest to God. The saying 'Let go and let God' is easily said but hard to do.

The idea of letting go control is closely related to faith in providence which is very prominent in the gospel of Matthew. Jesus says in Matthew that we are not to worry about clothes and food because our heavenly Father provides what we need (Matthew 6:25). In another place, Jesus reassures us that God has counted every hair on our heads. In the strange story of paying the Temple tax, Jesus tells Peter that God will give them the money they need to pay the tax. Jesus says,

> However, so that we do not give offence to them, go to the sea and cast a hook; take the first fish that comes up, and when you open its mouth, you will find a coin; take that and give it to them for you and me (Matthew 17:26).

The opportunity, or rather challenge, to have faith in God's providence comes to us continually in our lives: will what I am doing now bear fruit for others? Will I know what God wants me to do in a year's time? Will I be able to withstand the negative voices that often come strongly to me? What about the person who has told me that he wants to see me? I delayed in replying and now I wonder if that same person has lost interest in meeting me and it saddens me. In all these cases Jesus wants us to have faith that our heavenly Father will provide all we need and more.

Accepting Reality

In the Old Testament, the people grumbled that God had left them in the desert to die. In his dialogue with the Jews, John says, 'The Jews started to murmur in protest because Jesus claimed, 'I am the bread that came down from heaven' (John 6:41). Grumbling or murmuring is considered in the Old Testament as one of the major sins. We too complain when we lose faith in the larger self of which we are a part. We see ourselves as isolated and neglected even though we have chosen to rely on our little separate self. The contemplative attitude invites us to accept reality as it comes, believing that God is always looking after us. We are not to lose faith whether the experience we are presently feeling is comfortable or painful.

When we complain, we become unhappy and further isolate ourselves; when we accept what is there without judgment, we become peaceful. Here are a couple of examples where it is difficult to accept the reality facing us. I received a cheque from the Mill Hill Fathers for spiritual direction I had given to some of their students. I took the cheque to the bank and thought that the teller said to write my name in the payee line. It was wrong and I had to contact the Mill Hill Fathers and ask for another cheque. I knew it would be a long process and I was very resistant and I grumbled a lot. But when I accepted reality, the obstacles turned out to be blessings. I met Fr Jakob, one of the Mill Hill formators, who kindly brought cash in place of the cheque and who invited me to have coffee with him.

Another example was when the vehicle I was driving was hit in the back by another vehicle. The female driver of the vehicle which had hit mine said she would pay for damages and gave me her phone number. When I tried to phone her, however she hung up. I went to the police station with what details I had and the policeman said that it would be difficult to trace the owner of the other vehicle. I then went to the insurance and did all the things necessary to go through with the claim. I considered it an interruption and a great injustice. But I learned from this. Things came back to normal before long and my sense of being treated unjustly faded.

These difficulties can turn out to be blessings for us if we accept them. There is no need for us to impute blame on others. We can refrain from dualities and just accept what has happened.

When we accept what is there before us, we can receive insights: we can be open to the reality and wait for these insights to come. This happened when I was preparing some sessions for a group which was followed by a retreat for the same group. In preparing to do the task, we need to be receptive as well as active; then ways and means of accomplishing the task will eventually come.

We can accept our mistakes and failings in the past when they come into our awareness instead of browbeating ourselves: times when we blamed others for things going wrong; times when we refused to let others in our charge take responsibility for themselves; times when we were aggressive with others. In adopting a contemplative attitude, we can then accept these memories with tranquillity and self-forgiveness.

Benefits of Contemplative Thinking

Here in summary form are a few benefits of having a contemplative attitude:[63]

- We empty our minds of preconceived ideas and are thus more ready to receive the next experience of God.

- We face the paradox that everything just is, ourselves included.

- We find ourselves accepting more and more.

- We stop resisting new realities, new contexts, new beliefs, new people.

- We go to the depths of suffering and love and we accept it all.

- We live our lives from a place of non-judgment, forgiveness, love, quiet contentment with the ordinariness of our own lives.

So far, this chapter has tried to explain what a contemplative attitude is. We have ranged over the major elements of what is involved in the contemplative attitude. In the course of this discussion, I think it will have become clear

---

[63] Richard Rohr, *The Naked Now*.

to the reader that the contemplative attitude takes in many aspects of spirituality which we may already be aware of but under different names. For example, we all try to be non-judgmental, appreciative, humble, prayerful, compassionate. We try not to be envious, jealous, competitive, controlling, dominating, possessive. These are just some of the qualities we have discussed which we have shown are directly related to developing a contemplative attitude.

Finding A Detached Place within Oneself

The following list, also by Richard Rohr, gives some suggestions which move us towards developing this contemplative attitude. Rohr calls this list, 'Finding a Detached Place Within Oneself':

1. It must be without moral judgment, or you will tire of it.

2. It must be compassionate and calmly objective.

3. It names the moment for what it is.

4. It names my reaction without a need to praise or blame.

5. To see my reaction for what it is, it takes away this reaction's addictive and self-serving character.

6. It deflates my reaction and disempowers it from 'possessing' me.

7. Now I have a feeling instead of a feeling having me.

8. It maintains the good sense of 'I' but without ego attachment.

9. It actually fosters much deeper, broader, and more honest feelings.

10. It also gives me a strong sense of 'I' because there is now no need to totally eliminate or deny the negative part. (My full self is accepted.)

11. The truly destructive part of the negative is exposed and falls away as now unnecessary. To see the negative is to defeat it, for evil relies upon denial and disguise.

Here are the simple directives given by the promoters of centering prayer for those who wish to practise the contemplative attitude:[64]

- Sit quietly with your back reasonably straight so that for twenty minutes you will not have to move.

- Choose a symbol or word that names your intention to give your whole attention to the Mystery underlying all the thoughts and feelings going through you mind for this time. The word could be Love or Trust or God.

- If your mind wanders, gently bring your attention back to your symbol or word.

- Do this for the whole twenty minutes or for whatever time you have decided on. (The time could be as long as

---

[64] This list is given by Thomas Keating in many places in his books.

thirty minutes.) At the end of the time, you may move your body and finish by saying the Our Father either aloud or silently.

The Mentor as Model of the Contemplative Attitude

We will look now at the importance of the contemplative attitude for a mentor, that is, someone who models behaviour for others. I am using the term mentor to include teachers, religious formators and anyone in a position of influence over others who are younger than themselves. (Parents could even be included in this group.)

When the mentor is with the young person in the formation situation, he/she is modelling behaviour. We model what is the appropriate way for a mature person to act. The younger person is still learning and still impressionable. He/she may express anger badly or be self-pitying or manipulating. How does the mentor respond in these situations? Some situations/questions follow which we can consider:

- One of the students comes into the class late. She comes in late the next day. Do you act aggressively, calmly, moderately, firmly?

- You see that one of your charges has not done her work properly.

- You have just begun an overnight workshop with young people. It is the morning after you have arrived. One of them cannot be found when it is time to start the session.

- Your charge tells you that her accompaniment with you for the past year has not been very productive.

The mentor who has developed a contemplative attitude will first of all let the reality be there without judging. The person may be late for a very good reason. There may be a logical reason why the person is not there for the beginning of the workshop. When the young person tells you that your accompaniment for the past year has not been very helpful, you simply try to accept what has been said without becoming defensive. You allow the remark to be there and look at all sides of the question. In a discussion with the young person, you will speak quietly, listening to the reasons the other person has and giving your own views calmly but firmly. Having a contemplative attitude does not mean that you cannot think that one position is more accurate than another but that you have taken in calmly and non-judgmentally both sides.

Think of a situation when you felt angry. How do you manage the anger? How can you use angry feelings creatively and purposefully?

Think of situations when you felt you were not treated with respect by the younger person. Here are some possible remarks and behaviours you might meet:

- 'I don't care what you write about me in your evaluation.'

- 'Don't ever speak to me like that again.'

- 'You don't really care about me. You don't respect me.'

- The young person does not return your greeting when you greet them. This happens for several mornings.

How did you react? Do you really have to be treated with respect? We can learn to respond to these remarks and behaviours calmly and appropriately.

The mentor needs to be very positive. I remember teaching senior high school politics for the first time. The teacher who preceded me was a calm man who gently encouraged the students and got good results. I took his advice. I encouraged the students and affirmed any work they did which showed effort. I wrote encouraging remarks on the essays they gave me while also making suggestions at how they could do better. Beside me was a history class where the teacher was very demanding on the students. He interacted maturely with the students but constantly emphasised that they were not reaching the standards he expected. I did not spy on the class but could not help notice that he emphasised the negative rather than the positive. At the end of the year, my politics class did well while his history class results were not as good. If this teacher had emphasised the positive aspects of the students' work, I am sure they would have had very good results. At the same time, I knew another politics teacher who taught elsewhere who always spoke about the good things the students did. It even seemed to others who taught beside him that his approach was one-sided. But when the results came out, many of his students did brilliantly.

St Jean-Baptiste de La Salle, the founder of the Brothers of de La Salle, gave the following twelve qualities of a good teacher: dignity, calmness, prudence, humility, patience, wisdom, self-control, gentleness, zeal, vigilance, prayerfulness and generosity. All of these qualities relate closely with the contemplative attitude which mentors need to cultivate.

The Goal of the Contemplative Attitude

The following verses by Kirtana[65] speak of being present to the moment that is before us:

> Come without a thought
> About what's been or what's in store.
> Leave the world of mind behind you
> Like sandals by the shore.
>
> And trust me; trust the beingness you are;
> I breathed you here; I've carried you this far,
> And open to whatever is and see,
> Whatever is, is always only me.
>
> Not in imagined futures,
> Or in remembered pasts,
> But only here and only now
> Will you find a peace that lasts.
>
> So meet me, where the river meets the sea,
> Naked now, innocent and free.

This poem links the present moment with the one ultimate reality behind all reality, a Person, who says, 'And

---

[65] www.kirtana.com/content/meet-me

trust me'. We find the reality in every manifestation, that is in every moment. The primacy of the one ultimate reality is the foundation of the contemplative attitude. And when we find the ultimate reality, we will eventually experience the loving union for which we are all searching. We have to be constantly alert.

The following poem by Jane Tyson Clement describes the state of apprehension we are in before we encounter the ultimate reality. We imagine what this loving reality may want of us. We are afraid to stand before this loving presence. But then when the Master is actually there, our fears fade and we realise the love behind all the dualities of our lives:

> What would I do, O Master,
> if you came slowly out of the woods.
> Would I know your step?
> Would I know by my beating heart?
> Would I know by your eyes?
> Would I feel on my shoulder too, the burden you carry?
> Would I rise and stand still till you drew near
> or cover my eyes in shame?
> Or would I simply forget everything
> except that you had come and were here?[66]

These two pieces from Kirtana and Clements show us the goal of the contemplative attitude. It is simply to be present to reality and receive it in its richness.

---

[66] Quoted in Ronald Rolheiser *Internet Archive*, 12 June 2005.

References

Buechner, Frederick, https://wwwgoodreads.com/author/quotes/19982.FrederickBuechner.

Griffiths, Bede, *The River of Compassion: A Christian Commentary on the Bhagavad Gita*, Warwick: Amity House, 1987.

Brother Lawrence of the Resurrection, *The Practice of the Presence of God*, trans. Donald Attwater, Springfield, Illinois: Templegate Publishers, 1974.

May, G. *The Awakened Heart: Living Beyond Addiction*, New York: Harper Collins, 1991.

Rohr, R. *The Naked Now: Learning to See As the Mystics See*, New York: Crossroad, 2009.

Kirtana, www.kirtana.com/content/meet-me

Chapter Seven

Listening for God

WHEN WE TRY to have a relationship with the Mystery and to be aware of God's presence to us in our daily lives, it is almost automatic that we are to some degree moving in the direction that God's Spirit wants us to go. I say this is almost automatic but notice that, in this case, we have already decided to take God seriously and to get closer to God. We have stopped living without thought of the direction in which we are moving. John Cassian, the fourth century monk, says that, to be serious about our spiritual journey, three things are needed: first, we must give up living unthinkingly as though this is the way everyone lives. Second, we must take notice of our thoughts to see which way they are leading us. And thirdly, we must be ready to give up our taken-for-granted images of God so as to allow ourselves to become aware of God as God.[67]

In this chapter, I assume that we have developed this serious intention of not just doing good according to our own lights but of relating to God in a systematic and committed

---

[67] Margaret Mary Funk, *Thoughts Matter*.

way in our prayer. The alternative would be not to care where we are going or simply to try to live a spiritual life by obeying all the rules that we have been taught.

Listening for God in our Thinking

To listen to God, we first must trust that God is speaking to us in our hearts, in our life experiences and in our relating to others, in the wonder of the creation around us, and in the social movements that are prevailing in our culture. Our experiences in all of these areas of life produce a particular mood or feeling in us. First, our life experiences speak to us of God. One obstacle to hearing God in them is our attachment to wanting to be important. Margaret Mary Funk puts it this way: 'Who of us has not felt the surge of pride that is pervasively behind every one of our accomplishments and under every failure?'[68] We need to be able to find some space in ourselves to be free of this strong 'surge' within us. At first sight, it might seem impossible to find this freedom in ourselves. But even before this step, we may ask ourselves if it is really necessary to turn our lives around and to take this spiritual journey so seriously. After all, how many people are constantly aware of where their thoughts are heading? How can we keep the sense of God's presence with us constantly? Why not just do our best and hope that God is happy that we are not doing anything terrible and that we are trying to live peacefully with others?

---

[68] *Thoughts Matter.*

the person. He or she would have not felt encouraged by your response. In this case, when you felt discouraged and responded accordingly, it was the evil spirit prevailing in you.

Now recall a moment when you felt peaceful and someone called or phoned with exciting news. Then recall a moment when you were depressed and someone called or phoned with exciting news. In the first case, you would have felt very much in tune with the person and the person would have savoured the exciting news they had told you. In the second case, your response, if you had responded the way you felt, would have deflated them. Their excitement would have been strongly dampened and may have evaporated. We see here again how the two spirits can be within us and it is up to us to identify each and to follow God's Spirit and go against the evil spirit.

I remember, as a facilitator, going to two teachers in a particular school who taught religious education, and sharing with them some ideas about a topic they might consider offering their students. Both listened politely. The senior teacher then responded in a very guarded way. His voice was listless and as a result I felt the enthusiasm leaving me. Then the other much younger teacher responded saying that he thought that my idea was great and that he would love to develop a module of work around it. As a result, my confidence was restored and we continued the conversation enthusiastically. Even the older teacher then became enthusiastic to some degree.

This little exercise gives some idea of the difference between the voice of God's Spirit and the voice of the contrary spirit. God's Spirit encourages us, affirming that what we are

I am assuming that we believe that God does speak to us not just in our thoughts but in our moods and feelings. Listening for God's Spirit within us assumes that there is also another spirit contrary to that of God who also speaks and wants us to listen to it. We learn to distinguish between the two voices. We can tell the difference between the voices by the effect that they have on us. God's voice encourages us and the opposite spirit discourages us. The following is a helpful exercise to help us distinguish the two spirits or voices.[69]

God in our Moods

Recall a moment when you were feeling peaceful and someone called or phoned you in distress. Now recall a moment when you felt depressed and someone called or phoned in distress. In the first case, when you felt peaceful, you would have been very receptive to the distress of the person calling you. You would have been sensitive to the tone of voice you used so as not to disturb the person and you would have been encouraging in what you said to the person. In this case, it was God who was influencing us.

In the second case, when you were depressed, you would have felt like not showing much interest in the person's distress. You may have answered in a flat voice which did not help the person. In fact, your response, if you responded according to how you felt, would have been unhelpful to

---

[69] I received the following exercise from Sr Margaret Dwyer, RIP, in an email. It is one she had used when working on a facilitation team. Sr. Margaret did not give any details of who was on the team with her or who developed the exercise.

thinking and proposing is significant and worth pursuing. The contrary spirit discourages us and inclines us to move into our shells. Our self-esteem plummets and we trend to withdraw. The exercise shows us the working of the spirits in our relationships with others (one of the areas of life mentioned above where we need to try to discern God's voice). Cassian, we found, exhorted us to be aware of every thought that we have. In this exercise, that means noticing the thought that accompanies the encouraging or discouraging response we have for another person.

We can take the exercise further and notice how the spirits work in all our exchanges with each other. Here are some examples. Recently, I spoke to my sister, Margaret, about whether it was necessary to use nitrate spray if I think I am having angina pains. She said that they had checked my heart when I went into hospital earlier and it was okay. The pains are therefore not angina. I felt comfortable after that. Then I spoke to Grace, a health care nurse. She said that my sister was right but then at the end said that if the pain still persisted, to call an ambulance. That took me back to where I had started. It did not seem to be helpful. It brought back doubts that I was working to root out. In this connection, I remembered what happened at the end of a retreat I made years ago when I had decided to stay in Australia rather than go to West Africa. I was at peace with the decision to stay in Australia when I left the retreat, but doubts came later. I went to one person and my conversation with him reinforced the doubts and made me anxious and on edge. I was very unhappy and disturbed. Then I went to another and he said that I had already made my discernment which was to stay in Australia.

Immediately the peace, that I had felt originally, returned and it did not leave. This was for me a touchstone moment against which I could measure other similar experiences. I knew from this experience the tone and the feel of the way the Spirit speaks to me when I am discerning an important issue.

Soon after these conversations I had another with a Brother who was organising the visit of three Brothers from Africa. I had emailed him in a breezy reassuring way that I would help and that there would be no trouble. I was aware that he might have been anxious. He phoned me and asked if the pick-up from the airport had been smooth. I did not go into any detail and just said that everything was fine. I could tell that if I had shown any signs that I thought he had not arranged things well, it may have been hurtful to him and sapped his confidence.

In the couple of days following, I was particularly sensitive to the effect of my tone of voice on the other party in any exchanges I had and they on me. In the rehab. Hospital, I remember passing one of the physiologists who had worked with the group I was in. I greeted her saying her name and she gave me just a cursory nod in return. I noticed how this really made me withdraw momentarily into my shell. Then some time later, I passed one of the other physiologists and again I greeted him warmly using his name. Again, I got an even more distant nod from this person with whom I had felt quite close during the time he worked with my group in the program. These exchanges alerted me to the effect that we have on each other in exchanges of this sort. We can 'jab' the other as it were by our lack of interest or we can deeply encourage them by our warmth. We can potentially plunge them into discouragement and desolation or lift them into a sense of consolation.

I remember reading the autobiography of the famous Australian historian, Manning Clark.[70] He was talking about his own religious faith and how one particular childhood memory had influenced him and moved him away from believing. It was Easter Sunday and he had just come out of the church celebration. His defences were down and he said to one of the girls of his acquaintance, 'Let's have a game'. She looked at him and said, 'Who'd want to play with you!' and walked away. He stopped going to church after that.

These examples indicate how sensitive we can be to the reactions of others to us. John Cassian describes how a thought comes into our minds. In the cases we have been citing, it is a positive or negative remark that someone makes. Cassian advises us to notice what our feeling is to the remark. Does it incline us to be depressed or uplifted? We need to have the discipline to notice the effect and either to go with it or against it depending on where it is moving us. The Benedictine tradition calls this activity *diakrisis* or discretion.[71] Cassian is aware that two forces are at work, one moving us to life and the other to death. He tells us that we can choose to go with one or the other. It is clear that Manning Clark went with the negative movement in the remark with the resulting negative consequence of moving him away from any faith practice.

The two rival spirits work in both parties of an exchange.

---

[70] Manning Clark, *The Puzzles of Childhood*.
[71] Cf. *Thoughts Matter*.

In the one who makes the remark, there is the possibility of either encouraging or discouraging the other. In the one to whom the remark is addressed there are also the same two possibilities. Similarly in spiritual direction it may be a negative force or a positive one that prevails in each party.

Poems that Can Help Us Listen for God

In reading poems by the Sufi poet Hafiz, I noticed that different moods were being described. One mood was the brightness that the influence of God has and in other poems there was an alternative mood of confusion and commotion. Here is the first poem:

> Wherever God lays his glance
> Life starts Clapping.
> The myriad Creatures grab their instruments
> And join the Song.
> Whenever love makes itself known
> Against another body
> The Jewel in the eye starts
> To Dance.

In this poem we have the benevolent influence that is ascribed to God. It is like a mood that comes upon a person or a number of persons. Under its influence, people begin to celebrate and to sing together. They do this more or less spontaneously. When love is present in bodily contact, perhaps sexual contact, there seems to be a 'jewel' (a glint?) in the eyes of the two people. The people do not choose this mood but simply enjoy it. We can identify this action described as the glance of God with the effect the Spirit of God has on a person in what we call consolation.

Here is the second poem:

> God blooms
> From the shoulder
> of the
> Elephant
> Who becomes
> Courteous
> To
> The ant.

In this very simple poem, an elephant allows an ant to walk on its shoulder. Just in that place we are told God blooms. This is like saying that love suddenly appears and dominates the atmosphere of the two parties. The colossal separateness between the two of us and other characteristics disappears and the two are temporarily one.

The third poem contains a paradox:

> I have seen you heal
> A hundred deep wounds
> with one glance
> From your spectacular eyes,
>
> While your hands beneath the table,
> Pour large bags of salt
> into the heart-gashes
> Of your most loyal servants.

Here it seems to be God again who is acting. On the one hand, God heals numerous wounds with simply a glance. It is an effortless gesture from an infinitely gracious source, namely, God. At the same time as God is healing with this glance, God is also bringing great suffering into the lives of those who have been faithful to him. The poem is telling us that suffering can be a by-product of God's healing action. It must be that the suffering is necessary in order to rectify something. We are sure that this force that is operating is a loving one. God's action is loving but it does not always feel that way.

In the next poem, we see again the effect of the action of God:

> No conflict
> When the flute is playing,
> For then I see
> every movement emanates
> From God's
> Holy Dance.

Here the effect is harmony and oneness. It is as though everything and everyone is at one and coming from the one source. The immediate cause of this is the flute which calms and soothes. It seems the playing of the flute automatically has this effect.

The next poem tells us that a crazy mood can sometimes come over us:

> All the craziness of the empty plots
> all the ghosts and fears,

> All the grudges and sorrows
> have now passed.
>
> I must have inhaled a strange feather
>
> That finally fell out.

The person feels filled with a craziness that comes from nowhere. It might be that they wake this way and cannot explain the mood they are in. It may propel them into conflict with others, into destructive comments, into envy and even hatred. The person remembers grudges they hold and have not worked through, maybe sorrows of past failures that come to them and fill them with a sense of defeat. But this craziness goes just as fast as it comes and without the person doing anything. This seems to me a good description of desolation which comes from a source more powerful than us. St Ignatius says that we need to fight against such desolation but sometimes it will continue and we just have to wait for it to go. We have to hold on in patience.

Here is a very simple but powerful concluding poem:

> How do I listen to others?
>
> As if everyone were my Master
> Speaking to me
> His cherished last words.

This is how we would all like to listen to others. At our best, when we are experiencing consolation, we will listen in this way. Sometimes in a spiritual direction session, the director will feel totally immersed in what the other is saying and feel fully in tune with it. In our ordinary lives, it may be that we want to listen in this way but the other person does not allow us. The person we are listening to may speak obscurely or even negatively. But we must do our best to be in tune with the words of those who speak to us and bring the harmony and peace that our presence is capable of bringing.

Listening to God in Social Movements

Another important area where discernment of these two opposing spirits within us is necessary, is the social atmosphere. I have just been reading a book that my brother gave me titled *Keeping the Faith*.[72] I strongly resisted reading the book because I had others to read, but eventually I sat down to read some of it. In it the author, James Grant, comments on changes that are happening in society and particularly in the Catholic Church. Grant slowly moves into giving his opinions on how the church is going and says that we have to resist these movements. One is the emphasis given by the church to 'peripheral' groups and issues such as asylum seekers trying to enter Australia, unemployment benefits for those who cannot find employment, gay rights proponents, LGBTIQ groups, youth, resistance to accumulating wealth, etc. Grant claims that the church spends too much time on marginal groups and that it has little expertise concerning these groups. The church should devote time to advocating for higher employment rates, the pursuit of wealth, raising the standard of living for those who are already managing

---

[72] James Grant, *Keeping the Faith*.

adequately and focusing on high quality standards in areas which are going to raise the general standard of living.

As I read, a strong dislike for Grant's views developed in me. I felt that the views he was putting forward were the exact opposite of where the Holy Spirit was leading the church at this time. He seemed not to have heard of signs of the times of which Vatican II spoke. I also knew that people like my brother would be strongly influenced by this book. My aversion for the views put forward in the book grew. The important thing for me was to take notice of my aversion to these views and to check it out through calm reasoning as much as possible and to ask God to detach me from my own entrenched views.

An important movement that is happening in the world today is that of caring for the earth. Recently, I returned from Nairobi where I had been teaching courses in spiritual discernment and spiritual direction and counselling. I was spending most of my time reading in these areas and not thinking much about the spirituality of caring for the earth even though this was an important movement in my religious Congregation. I had become interested in care for the earth when Pope Francis' document, *Laudato Si'*,[73] had appeared a couple of years ago. But, on the whole, I was absorbed in my own intellectual preoccupations as I was sure was the case with my colleagues who were teaching scripture and other topics not directly related to earth spirituality. When I came back to Australia for an extended stay, I was challenged strongly by the way the Brothers in the community talked.

---

[73] Pope Francis, *Laudato Si'*.

I could not use simply scripture all the time. I was aware of using the term Jesus too much since others might think that I was focused just on the historical Jesus. I had to be sparing in the number of times I talked about God and I found it appropriate to add materials and prayers from other religious traditions such as Buddhism and Sufism. This is still an important question for me.

This discussion shows how difficult it is for us to change views and ways of speaking that we have held for a long time. How are we to know when to change? Richard Rohr looks at how the early church tried to discern where the Spirit was leading it as distinct from the prevailing cultural voices that prevailed around it.[74] Jesus himself at the beginning of his public ministry went into the desert to listen to the voice of his Father. He had to distinguish this voice from the voice of Satan who tried to deceive him into believing the prevailing attitudes to power and religion. The early Christians also found the need to go into the desert in order to hear God's Spirit speaking to them. They believed in being 'in the world but not of the world'. The early Christians also found it necessary to live in small groups in order to support each other. If they did not support each other, they would quickly accept the views of those around them.

This scenario is also ours today. We have to ask ourselves if we are able to listen to the Spirit speaking within us. A Nigerian proverb very simply makes a distinction between the two voices: 'When the world says, "Give up", Hope whispers, "Try it one more time"'. The voice of the prevailing culture

---

[74] Richard Rohr, *Daily Meditations* Internet, August 2018.

in our time tells us to rely on ourselves, to have our own personal interests at heart, to put ourselves forward and seek the limelight, that those who succeed are the really worthy ones. On the other hand, God's Spirit tells us to be patient, to accept suffering when it comes, to 'try one more time.' We will be helped to listen to God's voice by reading the Beatitudes and the teachings of Jesus on helping the marginalised, and on trusting God when we are persecuted, overlooked or discarded.

Dispositions that help us Hear God

At the beginning, we said that we have to believe that God's Spirit is with us. The first letter to the Corinthians tells us that human power is not what impresses God. We have to listen very deeply in our inner depths to realise that God's power is of a different nature. It is only when we rely on God that we will see 'the power of the Spirit' at work in us. When God's power is at work it may seem that we are weak and foolish (cf. 1 Corinthians 2:1-5). Paul says that 'the Spirit reaches the depths of everything, even the depths of God.' Paul goes on to say that 'we have received the Spirit that comes from God'. We, meaning those who have the life of God within them, see things from a spiritual perspective. In contrast, 'an unspiritual person is one who does not accept anything of the Spirit of God; he sees it all as nonsense'.

How do we get to be among those who can listen to the Spirit? First, we need to believe that we have the Spirit of God within us. How do we access this Spirit and live by it? This is where we can learn from the first Christians who knew that they had to live in supportive communities, and thus shield themselves from the influence of the prevailing culture. We have to develop a deep interiority which is not swept away by the false praises we hear from the culture. We have to read the scriptures and gradually take on this spiritual attitude which is contrasted with the unspiritual attitude that prevails everywhere.

In Luke's infancy narrative, we have good examples of those who are able to listen to this obscure voice within that is easily drowned out by the cultural voices.[75] Mary prays and listens to the angel speak to her; she visits her cousin Elizabeth who is, like her, filled with the Spirit. Mary, Elizabeth, and Zacchary are the key figures who model this deep type of listening. Mary 'ponders all these things in her heart'. She has the attitudes of patience, humility, love and kindness. She does not look for acclaim and success. She is one of the 'anawim', the poor little ones, who wait for God. One of their attitudes that is highlighted more than others is trustful waiting. She forgets herself and entrusts herself to what God does in the simple events of her life, finding no room in the inn, giving birth to Jesus in a stable, receiving the humble visits of the shepherds. Amidst of all these humble activities she is able to see God at work. She experiences the overshadowing of the angel, the joy of being pregnant and of finding her cousin Elizabeth pregnant.

We can imagine the sort of attitude that was present in Mary's heart at this time. It was obviously one of deep joy even when things were going outwardly wrong. What was

---

[75] Cf. Jacques Guillet, *Discernment of Spirits in Scripture*.

it like for her to ponder things in her heart? The song of the Medical Missionary Sisters (*The Visit*) is one way we might see it. Mary was going to meet her cousin with the knowledge that there was a special child in her womb. She knew also that Elizabeth, her cousin and friend, was also pregnant after it seemed impossible. The song expresses it this way:

> She walked in the summer through the heat on the hill.
> She hurried as one who went with a will.
> She danced in the sunlight when the day was done.
> Her heart knew no evening Who carried the Son.[76]

Mary was young and her heart was so full that she did not feel the heat. She walked on air, hardly aware that she was walking at all. She was full of the message from the angel. She came to the house of Elizabeth and as soon as the two met, a spark lit within them. The child leapt in Elizabeth's womb and Mary felt its reverberation. The next stanza of the hymn brings together Mary's extreme youth with the dignity of her motherhood and with the wondrous announcement to the world of the coming of God's son. It is as though all the stages of life are brought together in one moment.

The hymn finally reminds us that we too have moments like this when everything comes together and we feel carried into the bliss of union with the wind and the warmth. We feel that any burdens we carry are light and of little consequence. We know that we, like Mary, carry God and God's love to others.

---

[76] Medical Mission Sisters. See *medicalmissionsisters.org*

The following song, Love, make Your Way by Alana Levandoski,[77] has a similar message of being carried above all the burdens of life. We feel that the times of loneliness and of hurt are nothing because there is a power carrying us beyond them and through them:

> There is a light travelling through the dark,
> And it is beautiful like a hurting heart.
> Through the abyss, through this emptiness,
> The light... will come in.
> O love, O love, grow inside of us, O love, make your way.
> O love show the world that it bears Your holy name.

We feel a love inside us that is carrying us along, and this love is more powerful than any darkness. When we hear the song, we feel, just for that moment, a taste of an infinite love that sweeps us away beyond all cares. We do have these experiences when we listen to certain music and lyrics that go with the music. We are taken out of our normal world into a world that we sense is real and which is ours.

In the above reflections, we have begun to describe the effect that God's action has on us. What in the language of spiritual discernment we call consolation is based firmly on an incredible and infinite love that is present there at the heart of our lives but of which we are normally not aware or at least not in this vivid way.

When we touch this deep love within us as happens when we are deeply moved by a piece of music such as *The Visit* or *Love Make Your Way*, we are also touching into the Holy

---

[77] Alana Levandovski, *Love Make Your Way*, Youtube.

Spirit who is deep within our souls. Andre Louf says that the spiritual director always needs to keep in mind this reality in the person she is listening to.[78] The directee may be caught up at the level of his personality where he feels he has to keep the rules slavishly and this can lead to a total lack of freedom. If the director continues to listen patiently to him while not affirming this legalistic voice, then eventually the Holy Spirit begins to be heard. The point is that the Holy Spirit continues to dwell in our depths no matter what traps of the evil spirit we may have fallen into.

Silence is Essential

Thomas Keating also affirms the reality of the presence of the Holy Spirit in the depths of the person.[79] In centering prayer, if we stay with the symbol we have chosen, we will gradually move into deeper areas of ourselves until we reach the deepest area where the Spirit is present. At this level, healing takes place of past enslaving memories and hurts. I would like, for a moment, to look at what it is like when we move below our surface thoughts into these depths. Here we begin to talk of silence. The film *Into Deep Silence* gives us a little taste of what this silence is like. I remember seeing this film in a public theatre which was full. The others present as well as myself did not know what had hit us. Yes, we knew we were going into a religious film where there would be silence but we did not expect the deep silence which was created by

---

[78] Andre Louf, *Grace Can Do More*.
[79] Thomas Keating, *The Human Condition*.

the film. We saw monks going through their daily duties but with no sound track much of the time. We found ourselves having to choose to go into this silence or to leave. For me it was not until the film had been going for an hour that I realised that I was going to stay for the whole length of the film which was about two and a half hours. I was with my aunt and after the film we went and had coffee and gradually came back into the ordinary world.

I had another very profound experience of silence when, while staying in an Aboriginal community, Santa Teresa, in Central Australia, I visited what I thought was the art centre. It was a beautiful building. I entered and moved along a descending winding corridor at the entrance. I was expecting that there was going to be someone to direct me to where the paintings were, but I could see no one. I noticed that there a deep silence surrounding me. Eventually, I found an Aboriginal lady to whom I spoke. She did not reply to me immediately, and when she did, her voice seemed to be coming from that deep silence. She said little and I soon found that in that building there were no paintings on display. Instead one or two women were working on paintings and with no interest in meeting anyone. In that place I felt immersed in silence. It was the most powerful experience of silence I have ever had. It gave me a sense of what silence could be like.

Most of us are not really aware that there does exist this place in us from which thoughts and words and motivations come. But we all do possess this place. It is where we can hear the Spirit speaking to us. I have called this chapter 'Listening for God', not to God, since the process of discovering what God is saying to us is an indirect one. It comes only to the humble, the 'anawim' like Mary, who are open to God. The proud hear nothing of what God says.

The story of Elijah the Tishbite, is a sobering one (cf. 1 Kings 17-19). The first thing we hear of Elijah is that he prophesies to Ahab the king that there is to be a drought. Then Yahweh tells Elijah to go to the wadi Cherith where God will look after him. Ravens bring him food as Yahweh had promised and then the wadi dries up. The drought has come. Then he is told to leave Cherith and to go to a widow who feeds him with her last crust. Elijah then raises the widow's son who has died. We see here how Elijah is obedient to Yahweh, humbly waiting on Yahweh, and, as a result, though living in hardship, has power even to raise someone to life. Elijah so far is a model for us who try to listen for God in our lives. Then Elijah begins to change. He engages in a contest with the prophets of Baal and Yahweh allows him to have a great victory. He is full of confidence but also full of himself. As soon as Yahweh's power leaves him, he finds himself terrified of what Jezebel will do to him and he flees. He is at his lowest ebb until Yahweh comes to help him again. He goes into a cave where he is to wait for the coming of Yahweh. He is told to come out of the cave and wait for Yahweh. There is an earthquake but Yahweh is not in the earthquake. Then there is fire and Yahweh is not in the fire. After the fire comes 'a sound of sheer silence' (1 Kings 19:12). It is in the silence that he hears God. It is in this silence that we too will hear God.

In the silence, we will be able to see things objectively. We will be able to look back on our lives and recognise the distorted way we sometimes saw certain things. We will see how we saw things from our own small perspective and blamed others for what were our own failings. I noticed this tendency in an item in the media lately, the attack on the chief umpire by Serena Williams in the US Open Women's Tennis final. Williams abused the umpire for claiming that she had received messages from her coach's box during the match. Her attack on him took away the attention from the young Japanese player, Naomi Osaka, who beat her. The reports appearing the following day spoke of how wrong Williams' attack had been. We are all guilty of similar accusations of others at one time or another. The following poem by Leunig shows how sensitive we are to injustices against ourselves and how insensitive to the injustices we perpetrate on others:

> I am sad, I am sad
> For the whippings I've had
> In my weary old life.
>
> But I'm glad, I am glad
> That the cuts weren't so bad
> As the whippings I gave
> To my poor little slave.
>
> It is mad, it is mad
> How I flogged the poor lad
> But couldn't quite see
> That the poor lad was me.[80]

In the silence, in the depths of ourselves, we will be able to uncover the deceptions and the rationalisations. When the

---

[80] Leunig, *The Age*, Melbourne, 8 September 2018.

revelations come, what is needed is humility on our part, because in these revelations, God is speaking to us.

Knowing We Are Loved

We have spoken about the power of love in helping us hear the voice of God and then the power of silence. Along the way, we have seen examples of times when people have been unable to hear God's voice and have been caught in self-deception. I wish to conclude by suggesting that it will be very helpful to us to reflect on experiences of love we have had. Without feeling loved, I do not think we will get to the truth, that is, to hearing God's voice, amidst the confusion that may surround us.

In his book *The First Spiritual Exercises*,[81] Michael Hansen gives many very concrete prayer activities of recalling experiences we have had of God's love in our lives.[82] The first activity is to remember an experience of being really loved. We simply remember as vividly as we can the experience with the details of place, weather, conversation, actions and people and to relive the experience with all our senses. Hansen says that when we do this, we are able to bring this experience into the present. We actualise this experience of love here and now and again experience its effects. In the second activity, I remember an experience of being loved and feeling grateful. This is a slight but important extension of the previous

---

[81] Michael Hansen, S.J., *The First Spiritual Exercises*.
[82] The activities are of God's love coming to us through others as well as directly.

activity. When we are able to experience gratitude in this way we, at the same time, free ourselves from impact of the bad spirit which turns or attention on to everything that is wrong in our lives: meals with no taste, 'unnecessary' community meetings, people passing negative remarks, a sudden drop of energy, etc., etc.

The next activity is to remember an experience of being loved and of responding. In this case, we not only experience the love again, and feel grateful again, but we also find the energy to respond to such love in a loving way ourselves. A fourth activity is to remember an experience of loving friendship with a close friend. We see here a further progression where the love is not just occasional but prolonged. Hansen then invites us to remember a time when we felt the love of Jesus directly, then the love of the Father in the way that Jesus experienced that love. All experiences of being loved are experiences of the love the Mystery has for us. When we feel loved in this way, we are open to what God wants to say to us and are in a good position to be able to detect the negative voices that want to move us into ourselves and away from love and life.

Conclusion

In this chapter, we have focused on listening for God in our interactions with others. This involves being aware of thoughts that come from what others say and how they react to us, and especially being aware of our moods and feelings. We looked in less detail at how to discern God's presence in social movements. We did not look systematically at how moods and feelings opposed to God's action affect us but rather at those times when we feel certain of God's presence because of the love which spontaneously emerges within us. Along with these occasions we looked at times when we have had the experience of being loved. The other areas we covered were the dispositions of humility and openness needed to hear God and the help it is to be aware of silence that we can occasionally tap into.

References

Clark, Manning, *The Puzzles of Childhood*, Melbourne: Penguin Books, 1990.

Funk, Margaret Mary, *Thoughts Matter*, New York: Continuum, 1998.

Grant, James, *Keeping the Faith*, Redland Bay, Queensland., Connor Court Publishing, 2017.

Guillet, J., S.J. et al. *Discernment of Spirits*, Collegeville: The Liturgical Press, 1957.

Hafiz, *The Gift: Poems by Hafiz, the Great Sufi Master*, trans. Daniel Ladinsky, New York: Penguin/Arkana, 1999.

Hansen, Michael, S.J., *The First Spiritual Exercises*, Notre Dame, Indiana: Ave Maria Press, 2013.

Keating, Thomas *The Human Condition: Contemplation and Transformation*, New York: Paulist Press 1990.

Levandosky, Alana, *Love Make Your Way*, Youtube.

Pope Francis, *Laudato Si'*, Nairobi: Paulines, 2015.

Chapter Eight

Outwitting the Nagging Spirit

I WAS ATTRACTED to the reading for Sunday 23, Year B in Ordinary Time, from Isaiah. I will quote the reading here:

> Say to those with fearful hearts,
> 'Be strong, do not fear;
> your God will come,
> he will come with vengeance;
> with divine retribution
> he will come to save you.'
> Then will the eyes of the blind be opened
> and the ears of the deaf unstopped.
> Then will the lame leap like a deer,
> and the mute tongue shout for joy.
> Water will gush forth in the wilderness
> and streams in the desert.
> The burning sand will become a pool,
> the thirsty ground bubbling springs.
> In the haunts where jackals once lay,
> grass and reeds and papyrus will grow
> (Isaiah 35:4-7).

I thought of this passage in terms of the great encouragement it gives in face of the doubts that come to all of us at times. I just read a short chapter in the Saturday *Australian Review* which quickly sketches the stages of life of a smoker. At first, the smoker has 'the invincibility of youth' in stubbing his cigarette butt on the pavement. In his thirties, he continues to smoke without a thought. Ten years later the tests show that his chest is affected by the smoking but his lungs still function. Next, he is struggling for breath but he continues to smoke. Finally, he is told that the cancer he has is inoperable and he leaves the clinic but this time does not smoke. It is a sad little cameo which alerts us to the invulnerability we feel in our youth and how this sense gets unmasked as our lives go on. When we are young, we can keep any discouragement at bay because our lives are stretching out endlessly before us, but this factor is not possible as we get older. In our forties and fifties, questions come to us about how we are spending our lives and what will happen to us in the future. The professional activities we are engaged in occasionally do not seem so absolutely essential. There develop chinks in our armour. Eventually, we are confronted with questions which can easily lead us down a spiral. We read in the newspapers of beautiful young women who are mysteriously drowned after taking drugs or excessive drinking. If we are religious, we wonder where God is in all this. What about all the things we have heard about God's love? Is the mystery behind ordinary events really loving and gracious?

It was with these questions in my mind that I read the passage from Isaiah. Isaiah comes with an incredible promise that our fears will be banished because our God is coming. When God is present, Isaiah says, 'The eyes of the blind will be opened, the ears of the deaf be cleared', the lame will walk and the dumb speak. Then in the gospel of the same Sunday we see Jesus curing a deaf man by going through a series of actions with him. In Jesus God is here. In our own lives, the action of God is not so clear. We have to unearth it and then co-operate with it. We will look at some scenarios where the action of God was not immediately obvious but had to be recognised. Here is the first example. The community held a meeting which was to be devoted to the members sharing how they find living in the community especially in the areas of their personal spiritual lives. The leader had some initial material which he hoped would lead into personal sharing. Nothing much happened for a while and then the leader asked if anyone would wish to share how he was finding community life. Someone offered, saying that he felt isolated because of the way he felt Eucharist and prayer was being conducted. His contribution was just a start. What was needed was for someone to pick up on what he had said and interact in some way. A second member said how he was also uncomfortable with the way he himself led the prayer. He felt that others were not happy when he did so. As a member of the group, I felt that the ice had been broken and that we were starting to share in a worthwhile way. Here is an example, I think, of how someone's tongue was loosed and how God had entered the scene.

Were there any factors operating, trying to stop God from acting? Yes. These factors come from what I am calling the nagging spirit working against the action of God. First, there had been resistance to having a reflective meeting like this rather than simply a business meeting even though there was also a deep sense in many that there was a need to share personally. I met one of the community members that morning. This Brother came in and complained about the meals we had had that week. He said that yesterday's meal of pork pie was tasteless. I did not say anything. I should have asked him about the meal on Monday and on Sunday to help him see that he was generalising and thinking himself badly treated when it was quite false. His negative remark made me aware how easily we all see things negatively and as a result feel unhappy. He then said that he did not know why we were having a meeting that afternoon. All we had to do was be faithful to the ideas of the founder and that there was no need for a meeting. Just as the meeting was about to begin, one member said that another had phoned him to say that he was held up in traffic and would not be at the meeting. What was going on in the minds of the brothers involved? We can surmise that something in them was telling them that this meeting would accomplish nothing or that it would upset their ways of seeing things. My own sense that we would not get anywhere at the beginning was also a negative voice. We can see that this voice which is a nagging voice begins to operate against the action for change, in this case, the meeting.

Here is the second example. We had staying with us two young Brothers from Africa. They had a program they were attending but on the day before leaving they had a free day. I thought of the idea of offering to take them on a ferry ride to Williamstown. I thought of the cost involved, of whether they would accept and whether they would enjoy it. I approached them and they accepted my invitation. I then made some investigation on where to get the ferry and how to plan the day. I could not find all the details but thought that we just had to go ahead with the plan. During the night, I was disturbed with discomfort in my chest. (I had had a heart attack a couple of months earlier) I got up at 2.30 a.m. and did not sleep after that. I took spray and this disturbed me. I lay down a couple of times but felt discomfort and did not persist in lying down. But after I had some breakfast, I felt a little more stable. I talked to a Brother, Frank, in the dining room about whether I would go with the young Brothers and that was helpful. His encouragement and then another brother, Mark, said it was a great idea and assumed that I was going. I was worried that we would be late but I did not try to hurry the Brothers since I knew that might upset them. Mark suggested that we could come back by train and that would lower the cost.

We left and got to the place to get the ferry since people helped us with directions. The two visiting African Brothers, Amos and Nicholas, went back to get some more money on their Myki (public transport) cards and I stayed and had some time in the sun. We were early and I went to find a toilet and in doing so I had a look at Southbank. I came back and talked to the driver of the ferry who pointed out two swans and their babies to me. It was nice to sit in the sun and not do anything. We got onto the ferry with all the other passengers who were many. The atmosphere going over to Williamstown was leisurely. Everyone was relaxed and ready to talk to each other. Amos and Nicholas took a lot of photos and enjoyed the trip. We docked at Williamstown and I did not know if we would have some fish and chips or wait. But the decision made itself since Nick and Amos were both keen on fish and chips and we enjoyed them. We ate in a leisurely way and then made our way to the train which was further away than we expected. We found the station and were just in time for the train which was waiting at the station. It was good to come back this way through a big stretch of industrial Melbourne and an area which I appreciated seeing again. I enjoyed the city of Williamston too with its leisurely pace. I enjoyed being with the two young men. I could see that they appreciated my effort in taking them and in being ready to spend money on them. It showed me that people are the important thing and not money.

When I think back on it, I notice that the encouragement that Frank and Mark gave me earlier were very important. Their encouragement also proved to be well founded. If they had not shown their approval and affirmation, I would not have felt as confident. I also noticed that others were helpful. The train attendant who showed me the way to the bridge across the river to Southbank; the man I asked about the washroom in Southbank, the men we asked for directions to the train in Williamstown street, the shopkeepers at the fish and chip shop, the people on the ferry the man who sold us the ticket for the ferry.

That trip was an important one. There was much to enjoy, not least the beautiful sunny day. I particularly noticed young people during the day. They were enjoying their youthful energy and displaying it at every turn. They did not have to worry too much (like me) about losing balance on the tram;

they did not worry about whether they would have time to get off. I watched them with interest and with enjoyment. I was glad that they had all this energy. I saw the driver of the ferry and noticed that he was about fifty. There was another man who had a group of students who was also in his fifties. I thought of how this second man who had great energy would not have this same energy for long. I was sad that the ferry driver was smoking since I knew that it was bad for his health as he got older.

I wondered what my own feelings were as I saw all these younger people around me, some in their twenties, some children, some as I have just mentioned in their fifties. As I came home in the tram, it became clear to me what my feelings were. I was full of sadness that I do not have this youthfulness or this energy any more. I was sad but I was also grateful that I had had many years of youth and energy. I did not envy these young people their energy or their chance to live their lives which stretched out ahead of them. But there was sadness. I was sad, sad, that I am not able to walk briskly now or even to seem to be youthful. I thought of the lady in the wheel chair who came on the ferry and realised that she was worse off than me.

When I look at this experience, I see that a voice was trying to discourage me at many points saying things like the following: it is an unjustified expense; your health is not good and you can just put them on the ferry without going with them; things will not work out since you do not know the time of the ferry; you will not be able to find the place to get the tickets for the ferry; the two young Brothers will not enjoy it; there are too many decisions to be made. In this episode, we see the struggle between this nagging voice within and the positive voices which were mainly outside me. Adrian van Kaam speaks of life situations as life directives.[83] The life situation in this situation consisted of all the different things that were happening to me: my inability to sleep during the night, my meeting with the those who encouraged me, the tram ride to the city which put me in touch with real people going about their business, all the people on the tram who were with me, those who gave me directions to the ferry, the ferry ride, etc. This life situation was constantly giving me helpful directions if I was able and ready to listen to it. It was essential for me to hear these life directives if I was to escape the clutches of the nagging voice putting up supposedly good but in fact spurious reasons for not going on the ferry ride. All the positive things that happened to me during the experience that are recounted above, these would all have not have found the light of day if 'the Nagger' had had his way.

Experiences of Grace

Some further experiences where the life situation was offering life directives follow. I call them also experiences of grace since they were mediating to me God's voice. We will also see how there was the nagging spirit accompanying the grace and trying to subvert it. The first experience was when two people visited the community one Saturday afternoon. I heard Kevin, one of the community members, speaking to

---

[83] van Kaam, *The Dynamics of Spiritual Self Direction*.

them at the door while I was in the kitchen having tea. One was a female voice and my name was mentioned. I felt that Kevin was trying to 'fob' responsibility for them onto me and I did not want to meet them, but he brought them into the dining room and I did meet them. Kevin had been gracious to them and I too now welcomed them graciously. Other members of the community came in and I found that the visit was an enjoyable and enriching one. Later, I thought of the visit of the three angels to Abraham and Sarah in the Book of Genesis (Genesis 15) and of how important it was for them to be accepted graciously. Were not my two visitors also angels in disguise, sent by God? I would have missed all this if I had not made the effort to open myself.

On a second occasion, I woke up in a depressed mood. I felt that I did not want to continue with the chapter I was writing. I wondered if all this effort at writing was accomplishing anything. I went on with something else and ignored the depressed mood as much as I could. I waited patiently for my friend, Chris, to come to go with him to his house in Korweinguboora Forest. When we were together and talking and later walking, I felt better. We had two walks, one around the property and the other into the forest itself. As so often happens, it was only after we reached home and said goodbye that I appreciated the gift it was to be together. I was very happy especially that we had walked a fair way especially up a hill that kept ascending. But I also enjoyed sharing conversation with Chris and noticed that he was critical in some things but very open on others. I also enjoyed the photo collage of his wife, Jan, who died two years earlier. There were many things to be grateful for. My decision to put aside the nagger, my depressed mood, of the morning allowed me to enjoy the grace of the day with my friend that God was giving me. If I had listened to the nagging, it would have prevented the positive outcomes of the day.

A third visitation of grace that came to my mind was the day I spent with my friend, Kaye, visiting her and then going to a second-hand shop and buying some great clothes, thanks to her initiative. That day also left my very inspired and happy and grateful. On that occasion, the nagging spirit had not been very active except to say that the effort of choosing and trying on the clothes would be very tiring and in the end I might not have ended up with clothes that I liked. I recount these episodes of grace to show that when God is active, the nagger will also be active doing his best to undermine the loving and grace-filled action of God.

Directives from the Life Situation

We will look further at the importance of directives from the life situation. In a recent community prayer which I led, I was worried beforehand about how the material I was to present would be received. One of the community members had said that some of the language we had been using in our community prayer did not speak to him. I heard this after I had already prepared the next prayer. I put aside the fears. But a couple of hours before the prayer, the fears reappeared in sharper form. I mentioned this to a couple of the community members at tea and one reassured me that I should just go ahead. Another said that the brother concerned would not be at prayer since he had marked himself out for dinner that followed the prayer. Both of these comments reassured me and I felt very relaxed about the prayer as the time approached. I had prepared the chapel and the music for the prayer and ten minutes before the prayer, the Brother whom I thought would not be there, entered. He came to me and said, 'Tim, I will accept anything you present in the prayer. My comments about the language we use in prayer were a bit exaggerated'. Any fears I had disappeared and I went ahead. We can see the directives from the two brothers at the afternoon tea and then the comment of the brother in question immediately before the prayer cleared away the difficulties for me. All that was needed for me was to stay open to the situation.

Directives from within Oneself

Occasions have kept coming to me as I have been writing this chapter about the ways we have of overcoming the 'nagger' within as I have called him. I went to a family gathering to farewell a grand-niece who was going away to England for a year. I looked forward to the gathering and enjoyed it. I met my three grand-nieces and spoke briefly to each as well as spending time with another very old member of one side of the family I did not know well. I also found myself at table with a group of people only one of whom I knew and thought that it would be a difficult time. But, instead we had a very lively conversation about novels which most of us had read. On the next morning at breakfast, the thought came to me that this gathering was not so wonderful after all. I thought how some of the aspects had been difficult; my conversation with the old lady had gone on for too long; I had not had much conversation with the niece who was going away, etc., etc. These thoughts made me feel low. The 'special moments of grace' I have just described above now did not seem so special but ordinary. I thought that I had been exaggerating everything and idealising it. Then I recognised that here was the 'Nagger' coming to niggle away at me so as to undermine my joy and my insights about all these experiences. When I recognised the presence of this nagging voice its influence quickly left me.

The Nagging Voice in the Spiritual Direction Situation

We will look finally at two examples of the nagging spirit as revealed in a spiritual direction setting. Christian is a seminarian in his theology years. He says that when exams come up, he stops praying because he knows that he will not be able to concentrate. He has never been able to concentrate up to now when exams are coming and he knows this will continue. The director hears the nagging voice persuading Christian that prayer is impossible for him during exam time. He realises that the nagger has Christian in his grip but, unlike Christian, does not believe this voice. He invites Christian to tell him what happens when exam time comes around. Rather than hear Christian's interpretation, he wants to hear the stages that occur before the interpretation. He listens non-judgmentally and then asks Christian if he is prepared to try to pray a number of times during the exam time and report about what happened at the next direction session. Christian is happy to do this and, to his surprise, finds that he is able to pray after all. The director asks him how he feels towards God now compared to when he was not praying, and he reports that he feels closer to God now.

At a subsequent session, Christian says that for the whole month he had felt low at times but he could not put his finger on the cause. At the beginning of the month, he heard that soldiers were to visit his home village in West Africa and that meant that they could do harm to members of his family especially to his 18-year-old brother. He heard that the soldiers had come to the village and one of the neighbours had been killed but none of his family. He was relieved but he was perplexed that the fear had not left him. He kept talking and remembered that he had had a recurring dream that had disturbed him. The last dream was about a time when he was with a friend in his home village and they were chased by a lion. He had climbed a tree but the tree was not very tall and not very strong. He was above the lion but he did not seem very safe. He took the dream to mean that God whom he relied on was not able to defend him from the strength of this lion who was out to kill him. The director suggested some interpretations of aspects of the dream: that the lion represented a part of Christian himself and that the tree did not represent God but was also a part of himself. This meant that he himself was not very strong but God was still strong. The lion represented a part of him which he did not want to face. But if he faced it, it would lose its fear and its hold over him. The director asked him how he felt after thinking of the dream in these terms. He said that, even as the director was speaking, he could feel the fear leaving him; the tight grip that the fear had was quickly disappearing. He was certain that the fears would vanish further when he prayed. He felt so much better. The fears had already lifted. The dream now had a different meaning for him. In this example we see another manifestation of the nagging voice and of the power that that voice can have until it is confronted.

Here is a second example. Sr. Irene who was in her forties had been fearful of coming to do studies in spirituality and at first felt out of place being with students who were much younger than herself. This fear had gone and she now felt comfortable with the younger students. She felt accepted by them and was comfortable in the classes now. She could now see that this is where God wanted her and she felt grateful to God for bringing her here. But then another fear appeared on the scene. Exams were coming up and she was afraid that she would not be able to do them. The director asked her how she had managed in exams which she had done when she last studied. She said that she had done well. He then asked if she could understand the material in the courses and if she was spending regular time at study. She again replied in the affirmative. The director then suggested that she talk to God in prayer about her fears and she agreed. Here is a further exam of the nagger. It is clearly nagging in this case because this area of anxiety had been a source of pain in almost the whole of Sr Irene's life. The nagger had now been unmasked and wounded, if not killed, by the challenge he had received in the session.

When does the Nagging Stop?

So far in the examples I have given, the nagging spirit started to lose its power as soon as it was recognised. There are other occasions when we recognise the nagging spirit but, no matter what we do, the nagging continues. What are we to do? Has the nagging spirit now defeated us? This is not true since we all have experiences where everything looks black and when there seems no way out for us. Jesus felt this on the cross when he cried out, 'My God, my God, why have you forsaken me?' We can be besieged by very strong desolation. We may think, 'God does not want me to succeed in order to strengthen me'. We realise at some level that God does not work this way but the statement still seems to have some truth to it. We go about our business but the thought hangs on and will not go away. It may seem that a curse has been put on us, sapping us of our confidence. We tell ourselves that these thoughts are false but they keep affecting us. We do other things, go for a walk, but the thought keeps coming back. We know we just have to go ahead with what has to be done. This is not an unreal scenario.

We can be attacked by even more extreme thoughts: that this time we definitely cannot go ahead with what has to be done. We feel the energy ebbing from us. This seems the strongest attack we have ever experienced. It is hard for us to believe that these thoughts are lies. We know we just have to hang on for grim death to the belief that this is the nagging spirit who is attacking us. We go ahead with the task to be done and get through it. The next time we have difficulties that we do not foresee. Someone who was formerly co-operative now seems to be working against us. When we interact with those involved, enough good things happen to encourage us, but there are still doubts in our mind and the same desolation comes the next time we approach the task.

These experiences of desolation may continue for weeks and months. When will the nagging stop? The answer is that we cannot stop the nagging coming from the evil spirit and which we otherwise call desolation. The nagging will continue until God stops it in God's own time and for God's own reasons. Rules 7 and 8 of St Ignatius' first set of rules of discernment give us direction here. Rule 7 says that we are to notice that we are in desolation (that the nagging spirit is working) and that we are to resist even though we feel no consolation. We are to remember that we are able to resist 'with the divine aid, which always remains with (us) even though (we) may not clearly perceive it'. The rule continues: 'For, although the Lord has withdrawn from (us) his bubbling ardour, surging love, and intense grace, nevertheless he leaves enough grace to go forward to eternal salvation'.[84]

The following rule, Rule 8, directly addresses the question of when the nagging will end:

> Let him who is in (spiritual) desolation work at holding on in patience, which goes contrary to the vexations that come at him; and, while taking unremitting action against such desolation, as said in the sixth rule, let him keep in mind that he will soon be consoled.[85]

---

[84] See Jules Toner, *A Commentary on St Ignatius' Rules for the Discernment of Spirits*, St Louis: The Institute of Jesuit Sources, 1979.
[85] Jules Toner, *A Commentary*.

Ignatius is telling us here that we are to wait in patience, a patience that we sometimes do not think is possible. We are to continue to believe that God has not forgotten us and that the desolation will soon turn to consolation. We are to realise that constantly in our lives there is an alternation between consolation and desolation. When we are experiencing consolation, Ignatius tells us to prepare ourselves calmly for the time when desolation will come and that when we are in desolation we are to encourage ourselves that consolation is not far away.[86]

Eventually the nagging will stop. We find again that God takes us by the hand and we feel confident again. God speaks directly to us most directly when we are weakest. God lets us go to this point where we feel on the brink of annihilation so that She can show Her power and love. God comes from nowhere without any preparation.[87] God fills us with joy and certainty and lets us see what is the way ahead which, until then, had eluded us. Doubts about ourselves depart. We stop relying on ourselves and our attention moves to God and to the presence of God in the situation. At these times, we know, and do not just believe, that God will not abandon us or leave us flagging. We also know that God will work in God's own way and that we cannot control or force her to act. God comes because of his love and generosity and out of total freedom.

These experiences of being close to the limits of our resources are not uncommon. When Ellen Johnson Sirleaf,

---

[86] Jules Toner, *A Commentary*.
[87] See Jules Toner, *A Commentary*, Second Set of Rules, Consolation without previous cause.

the former President of Liberia, was interviewed on BBC some time ago, she described how she was near death as a government minister in Liberia in the 1970s and how she faced it. Her attitude was calm as she spoke but it was clear that she had been 'on the edge' and that she had had to summon all her human and divinely-given resources to face the danger. She said how, at many other times, her job as a minister and later as president had been difficult. St Teresa of Avila in her *Life* speaks about her experience of going ahead with her first profession even though all her feelings were against it. After the profession she experienced strong consolation and she learned that we need to face unpleasant situations with courage and determination. Later in her life, Teresa told her sisters to face these sorts of trials with 'determined determination'.

Returned soldiers also face trials that take them to the brink. I heard how US veterans find health and calmness in dressing up in costumes and playing parts in Shakespearean plays. The words of the plays arouse spiritual energies in them since the words remind them of the struggles and hardships and dangers they went through in their war experiences. We need not just courage but creativity to face the challenges we experience in our lives.

Scriptural Passages that Oppose the Nagging Spirit

Isaiah 64 speaks of a situation where the people start to lose hope. The passage asks: why have you left us to our own devices? why have you left us to be unfaithful to you? We too in these situations can admit how hopeless we feel and how helpless we are and then we can implore God to come and save us. In desolation, we start losing hope or we may have already lost hope. We ask God to bring us to a land where his face can shine on us. We can pray, 'Lord, I know you are there, come to console me and to save me'. We can also use this formula on ourselves: 'Change your ways! Turn around from the path you are taking which is the path of desolation and at least act as though you believe that God is with you'.

This is the theme of redemption in the Old Testament. A redeemer in the Hebrew language is one who rescues us when we are in danger from the enemy or if we are captured. The redeemer brings back the captives. When we are experiencing desolation, we are captive to the devil, our archenemy.

In order to stay awake and to change our ways, we have, in spite of our culture, to stop being impatient and be patient instead. In desolation we need patience. God will come at a time that we know not. This is certainly true. Our culture tells us: If it is not working, drop it: a plan, a sports coach, an idea. We want instant results but instead, we must witness to patience to our brothers and sisters.

In desolation we are in a battle. Romans 13 says, 'The night is nearly over and the day is at hand. We have to wake and to stay awake!' This is an important piece of advice when we are in desolation. We are to stay awake to recognise the thoughts that are coming to us to notice those that are coming from the devil. We are to remember them as quickly as possible and reject them.

Before doing something significant, we are in a period of waiting. We do not have to think that we are supposed to feel a certain way: calm or whatever. We can, however, feel and work with what we are feeling. The Lord comes and ransoms the captives, the slaves, those imprisoned, that is, us. The desolation need not stop us enjoying a snack or a walk. During these times the desolation may be strong but it is neutralised by the walking and our purposefulness. When we come back, we spend a little time preparing to do what we have to do and then wait. We then go to the classroom (if it is a teaching situation). We may quickly realise the students are very settled and their mood shifts to us. We too now feel settled and comfortable. Almost all the nagging has disappeared. The reason is that we have paid attention to the mood of the life situation that is before us.

In his homily, the deacon, an African, on this occasion spoke of how we expect things to be easy. When Africans come to religious life, they think this. Someone phoned him just after that person's final profession and said that he feared he had made a mistake in making final vows because the community seemed against him and everything was getting him down. The deacon told him that he had not made a mistake and that now he was taking up his vocation seriously. Now it was real and he needed to go ahead courageously.

When things are going along very smoothly and there are no difficulties and everything seems easy, it is time to be vigilant. We may be going the wrong way. This was the message a general superior gave at a final profession of some of her sisters. She told some of her own story: that during postulancy she wanted to leave. Then when it came to going to the novitiate, she felt she should not go and her parents did not want her to go. She settled down but things did not become suddenly easy. In fact, she said that her whole religious life had never been easy but, in the difficulties and the struggles, she had found joy. Jeremiah in the Old Testament said yes to God's call to be a prophet and he thought it would be straightforward: he would preach the word of God to the people and they would accept. But he found that the message he had to give was one of violence and destruction because the king of Judah wanted to co-operate with the king of Babylon. We too start enthusiastically like Jeremiah but soon find that we have to do unpopular things and we come across opposition from places where we do not expect. This was the way Jesus experienced his call and his journey too. He had to accept and not give in to the temptation of Peter that he would not have to suffer. He strongly turned away from Satan in the desert and to Peter saying: 'Get behind me Satan because what you say is not what God says' (Mark 8:32).

It is when we encounter difficulties, including desolation (the devil's biggest weapon), that we are taking up the life of a follower of Christ. It is not a sign that God has deserted us but is a step that we are taking towards Jesus. It is something actually positive. When we take up this responsibility and accept this cross, our faith will grow. If everything was always smooth, we would never grow in faith, hope and love.

In the gospel story of Jesus and the centurion (Luke 7:1-10), we are struck by the faith of the centurion to which Jesus responded. He truly believes that Jesus would cure the slave. This is the faith that Jesus is calling on us to have in times of desolation. We are to go ahead, believing like the centurion with all our heart that Jesus will answer my desperate prayer for help. A footnote on Matthew 8:5 in the Jerusalem Bible tells us that the faith that Jesus asks from the outset of his public life (Mark 1:5) is 'that act of trust and self-abandonment by which people no longer rely on their own strength and policies but commit themselves to the power and guiding word of him in whom they believe' (cf. Matthew 21:25; Luke 1:20, 45).

Everything is Made New

In Matthew 19:23, Jesus says, 'In truth I tell you, when everything is made new again, and the son of man is seated on his throne of glory, you yourselves will sit...' All is made new though we still have to wait for the completion of the newness which will be on the last day. But it was happening there and then at the beginning of a new semester. Beneath the appearances things are being made new. The new is always happening. We can see things with new eyes. Jesus brings about newness and changes that we cannot always see. This is the way we can approach challenges and things that we might otherwise fear.

The resurrection tells us that we are not totally hemmed in by events that have happened. God brings about the new in us as he did at the resurrection and he does the same things in our own lives whenever the new happens which is beyond our understanding and beyond what seems to be possible.

The parable of the talents (Matthew 25:14-30) tells us to focus on the gifts we have and to use the gifts. We are happy when we are given gifts, but we are happier when we use them. In the world of the spirit, there is no scarcity; it is the land of abundance. The Lord wants us to use the gifts he has given us because they are genuinely ours; he wants the gifts to bloom. In the parable the stewards think that the lord is harsh; in fact, he is not harsh but passionate. If we do not use spiritual gifts they will evaporate ('Take the talent from him and give it to the one who has five talents'). The more you give away, the more you will get. That is how things are in the spiritual world.

See also what Jesus says about gifts, 'Give and gifts will be given to you, full measure, pressed down and flowing over will be poured out; for the amount you measure out is the amount you will be given back' (Luke 6:38).

Suggestions and Activities to counteract desolation

Here are some activities that can help us be free of the nagging spirit:

1. Think of experiences of consolation and let them nourish you.

2. Reject the thoughts coming from the desolation.

3. Be active: e.g. for a walk; use your power of thinking.

4. If having to do something, open yourself to what is around you, the people and the attitudes and moods. Pay attention to people around you before the event: note their friendliness and good will.

5. Sing encouraging hymns to yourself
   'You alone are my strength, my shield,
   To you alone will my spirit yield...'

6. Process our negative memories and counteract them by remembering positive things.

7. Manage our idealism, perfectionism: we will never be perfect; we will always be experiencing some opposition. We don't have to have a standing ovation after every talk or presentation. Don't let our imperfections frustrate us. Be patient with our weaknesses and don't overrate them.

8. Let go of the things we cannot control e.g. mistakes that students make (inattention, laziness, drowsiness, lack of understanding). Address these when necessary in a friendly, non-judgmental way. Focus our areas of responsibility. Take responsibility where we can and leave the other areas that we can do nothing about.

9. Celebrate small gains. It is false to think that unless we do something big it does not count. Remember that Jesus spoke of tiny mustard seeds, a little yeast with the dough, the little flock, a secret deed and a simple cup of cold water.

Conclusion

The main focus of this chapter has been to examine how the spirit opposed to God works to deceive us in our lives and how we can withstand this deceitful and nagging force. We looked in some detail at the way the nagging spirit works to undermine our peace and take away our joy. We took many examples of the nagging spirit to see how varied its approach can be. Our first task is to recognise the voice. Just to recognise it and to steel ourselves to disbelieve the voice, brings good results. We are not to be frightened, not to back away because when we do, the nagging voice becomes more powerful. Exposing it takes away much of its power. Reflecting on scripture is a good way to unmask the nagging voice. We must also have in our minds continually that God's Spirit is at work in our life situations. Constant vigilance is necessary.

References

Alison, James, *Raising Abel: The Recovery of the Eschatological Imagination*, New York: Crossroad, 1996.

Louf, Andre, *Grace Can Do More: Spiritual Accompaniment and Spiritual Growth*, Kalamazoo, Cistercian Publications, 2002.

St Teresa of Avila, *Life*, in *The Collected Works of Teresa of Avila*, trans. Kieran Kavanaugh and Otilio Rodriguez, Vol.1, Washington, D.C.: Institute of Carmelite Studies, 1976.

Toner, J., S.J., *A Commentary on St Ignatius' Rules for the Discernment of Spirits*, St Louis: The Institute of Jesuit Sources, 1979.

van Kaam, Adrian, *The Dynamics of Spiritual Direction*, Denville: Dimension Books, 1976.

Chapter Nine

The Wind Blows Where It Will: Recognising the Spirit's Action Today

IN JOHN'S GOSPEL, a Pharisee named Nicodemus comes to Jesus by night to find out who Jesus is and where he comes from (John 3:1-21). Jesus and he enter into a discussion where Jesus speaks about being born of the Spirit. Nicodemus takes Jesus' words literally about being born again of the Spirit. Jesus says that the wind (the Spirit) will not give any signs but will blow wherever it wills (cf. John 3:8). This further puzzles Nicodemus since he wants things to be plain. We are like this also today and often we take it for granted that we know where the Spirit is moving. This was certainly the case in the church before Vatican II. The pope at that time had supreme authority.[88] The bishops and priests were the ones who knew what God wanted since they were the ones who had studied the Scripture and the laws of the church. It

---

[88] See Paul Collins, *Absolute Power: How the Pope Became the Most Influential Man in the World*, New York: Hachette Book Group, 2018.

was expected that a Catholic would consult the priests about interpreting a Scripture passage or a law of the church such as sending children to Catholic schools. The priest interpreted the laws of abstinence on Fridays and any questions about who a Catholic could marry. But here in this passage Jesus is telling us that we cannot understand what God is doing simply by knowing laws.

In the church before Vatican II, that is, before 1963, the emphasis was on God being supernatural, that is, above the created world. God was powerful and had very powerful commandments to ensure that people acted according to the laws of the church. In the area of morality, there was an almost total identification of the church with God. The laws were clear and failure to obey the laws brought very strong punishments. Not going to Mass on Sunday was considered a mortal sin and if a person died in mortal sin he/she would go to hell. There could hardly be a worse punishment! The authority of the church was so strong because there was a general belief that God did act in this way even though God was also loving. The sharp difference between the supernatural and the natural made it easier to think that God could make laws like this.

Before the Council, belief in God was strongly interwoven with social beliefs. Everyone in the Catholic Church shared these beliefs. It was almost unheard of that someone who was a Catholic did not share them. People felt secure because everyone believed the same things and, as long as one obeyed the commandments, fear of the all-powerful God was kept at bay. In the late sixties, a Jesuit priest, Fr Alphonso Nebreda, visited Australia from the East Asian Pastoral Institute in

Manila with a message that helped people become more self-aware. He said that when he went to Japan as a missionary he was amazed to find that no one in Japan shared the same Catholic beliefs about God as he had. This was amazing to him since in the Philippines, his own country, everyone believed them.

Those who can remember the church before Vatican II will recognise the truth of the presentation given above. Since that time, there has been a great shift in the church's attitude to authority and to its relationship with the world as well as very great changes in society. At Vatican II, enormous changes were made to the teachings of the church and there was wide expectation that the church's attitude to its own authority would change. But instead, under the influence of Pope John Paul II and Cardinal Ratzinger, later Pope Benedict XVI, there was a return to insistence on the ministerial priesthood and its distinction from the laity. These two leaders in fact were afraid to implement the changes advocated by the Council fearing that the church would be weakened.

In the wider culture, enormous changes have taken place since 1960. Emphasis is now put on the self and on how people experience things subjectively rather than on what objectively happens. There is emphasis now on feeling. It is the individual now who is considered important. The collective life of the church has been almost totally lost. The authority of the church has been greatly weakened. Catholics now make up their own minds about what is right and wrong.

According to Charles Taylor, there are two types of sensibility which are present today. One is what he calls a stifling moralism. The other is a trust in 'the first promptings of love'.[89] Most people today have an abhorrence of moralism. They hate being told what they can do and cannot do. This does not necessarily mean that they do not care what is good and bad but that they do not want to be told. Attitudes to homosexuality and gay marriage have changed. The general consensus now is that, with regard to moral matters, people should not be treated in an infantile fashion but as adults. They may need guidelines but not be told what to do as though they were children.

The First Promptings of Love

What people do respond to today are those who in their lives show a spontaneous love for others, who 'trust in the first promptings of love'. St Thérèse of Lisieux continues to be hugely popular because her love was so evidently genuine. People are not turned off when they hear her say:

> I would wish to be flayed like St Bartholomew; to be plunged into boiling oil like St John; I desire like St Ignatius of Antioch to be ground by the teeth of wild beasts so as to become a bread worthy of God. With St Agnes and St Cecilia, I would present my neck to the executioner's sword, and like Joan of Arc at the burning stake, murmur the name of Jesus...[90]
>
> Love alone is capable of setting the other members (of the body) in motion and if love were ever to die out, then the apostles would cease to proclaim the gospel and the martyrs refuse to shed their blood.[91]

---

[89] Charles Taylor, *A Secular Age*, Cambridge, Mass.: Belknap Press, 2007.
[90] St. Therese of Lisieux, *The Story of a Soul*.
[91] Ibid.

Rather than being turned off, they are moved by the genuine love that Thérèse had and want to hear more. Their cynicism is challenged and they are likely to be inspired to change their own lives. No one today scoffs when they read chapter 13 of Paul's first letter to the Corinthians:

> Love is patient, love is kind. It does not envy, it does not boast, it is not proud. It does not dishonor others, it is not self-seeking, it is not easily angered, it keeps no record of wrongs. Love does not delight in evil but rejoices with the truth. It always protects, always trusts, always hopes, always perseveres (verses 4 to 7).

When we hear the following words of Mother Teresa, we are probably not put off by the piety but moved by the fact that it is clear that Mother Teresa clearly believes it:

> Pain and suffering have come into your life, but remember pain, sorrow, suffering are but the kiss of Jesus – a sign that you have come so close to him that he can kiss you.[92]

The saint who has probably been most inspirational throughout the history of the church and who continues to be today is St Francis of Assisi. George Bernanos, the famous novelist, compared the reaction of Francis with that of Luther to the scandals which both saw in the church of their day. Luther revolted and left the church. Francis would have been just as horrified as Luther at the immorality and greed of priests but he did not revolt. In fact, he continued to love the church. Bernanos says:

---

[92] Mother Teresa, https://www.brainyquote.com/authors/mother_teresa

Instead, he threw himself into poverty, immersing himself in it as deeply as possible along with his followers. He found in poverty the very source and wellspring of all inspiration and all purity. Instead of attempting to snatch from the church her ill-gotten goods, he overwhelmed her with invisible treasures, and under the hand of this beggar the heaps of gold and lust began blossoming like an April hedge.[93]

In her book, *The Quest for the Living God*, Elizabeth Johnson presents very positively the Hispanic church in the U.S.[94] While it is very much part of the Catholic Church, it has very distinctive characteristics. It certainly comes under Taylor's category of having a festive and devotional emphasis. It is happy to have priests or bishops lead its ceremonies but is happy also to have ceremonies where there are no priests. Its ideas about God come out of the people's experience, not from church dogma. It is born out of the oppression and poverty of indigenous peoples by the European and American conquest. It has similarities with the church before the Second Vatican Council. This indicates that it is very strongly ingrained in the people and where God is found in the community. One of the chief devotions of the Hispanic church is to the Virgin of Guadalupe who appeared to a peasant, Juan Diego, in the hills outside Mexico.

Latino theology emphasises the faith of the poor. The Virgin of Guadalupe is a symbol of divine love present in the Latino world. The Latino church goes against the trend in

---

[93] Quoted in *Magnificat*,
[94] Elizabeth Johnson, *The Quest for the Living God*.

the Western world that religion is losing its appeal. Rather, it indicates that some aspects of religion are very resilient and do not depend on a strong clergy or church structure.

The Hispanic church indicates that the Spirit blows where it wills in not following the trend of a lessening of religious practice. We have seen that the Spirit is present and active in devotional and festive aspects of religion. Throughout the world, there is great interest in world youth days, in pilgrimages, in the lives of striking figures such as Pope John Paul I, Mother Teresa (now Saint Mother Teresa) and our present Pope Francis. However, we must return to the reality that in Europe, to a lesser extent in the U.S. and in countries like Australia and Canada, huge changes are occurring in church practice. The diminishment of religious practice in these parts of the world began long before Vatican II but the effects in much of Europe and in Australia and now in the U.S. have only become obvious in the last twenty or thirty years. In these areas, the church is in crisis. Reactions to the crisis are being seen clearly in the recent opposition to Pope Francis coming not from opponents of the church but from within the church itself. We have seen how Pope John Paul II and Pope Benedict XVI (formerly Cardinal Ratzinger) opposed the changes begun with Vatican II. They insisted on a strong distinction being made between laity and clergy. They opposed any debate on the church's teachings on sexual morality, divorce, marriage, homosexuality and married clergy. They wanted the church to remain as it was. Then five years ago a new pope was elected, Pope Francis, who holds very different views.

Resistance to Change

Pope Francis has promoted open dialogue within the church. At a synod on the family, he encouraged all bishops to speak their mind about any issue they wished but also to listen humbly to the views of others. The prohibition on discussion on married clergy was lifted. Pope Francis has spoken strongly on what he calls the evil of clericalism which keeps the clergy as a privileged class in the church. He emphasises a baptismal ecclesiology where all those who are baptised are equal. Richard Gaillardetz explains in a 2018 article in *The Tablet*:

> Francis has time and again emphasised the Council's teaching that all the baptised possess a spiritual instinct for the faith, a *sensus fidelium* (*Lumen Gentium*, 12) which can contribute much to the life of the church. This retrieval of the Council's teaching is central to his call for a synodal, listening church.[95]

Here are the details of the opposition of clerics to Pope Francis. Four cardinals challenged the Pope's teaching officially asking for clarification of some of his positions. The prefect of the Congregation for Divine Worship openly went against the wishes of the pope for liturgical reform; the retired Archbishop Carlo Maria Vigano publicly accused the Pope of covering up charges against an American archbishop for harassing seminarians and priests. These challenges to Pope Francis indicate clearly that many within the Vatican do not want the changes originating with Vatican II that the

---

[95] Richard Gaillardetz, 'Francis under Fire,' *The Tablet*, 22 September 2018.

Pope is now officially being challenged by church leaders. They do not want lay leadership in the church which would weaken their power; they do not want to emphasise the missionary nature of the church. Pope Francis insists that power and security will not give life to the church.

Why is it that many within the church do not want the changes that are so necessary if the church is to be credible to people today? The answer must be that they feel threatened. They want to hold on for dear life to their control. They identify their power with divine power. They think that the church has withstood the Vatican II changes for the last fifty years, so why can't the resistance continue successfully. If they allow the changes to come, the church will be overthrown by stronger powers. It will cease to be the church. The reason for resistance is fear. Leaders do not want to be vulnerable or weak.

What Pope Francis and his opponents probably share is a desire that the church will survive. His opponents want it to survive by clinging on to its glories of the past. Pope Francis believes that it was the Holy Spirit that was very clearly present in the changes made at Vatican II and believes that church leaders and especially himself need to have the courage to enter into the changes which has, at its centre, honest dialogue with the wider society to whom the church believes she is sent. Francis wants priests to go out to the homes of people and to their workplaces and interact with them. He does not want the church to look good by having its buildings full every week and to be seen to be successful. Rather he says:

If something should rightly disturb us and trouble our consciences, it is the fact that so many of our brothers and sisters are living without the strength, light and consolation born of friendship with Jesus Christ, without a community of faith to support them, without meaning and a goal in life.[96]

Francis does not see those who are not going to church or who do not agree with the church as enemies but as people who need the support that the church can give them. He does not want to make their lives harder by imposing something on them but of giving them something that will make them happy. In this following statement, Francis acknowledges that those who are resistant to change are motivated by something good, that is, what they think is the survival of the church:

> More than by fear of going astray, my hope is that we will be moved by the fear of remaining shut up within structures which gives us a false sense of security, within rules which make us harsh judges, within habits which make us feel safe, while at our door people are starving and Jesus does not tire of saying to us: 'Give them something to eat' (Mark 6:37).[97]

Francis here paints an accurate picture of how church leaders resistant to change are seen by people at large. If the church is to be effective it must be ready to dialogue with others on an equal level; it must stop being or giving the

---

[96] Pope Francis, *The Joy of the Gospel*, 49.
[97] Ibid.

impression of judging others for their shortcomings; it must stop using language that no longer registers with people.

In this chapter, we are concerned with trying to recognise where the elusive Spirit of God is working in the world today. We have looked at how there are two views within the church. One sees the Spirit as moving the church to be open to the world and ready to change; the other thinks that the Spirit is calling the church to be defensive and to hold on to what it has. When we put it in these terms, it seems that the position of Pope Francis is more likely to be right. How then is the church to interact with the wider world? First, it must acknowledge that the changes that have happened over the last thousand years.[98] The attitude of people to God and to the supernatural has changed. One of the main changes has occurred in the way that God acts in the world. Charles Taylor shows how the sense of a God who is transcendent and who acts outside of human activity has disappeared to a great extent.[99] Human beings today in the Western world are more open to immanence than to transcendence, that is, to a power beyond the human but working within the human. Taylor calls this 'the immanent frame'. Except for particular spiritualities such as that within the Hispanic church, people are not very open to miracles as they used to be. Appearances of Mary can be very influential to certain communities but not to people in general. When we read the miracle stories in

---

[98] For a treatment of the changes in the church since medieval times see, D'Orsa, Jim and Therese, *Explorers, Guides and Meaning-Makers: Mission Theology for Catholic Educators*, Mulgrave: John Garratt Publishing, 2010.

[99] Charles Taylor, *A Secular Age*, Cambridge, Mass.: Belknap Press, 2007.

the gospels today, we find it hard to believe that the miracles happened exactly as they are described in the gospels. The reason is that human minds today believe that God works within the immanent frame rather than outside it. People are sceptical of outside interventions from God.

Taylor speaks of 'the immanent frame' from which the modern world looks at reality. This, he says, is an invention of the West rather than something that accords with reality. It allows people to set aside the idea that the world is created. Taylor rejects this approach and investigates other ways of approaching the reality which we call God within the created order. One way is through poetry and literature. Today, there is a return to interest in an order of reality beyond the mere prosaic and mundane. People long to explore this reality and are very open to hearing new ideas about it. One way is through novels. In her historical novel, *The Lieutenant*,[100] Kate Grenville tells the story of a young Englishman, Daniel Rooke. He is different from other young men and has a great capacity to study and to be by himself. He discovers, with the help of a mentor, that he has abilities in mathematics and astronomy. He decides to join the merchant navy and after one journey to the New World, he finds himself assigned to the first fleet to go to Australia. As a member of the navy, he is also a soldier although he has no interest in fighting or using weapons. One of the first issues to be dealt with in the new colony is relations with the indigenous people. As part of his study of astronomy, Rooke is assigned to study the stars in a hut on his own. While he is there, Aboriginal people come to visit him

---

[100] Kate Grenville, *The Lieutenant*, Melbourne: Text Publishing, 2008.

and he sets up good relations with them. Men and women and children come. Rooke is interested in learning some of the language of the Aboriginals and develops a relationship with one of the girls, other children, but on one occasion she comes on her own. She indicates that she is wet and Rooke offers her his coat but realises that she has never worn clothes and that she would get dry quicker without the cloak he offered her. We are not told the age of Tagaran, probably deliberately, but she is definitely a child. And the relationship between her and Rooke is not a sexual one.

Rooke learns much language from Tagaran and she from him. On one occasion she comes to him and tells him that she has been hit by a white man. She expects Rooke, her friend, to do something about this ill treatment, but Rooke knows he can do nothing. Any complaint he could make would be ignored. Relations between the whites and the Aboriginals are at first okay but there is always danger of misunderstanding or of violence from one of the parties. The first incident happens at this time of a white man, the major's game keeper, being speared by an Aboriginal. The whites decide that the punishment for this will be to take the culprit along with six other Aboriginal men and execute them. This, they say, will teach the Aboriginal community a lesson. Rooke is assigned to be one of the party to find the men to be killed. In the meantime, his relationship with Tagaran has become closer. This relationship is more intimate than any relationship he has ever had except with his sister. It is a friendship which means a lot to him and he knows that being part of the team to capture the Aboriginal men will destroy the friendship.

When Tagaran comes next, he tells her as clearly as he can that there will be a raid on the men and he says, 'I would like you to tell Wagarun (the Aboriginal leader)'. At this, Tagaran looked straight into his eyes. She understood; he could see that. Not just the words but the significance of him having said them to her.[101] He enjoyed using her language to tell her this and noticed the pleasure he got from the melodious sound of the Aboriginal words. Then he reflects:

> He could hear a bird above them chattering as if scolding the dry whisper of the leaves. Everything was going on as it always had. For centuries, for millennia, the forebears of that bird had sat out there and the forebears of those leaves had whispered in that breeze. Only in here were things changed.[102]

He then tells her that he will be one of the party that will hunt and capture the men. Again, she understands this. He finds it is a relief to say this to her but it is also a risk since he does not know how she will take it. Then he says to her:

> 'What is to be done, Tagaran? What is to become of us?' She went over to the fireplace and held out her hands to the coals. He thought it was her polite way of ending their conversation. But then she turned back to him and held out her hands for his. She pressed his fingers with her own. He felt her skin warm and smooth... Everything in his life had come down to the sensation of her fingers against his. The person he was, the history he carried within himself, every joy and grief he had

---
[101] *The Lieutenant*, 254.
[102] Ibid.

ever experienced, slipped away like an irrelevant garment. He was nothing but skin, speaking to another skin, and between the skins there was no need to find the words.[103]

In describing religious experiences within 'the immanent frame' of the modern mind, Taylor speaks of the experience of fullness. It is an experience 'of the world imbued with meaning, beauty and connection.' The person today sees such an experience as subjective but also objective, that is, an experience of the world as it is. To describe the world this way means that the immanent frame can be maintained but the excitement of something beyond the human can also be experienced.

In the description of Rooke's experience with the Aboriginal girl, Tagaran, Grenville speaks within the immanent frame. Taylor does not lament that people today speak in this way. To speak in terms of transcendence of this world which is done from a faith perspective would be a more complete admission of the reality of God. But this absence is something to be expected and not bemoaned. Let us look at the difference between interpreting an experience as one of fullness within the immanent frame with an interpretation of the same experience from a faith perspective.

Believers agree that God normally works within the immanent frame. But the way they talk about an experience of fullness is different. A Christian would see the experience of Daniel Rooke with Tagaran as having many dimensions: cultural, historical, psychological and spiritual. We all have experiences of union or love or something beyond our own

---

[103] Ibid.

human powers. When we look at God's intervention in the history of the Israelite people in the Old Testament, we look first at what happened. We do not think that the events happened exactly as they are described. What happened at the call of Abraham? Abraham probably had a feeling inside him that his people needed to leave the place where they were if they were to survive. But the people eventually interpreted this event in terms of Yahweh choosing them. Similarly, the Exodus from Egypt, that is, the escape from Egypt and the crossing of the Red Sea was a series of actual events. But the people interpreted them as God intervening in order to save them. We continue today to interpret events from the viewpoint of God's activity in our lives. What then is the advantage of believing that God is specifically at work in these events? What is the advantage of giving a distinctive religious connotation to certain happenings?

In one of his books, William Barry reflects on this question. He gives the example of a family at the death of a loved one. The various members of the family gather in the house and speak of their memories of this deceased person. They remember the goodness of the person. They are happy to be together and gain consolation from each other in the stories they tell. A believer might say that God is actually present with these family members as they gather. Does it matter that the name of God or Jesus is not mentioned? Yes, says Barry. Without seeing God's presence in this experience of being consoled and strengthened, there is something missing. It is an incomplete experience and the meaning of the event is not examined. Think of all the richness of ideas and teachings in the Catholic Church that surround the event of death: the death of Jesus and his resurrection from the dead; the idea that this present life will be transformed; God's overcoming of the forces of evil and death; God's forgiveness of the person's sins. Unless the word God is mentioned none of these rich thoughts and realities are mentioned. St Paul deals with death and the afterlife in his letter to the Corinthians. After dealing with Christ being raised from the dead he says: 'Then the end will come, when he hands over the kingdom to God the Father after he has destroyed all dominion, authority and power. For he must reign until he has put all his enemies under his feet. The last enemy to be destroyed is death. For he 'has put everything under his feet'. Now when it says that 'everything' has been put under him, it is clear that this does not include God himself, who put everything under Christ (1 Corinthians 15:24-27).

Such a positive vision of the end of the world and the end of our own lives gives us hope we would never have reached without the mention of God, that is, without religious language which goes beyond just the immanent frame.

Conclusion

Great changes have occurred in the last hundred years and more with regard to religious belief. People no longer go to church in the same numbers as they used; they do not follow church leaders as they used; they no longer understand much of the language that the church uses. On the other hand, people today are searching for something more than just everyday life. They want meaning, they search for solitude, they learn techniques for meditation. We must see what has happened with decline of religious practice in a larger context. The Spirit blows where it will and is doing so in the world today. In accordance with the action of the Spirit, we too must be open to change and embrace it because God is always doing something new.

The Spirit is moving the church to move into dialogue with those not belonging to a church. Pope Francis says that the role of the church is to offer those outside the consolation of a community of faith. From this point of view, it is a cause of sadness that people do not belong to a church. The answer, however, is not to judge them but to remember that the Spirit blows where it will. Those in the church need to see the good things that are happening. It is a cause of rejoicing that there is so much interest to day in religion today even if it is within 'the immanent frame'. If the churches are empty, this may not be a bad thing. It may be better for people ask themselves if they really want a relationship with the transcendent dimension of life. Karl Rahner said that the church of the future will be a church of mystics. Many of those who filled the churches in the past were there not out of conviction but out of habit. They were simply cultural Christians. Bonhoeffer said that religious language such as salvation, heaven and hell were overused and that such terms should not be used for a period of time so that they could regain some of the meaning that they formerly had.

One very important development among churches is the dialogue that is happening between them. An article in *The Tablet* speaks of an artist, Nicola Green, who in the last ten year has been present at meetings of faith leaders and portrayed them in ways so as to provoke thought about their work. She saw leaders of different faiths working side by side on issues. One of these meetings was between the Dalai Lama and the then Archbishop of Canterbury, Rowan Williams. Others have included Pope Francis and other Catholic leaders. She says, 'They're not saying they think the same, and they're not trying to compromise: instead, they're trying to work out how they can sit alongside someone with whom they have a different belief'.

The dialogue that is taking place with leaders of the different churches and faiths is certainly the work of the Spirit in the world today. There is a greater respect for the freedom of others in what they believe. The situation today of people's relationships with churches does not mean that we should not work to improve things. The Spirit does not seem to be working in those within the church opposing Pope Francis. Gaillardetz is right in saying:

> But many of Francis' critics are resisting his leadership and even calling for his resignation because they discern in his papacy the bold, reforming vision of Vatican II, to which they may pay lip service but would prefer to see emasculated. The success of this pontificate likely represents the last best chance for decades to come for the decisive realisation of the vision of Vatican II.[104]

---

[104] See Gaillardetz.

References

Allison Jr. Dale C., *Death Comes: Death, Imagination, and the Last Things*, Grand Rapids: William B. Eerdmans, 2016.

Barry, W., *Spiritual Direction and the Encounter with God: A Theological Enquiry*, New York: Paulist Press, 2004.

D'Orsa, Jim and Thérèse, *Explorers, Guides and Meaning-Makers: Mission Theology for Catholic Educators*, Mulgrave: John Garratt Publishing, 2010.

Gaillardetz, Richard, 'Francis Under Fire', *The Tablet*, 22 September, 2018.

Grenville, Kate, *The Lieutenant*, Melbourne: Text publishing, 2008.

Johnson, Elizabeth, *The Quest for the Living God*, London: Continuum, 2011.

Taylor, Charles, *A Secular Age*, Cambridge, Mass.: Belknap Press, 2007.

Moorhead, Joanna, 'Faces of Faith', *The Tablet*, 22 September, 2018.

Magnificat magazine, Yonkers, NY, USA.

Chapter Ten

Walking Humbly with God

IN CHAPTER 6 OF THE PROPHET MICAH there is a dialogue between God and the people where God asks: 'O my people, what have I done to you? In what way have I been a burden to you?' (Micah 6:3). The people are contrite when they hear this lament of God and want to know what they can do to console God. They say,

> What shall I bring when I come before the Lord
> And bow down before God the most high?
> Shall I come with burnt offerings
> With sacrifices of yearling calves?
> Will the Lord be pleased with thousands of rams,
> With ten thousand streams of oil.
> Should I offer my first born for my sins,
> The fruit of my body for my wrongdoing? (Micah 6:6-7)

And here is the answer coming through the prophet:

> You have been told, O mortal, what is good
> And what the Lord requires of you:
> Only to do justice, to love mercy,
> And to walk humbly with your God. (Micah 6:8)

The people are genuinely contrite and sincerely want to pay some compensation to God. They think of all the difficult, even heroic things they might do: offering animals; and then the seriously harmful thing of giving their first-born child for their sins. God rejects these suggestions. Instead, God wants them to walk humbly with him, God. The people think in terms of heroics. The suggestions they make are not realistic and have little or no chance of being implemented. God does not ask for this.

It may seem that the people are being incredibly generous whereas they are actually listening to a voice that wants to keep them far from God and far from living the lives that God wants of them. We too get grandiose ideas in our heads which take us away from ordinary reality. God, on the other hand, wants us to go about our lives humbly and to resist these false desires which will only discourage us and probably lead us back to being unfaithful to God.

At the bottom of these seemingly good thoughts of the people is self-centredness. We think of how heroic we will be, of how we will be better and more generous than anyone else. Our focus is not on God but on ourselves and our attitude is not humble but proud. In his book, *The Dynamics of Spiritual Self Direction*, Adrian van Kaam speaks of how our life situation proposes life directives to us. God, he says, speaks to us mainly through these directives. The first aim of humility is to respect the limits that God puts upon us as human beings. Humility means accepting who we are and living within these limitations. We grow in humility not by assiduously cultivating the exceptional virtue of humility which few possess, but simply of entering into our lives trustingly and gratefully.

From this perspective, most people have a good deal of humility. Almost everyone accepts their life situation to a fairly high degree. We get up in the morning and go to work or to whatever we have to do. We accept a lot of drudgery during an ordinary day. We look forward to going out to celebrations, to spending time with friends, to having holidays. We go through childhood and accept this time of our lives, then adolescence, then young adulthood. We spend a good many years from thirty to sixty or seventy within the limitations of our responsibilities and our abilities. By the time we get to our late sixties and seventies most of us are able to spend our time profitably without having to be constantly entertained. Accepting our life situation and trying to listen to the directives coming from it are the basis of the virtue of humility. What we call humility may have other elements but this listening as well as we can to our life situation is the basis.

So first there is the situation we are in which we can accept or reject. Here are some examples of limitations. The day is cold and windy; there are no oranges in the house; someone is unresponsive to me; I don't feel well; I have a heart attack; I have DVT and spend time in hospital; I get swelling in the legs; I am old and do not have the strength I used to have; I lose my good looks; I am not as intelligent as others I admire; I do not relate well; I have a quarrel with someone I care about; I lose something that is very important; I do not have the use of a vehicle and am restricted in my movements; I have back problems which restrict my walking; I wake up feeling in very low spirits.

The way to be humble is to accept these limitations as well as we can. Grumbling is considered in the Old Testament to be a major sin: think of the people who complained to God in the wilderness and who wanted to go back to the fleshpots of Egypt; or of the scouts that Joshua sent to reconnoitre Canaan who came back and said that the inhabitants were giants and who painted an impossible picture of entering the land. We have times when we feel like grumbling. When we do, we are not humble but proud. We can also cultivate a sense of thanksgiving for all the life situations we are in. When we do this, we are accepting the gifts God gives us along with the inevitable limitations. We can cultivate humility by being attentive to the life situations and accepting them when they are difficult and being thankful when they are congenial.

Let us take some examples of life situations being accepted. Someone has had a heart attack and been through an operation and rehabilitation. How well has she accepted the fears that the pains in her chest may signal another heart attack? How patiently has she engaged in the rehabilitation program activities and been patient in noticing the gradual improvement in herself? Does she keep working at improving her walking and other activities that exercise the heart? I am in a tram which is quite crowded; the driver announces to the passengers that the tram will end at this stop rather than continue the final three stops. Do I join in the complaints of some passengers who make nasty remarks to the driver as they leave the tram? I notice that most people accept the slight inconvenience.

These are some examples of the choice that we have to accept the life situation through which God speaks to us or to reject it. In order to be aware of God's voice in them, we need inner quiet and simplicity. We can practise accepting what is there instead of expecting it to be some other way. We can let situations speak freely to us. We can remind ourselves that the divine voice is speaking in all these ordinary situations.

Seeing our life situation as the way through which the divine speaks to us is to see that the spiritual is in the everyday and not somewhere else. We can gradually develop trust in this God who speaks to us in this ordinary way. Our lives consist also of specifically religious things such as prayer and listening to religious songs together. I watch a song on TV which moves me deeply. I notice the great fervour that those in the film clip have as they sing and how they repeat again and again the melody and the words which move me so much. I want to hear the song again and I do not want to leave from there. This is what it was like for the three disciples, Peter, James and John, who experienced Jesus transfigured on the mountain. Like these three disciples and even Jesus himself, we have to come down from the mountain. The purpose of the experience of the song was not to take us out of our ordinary life situation but to help us to return to it with greater zest and enthusiasm.

The life situation is not always pleasant. We can get on well with someone and feel we are close to that person, and later find that the person did not feel as warmly to us as we felt to them. Or it may seem that way. Our task is to look as honestly as we can at the actual situation without exaggerating it. It may be that that person did feel warmly towards us but those feelings have changed over time. Teachers have this experience. They may have a very powerful influence on their students while they teach them, but gradually this influence lessens. Our task is to be in the situation and to respond as lovingly as we can. To do this, we need to put aside our fear of being hurt.

Van Kaam believes that the appropriate response to a situation can arise spontaneously.[105] We begin to do something such as write a chapter or prepare a prayer. As we go through the process of interacting with the ideas and sources we have available, the way forward with the chapter or the prayer often becomes clear without our knowing exactly how. In order to open ourselves to the situation to see what directives it is giving us, we may need to put aside 'the vital life of passion and desire'. Van Kaam suggests that this passion may fade when we are gently present to the situation without trying to control the outcome.

The elder son in the parable of the prodigal son is an example of someone who rejects the disclosures from the life situation. The situation of the return of his younger brother and the loving forgiveness of the father invite him to come into the feast and to celebrate with the whole household. He refuses to join in the joy of the celebration even though his father praises his faithfulness and pleads with him to come in to the feast. The reason for this son's refusal is his focus on himself. Julian McDonald comments on this refusal:

> The elder brother is too stuffy, too full of his own righteousness to allow his father's passion and tenderness to touch him. He will not let his father's infectious joy distract him from his fixation with duty. And he cannot

---

[105] Adrian van Kaam, *The Dynamics of Spiritual Self Direction*, 49.

accept that it is his own inner anger and self-pity blocking him from softening. He can't even acknowledge that it is his own brother who has returned home. Instead, he spits at his father a stinging insult: 'Then, when this son of yours returns after squandering your property with loose women, you kill the fatted calf for him'.[106]

The son insulates himself from the situation by his judgmental attitude to his brother and to his sense that he has been treated unjustly by his father. He refuses to open his heart and gives himself many reasons for not doing so. Psalm 95, the psalm which opens Vigils in the Prayer of the Church begins, 'Today, if you hear his voice, harden not your hearts'. This is what the elder son refuses to do.

Van Kaam speaks of erratic heroism.[107] By this he means the tendency we all sometimes have to be dissatisfied with the present situation. If we are married, the thought comes that we should be more dedicated to God and hence unmarried as St Paul advises in 2 Corinthians. If we have taken vows in an active religious congregation, we think we are not doing enough and that God is calling us to become contemplatives. If we are teachers or lecturers, we imagine that we should be doing some form of manual work. We feel guilty because our standard of living is too high even though we are not living extravagantly. We see poor people in the slums of Kibera in Kenya and we feel guilty for not living lives of poverty like them. We think of famous people who have been at the top of their field such as actors, writers. For some

---

[106] Julian McDonald, Unpublished Commentary on Sunday Readings.
[107] Adrian van Kaam, *The Dynamics of Spiritual Self Direction*.

reason, we are not satisfied with them because they have not published more. Nothing is ever enough for us.

Another form of this temptation is to be dissatisfied with the gifts that we have. We think that we should be more successful or more famous. We have a gift to write but we fail to find a publisher and therefore we stop writing altogether instead of developing the gift that we have, even though it may not be as big a gift as someone else's. We offer a course and there are few who take the course. There is a tendency for us to downplay the good that we do or the achievements that we have. We become very discouraged that we are not as successful or as popular as someone else. We think that when we give a class or a talk that we should receive a 'standing ovation'. In all these ways, we are failing to accept humbly the lot that the Lord marks out for us through the life situation in which we find ourselves.

Ways of being out of touch with the life situation[108]

Being preoccupied with an idea or ideology can put us out of touch with the life situation. In a feature in the *The Age*, 25 September 2018, Zoe Strimpel says that 'the din of outrage about sexism, homophobia and racism is at fever pitch' just at a time when these three evils are at their weakest. She refers to the #Me Too movement where women are encouraged to bring up cases of sexual abuse or harassment against men. She is not against this movement but rather the abuse of it. The

---

[108] Marko Rupnik, SJ, *Discernment: Acquiring the Heart of God*, Boston: Pauline Books & Media, 2006.

proponents of #Me Too are often opposed to due process or to listening to the men's side of the story. Strimpel claims that in their defence of women's rights to expose sexual abuse, they use emotionally abusive behaviour themselves. They seek to silence any voices that try to put accusations into perspective and give as an example the opposition to Woody Allen's wife and former adoptive daughter, Soon-Yi Previn, who defended Allen against accusations that he had been abusive to her. She speaks about 'the growing intolerance of viewpoints other than left-wing orthodoxies'. We remember the McCarthy witch hunts in post-war USA against anyone suspected of sympathy with Communism. As a result, hundreds of people were unjustly accused of being Communists. The reason for these accusations and injustices is that the perpetrators get an idea into their head and this becomes the truth rather than seeking for the truth in the life situations in which people find themselves. They refuse to seek out the truth gradually and piece by piece and, instead, claim to have the truth in the ideology that they are using.

We can be passionate about the point we are making and not listen to the viewpoints of others. We defend a thought to the bitter end. We get over excited in putting forward our cause. Our focus is on the cause and not on God or on how others will benefit. We become wilful, wanting one thing regardless of anything or anyone else. There is a lack of love in the way we say things and relate to others. We blame others when relationships are not going well. These are all ways in which each of us tends to replace the truth that resides in the life situation with an idea.

We can fail to accept the directive from our life situation

by giving undue importance to our feelings. We focus only on the inner warmth we feel when we make some sacrifice. We get hooked on feelings and inner experiences. When we have a conflict with someone, we find it devastating; we are excessively hurt when someone does not respect us or give us the attention that we expect. We become attached to the pleasure we get from our work. The important thing, however, is not whether we feel emotionally 'charged' and close to others but whether we are doing our job as well as we can and doing what is ultimately best for others as far as we see it.

Men fail to see accurately the life situation of women and as a result make sweeping judgments about the attitudes these women have to them. 'Miss Temptation', a short story by Kurt Vonnegut,[109] begins with a description of Susanna who is living in a small village one summer while performing at night in the community theatre nearby. In the afternoons, she shows off her beauty by walking barefoot through the town not talking to anyone except to buy a New York newspaper at the drugstore. After this routine, she returns to the room above the firehouse where she stays. A young man, Fuller, notices her each afternoon and is attracted to her but thinks that she would be too 'stuck up' to talk to him. He thinks that women like Susanna are beyond the likes of himself.

One day, after she buys her newspaper at the drugstore, he confronts her about the way she walks down the street

---

[109] *Miss Temptation* by Kurt Vonnegut was published in *The Saturday Evening Post* in 1956.

like a temptress. Fuller criticises all women saying they are all the same. Susanna thanks him politely but does not know why he criticises her like this. But the next day, Fuller finds out that Susanna did not go to the theatre that night and did not pick up her papers. Fuller is surprised but pleased that his outburst to her might have been the cause of her not working that night. The drugstore owner challenges Fuller to take her papers to her. He goes to her house and is ushered in. He finds that the room is very ordinary and nothing like what he had expected and Susanna is dressed in very ordinary clothes. He realises that Susanna is just an ordinary young woman struggling to be accepted by others and without any airs about herself. Susanna invites Fuller to walk down the street with him on her usual walk. She changes into her showy outdoor clothes and they walk together down the street.

Fuller had been unable to interpret the situation involving this young woman. Instead of seeing what was there and reacting appropriately, he imagined her to be an arrogant, uncaring and irresponsible flirt. Instead, her life was commonplace like his and her struggles just as difficult for her as his own were to him. The whole episode forced him to see reality in its ordinariness and to respond to it accordingly.

Listening to Scripture

We have been seeing how a basic step in humility is when we accept the directives that come to us from our ordinary life situation. We can find ourselves being out of step with ordinary reality by being preoccupied with a cause such as feminism or racism and by giving undue importance to our feelings. We have seen also in the short story of Kurt Vonnegut how our prejudices and sensitivities can remove us from seeing what is actually there before us. The book of Proverbs can help us be in touch with what the ordinary situations of our lives require of us. Proverbs simply speaks about doing good to others: doing a kindness to someone if we can, not plotting harm against the person next door, not picking groundless quarrels with someone who has not done us harm, not being violent (3:27-34). As we read through these simple demands, we see that they require us to hold back our feelings for others and our tendency to put ourselves first and to look at what the situation requires of us. It does not require us to be heroic. We do not have to be different from anyone else but just to treat others as we would like them to treat us. The reading shows that there are plenty of ways that we can and are inclined to do harm to others. In some ways they do not seem demanding, but they indicate that we are to show good will and give practical help to others. These good actions of ours will come from the love that is in our hearts.

Psalm 14 speaks about the upright person who does what is right. Doing right has a high profile in the book of Proverbs and in this psalm. Just doing good is often contrasted with total dedication to God but this is inaccurate since doing good and being just are very significant ways of loving. We show that we love though these good actions. Then the gospel, Luke 8:16-18, is about using the gifts we have to bring about greater life for others. It is a very important message because it tells us to use the gifts we have and not to hold back which is the temptation we have. We are to look at what the situation requires. What is needed? Do we have the ability to do what is required? It may require simple generosity on our part or on overcoming our reluctance to put ourselves forward. Consider the wisdom of these further verses from chapter 21 of the book of Proverbs:

> To do what is right and just
> is more acceptable to the LORD than sacrifice (verse 3).

We are inclined to do what is heroic, but we are told in this verse and constantly in scripture that doing what is right is better than sacrifice. Offering sacrifice is often done to show ourselves off rather than to help someone else. Doing what is right comes from the love that is in our hearts.

> Haughty eyes and a proud heart –
> the unploughed field of the wicked – produce sin (verse 4)

Our eyes are haughty and our heart proud when we lose touch with the ordinary situation of our lives. We flee in our imagination to how important we will be if we do this or that and how much we will be admired, how famous. The verse tells us instead that the Lord wants us to keep our feet on the ground and to just do what is needed without looking for special acclaim:

> The plans of the diligent lead to profit
> as surely as haste leads to poverty (verse 5).

We are to be diligent going through all the little steps that are needed to carry out the task. If we are writing a chapter, we have to plan first and write one sentence at a time. If we want to build a library, we have to start with a few books without imagining that thousands will miraculously fall into our laps.

> A fortune made by a lying tongue
> is a fleeting vapour and a deadly snare.
> The way of the guilty is devious,
> but the conduct of the innocent is upright.
> The wicked crave evil;
> their neighbours get no mercy from them (verses 6, 8, 10).

Many who start off in their career are seduced into taking short cuts that will put money in their pockets and a stylish car in their garage. The short cuts they take are dishonest and may land them in prison or make life harder for others who refuse to take the short cuts. The liars and the dishonest will flourish for a time, but they will not be finally happy.

> Whoever shuts their ears to the cry of the poor
> will also cry out and not be answered (verse 13).

When we shut our ears to the cry of the poor, we are refusing to accept that others need our help. We refuse to respond to the cries of those who do not have enough or who have crippling burdens. The verse tells us that we will too find ourselves at some time crying out for help and no one answering us. Why? Because we failed to respond to what the situation required.

The Changing Life Situation Today

Recently, I saw on the table in the community dining room a booklet for the Requiem Mass of a lady whose picture was on the front. I did not know her but found her face very open and loving. She seemed to have been a person who came to have love for others in her heart. That got me thinking on the way that married people, who have no other ongoing formation apart from what they get in their parish, still grow in their faith. I think of my brother and his wife who are in that situation. They get some nourishment from their parish from what he tells me. My sister gets input from her reading and from her conversations with her daughter and from others including myself. I think of my mother and father and the limited resources they had. This reflection simply tells me that God works in the institution of the family which is everyone's first community and provides for each of us in very ordinary but powerful ways. We may overestimate the importance of the parish because we expect God still to be working there, whereas for many people, God is working elsewhere.

Pope Francis has told priests in parishes to go out to people and meet them in their homes and places of gathering.[110] That is where I found myself at the celebration for my sister's birthday. I am in touch with family members and others today to whom the gospel has not reached in ways I used to expect. What is my attitude? In the past, there was undoubtedly some disapproval to those who do not go to

---

[110] Pope Francis, *The Joy of the Gospel*, Nairobi: Paulines Publications, 88-91 et passim, 2013,

church. Today, priests are not always referred to positively or even respectfully. People do not care what official position you hold but whether you are able to relate on an equal basis. If you can do that, there is a chance that church-goers will have some influence over others such as those at the restaurant table that night.

In the past, the attitude of the clergy and religious was often not one of humility but of pride. There was little awareness that the church had lost authority and credibility for many people.

Luke 7:24-35 speaks of the humility that church people need today in the religious atmosphere they find themselves. The disciples of John come to Jesus and ask him if he is the one to come. Jesus tells them clearly that he is. John belongs to the old dispensation and a new one has now arrived. The church of today that is now being challenged and which no longer has the authority in the society which it formerly did is in the same situation as John the Baptist and belongs like him to the old dispensation. We have to acknowledge the goodness of the old but put it aside because there is now a new dispensation which God is now creating in the attitudes that I encountered in the family gathering for my sister. I, as a religious Brother, have to be with the people where they are and acknowledge that God is in this group. We have to adjust to the 'new wine' of the kingdom.[111] We are respectfully but firmly put in our place as belonging to an era now past if we insist that the practices of the past still hold the same weight that they had. By contrast, we are in a new period

---

[111] Brendan Byrne, *The Hospitality of God*, 82.

of blessedness since God is working in all the people of this present time in the efforts they make to be faithful in their marriages and in their good actions to help others and see beyond just the love they have for their families.

In this gospel, there are not only the disciples of John and the disciples of Jesus, that is, those who believe what Jesus proclaims, but also the Pharisees who reject what Jesus proclaims. Here I find Brendan Byrne's commentary helpful. He says they are not so much condemned as pitied (74).[112] They hear the music and the dancing like the elder son in the parable of the prodigal son but are unable to join in. Today, we are being called to rejoice in what people are doing in their groups in families and in work groups, etc. and not in their church groups. We have to rejoice in the good that is being done and not bemoan that things are not the way they used to be. The days of John the Baptist are gone. God is now doing a new thing.

In order to hear what God is doing now, we have to be humble. We have to adjust ourselves to the new situation in which God is working and be ready to leave aside old expectations that are no longer in touch with this situation.

---

[112] Brendan Byrne, *The Hospitality of God*, 74.

The Wider Situation of the Earth[113]

We have seen the necessity of adjusting to the Christian historical situation in which we currently find ourselves. We will look now at a still wider situation, that of the cosmos which we inhabit and of the crucial importance of making the necessary adjustments to enable that cosmos, which includes our earth and solar system, to flourish. One of the major factors that is threatening the solar system is global warming. It is caused by the global economic activity that has escalated in the world in the last few decades. The use of chemicals has expanded enormously and these chemicals are being emitted into the atmosphere, 'chemicals', says Thomas Berry, 'that nature knows nothing of and cannot deal with in any satisfactory manner'.[114]

Toxic substances and greenhouse gases have been released into the atmosphere thereby depleting the ozone layer that shields the earth from ultraviolet radiation. Berry says the situation is caused by setting human economy against the earth economy. He says there are four basic establishments that govern world development, namely, the world government, the corporations, the universities and the world religions. What has happened is that the corporations which exist in all parts of the world and which have enormous financial resources have come to dominate the other three establishments. The market economy has gradually inveigled its way into the other areas so as to make

---

[113] I am relying here on the insights of Thomas Berry, *Evening Thoughts: Reflecting on Earth as Sacred Community*.
[114] See Thomas Berry, *Evening Thoughts*, 101.

those areas dependent on financial aid from the corporations. The result is that voices which would otherwise be heard from governments, universities and religious institutions are half-hearted for the most part. This situation has been challenged lately. There has gradually developed because of information coming from environmental scientists that the planet which we inhabit is in danger of collapsing.

Berry describes the situation in these terms:

> This uncontrolled drive toward exploitation has now so ruined the soil, so emptied the seas of marine life, so devastated the forests, so polluted the atmosphere, so endangered the various species of plants and animals, so disrupted the hydraulic cycle, so wasted the countryside with road building, shopping malls, and parking lots that finally some alarm must be shown for the consequences to all forms of life on the planet. This is especially the case for global warming and all its deleterious effects on the life systems of the planet.[115]

In the last three decades, there have been Earth Summits beginning in Rio de Janiero in 1992. Through the efforts of a few, gradually a large swell of opinion around the world has challenged that authority of the corporations. There is much passion among ordinary people to use more eco-friendly forms of power, and to stop the use of gas emissions into the atmosphere. Legislation has been made in many countries to forbid the use of plastic bags, to stop using certain devices which especially pollute the Earth. The autonomy of the corporations is now being challenged in ways which give

---

[115] Berry, 103-104.

hope that our attitude to the Earth we inhabit will be changed.

More deeply-held attitudes must also be changed. We must get to the point where we see that human well-being 'depends absolutely on the flourishing of the life community of the planet'.[116] Fundamental elements of theology of the religions must change. Until now, Christians have seen the coming of Christ as the whole of the incarnation of God in the world. Now we must see that the earth itself is the primary revelation of God before Scripture and before the coming of Christ. Our attitude to the doctrine of Incarnation needs to see the coming of Christ as the climax of the revelation of God in the created world.

To walk humbly before our God today means to believe that our attitude to the Earth must change. We need to have a wider view of how God works in our lives to include not just our personal situations but also the situation of the Earth which God has given humankind.

The Degrees of Humility in the Rule of Benedict

We have seen, so far, the strong temptation of human beings to want to be special or heroic. We do not like being just ordinary. But instead of being heroic we are called by God to accept the ordinary situations of our lives. This requires that we do not constantly grumble that things are too hard, or that we have been treated badly compared with others. We are called to move the focus away from ourselves in

---

[116] Berry, 105-106.

being aware, as much as we can, of the changing historical situation such as the one we are in today where old structures of church attendance and of following strictly the authority of priests and bishops are changing. We found that we need now to look at more basic structures of family and family ties to find where God is most at work in people's lives. We saw the tendency to judge others according to ideologies of feminism and racism and preconceived ideas rather than looking at what is really happening. These points tell us that being humble before our God means taking the focus off our own self-importance and what we want, and looking to what God and others want of us as disclosed in our life situations.

We will look, finally, at the approach of the Benedictine Rule which gives twelve degrees of humility.[117] The degrees in abridged form are as follows:

- Focus on God rather than on ourselves and be careful not to forget God (first degree).

- Focus on doing God's will; make God's will our own will. Are we putting God first in our lives? Are we really seeking God? Give thanks to God rather than to ourselves for the good things that happen (second degree).

- Stop thinking that we have within ourselves the answers to our problems and admit that we need to seek help from

---

[117] I am using here material from Hartmann, Steele, OCSO, Humility in the Thought of Benedict: A Talk given to the Employees of the Archdiocese of Melbourne, 2012.

other people. In the case of monastic life, that will be an elder or the abbot (third degree).

- Be patient when we are treated badly or when we are given a job that is beyond us. Some things just have to be endured (fourth degree).

- Reveal what is going on inside us to someone. In the monastic situation, this will be the abbot. When we unmask our shame, it ceases to be shame (fifth degree).

- Be content with the poorest and worst of everything. The meaning here is to love ourselves for who we are not for what we do or what we have (sixth degree).

- When we continually fall into the same fault no matter what we do, go to our room and admit to God that we are helpless to free ourselves of this fault. This degree is a crucial one which, in the monastic situation, will lead the monk to realise once and for all that he is a sinner like everyone else and will never be better than others. When he does this, his attitude will soften towards himself and towards others (seventh degree).

- Do nothing except what is required by the rule, that is, admit that you cannot live as a loner and needs help from others (eighth degree).

- Restrain your tongue, that is, refrain from constantly talking, and listen to what others have to say (ninth degree).

- Refrain from being quick to laugh at others but rather be sympathetic when someone makes a mistake (tenth degree).

- When we speak, speak gently and with few words (eleventh degree).

- Finally, don't just be humble of heart but also be humble in appearance, that is, don't make ourselves look better than we are (twelfth degree).

We have not had time to spell out the implications of these degrees of humility, but we can see that the degrees are about putting God first in everything and gradually pushing oneself further and further out of the centre. In going through these degrees, we become less and less attached to our false image of ourselves and become more and more who God wants us to be. Benedict's degrees of humility lead us to a very similar place as the rest of what has been said in this chapter, namely, to walking humbly, hand in hand with God.

References

Berry, Thomas, *Evening Thoughts: Reflecting on Earth as Sacred Community*, San Francisco: Sierra Club Books, 2006.

Byrne, Brendan, *The Hospitality of God: A Reading of Luke's Gospel*, Strathfield: St Pauls, 2013.

Hartmann, Steele, OCSO, Humility in the Thought of Benedict: A Talk given to the Employees of the Archdiocese of Melbourne, 2012.

Miss Temptation by Kurt Vonnegut. https://padlet.com/alexandra_rigdon11/t0fj3mm0uimm

Pope Francis, *The Joy of the Gospel*, Nairobi: Paulines Publications, #'s 88-91 et passim, 2013,

Rupnik,Marko SJ, *Discernment: Acquiring the Heart of God*, Boston: Pauline Books & Media, 2006.

van Kaam, Adrian, *The Dynamics of Spiritual Direction*, Denville: Dimension Books, 1976.

Section 4
Spiritual Themes

In teaching a course on spiritual direction mainly for those seeking to avail of spiritual direction themselves, I quickly realised that the area of sinfulness is an urgent topic to address. I have included it here because if we put sinfulness aside, there will be a huge, largely unconscious, obstacle to our spiritual growth that will block or path. I use the poem The Hound of Heaven *by Francis Thompson. Some may be put off by this poem. If so, I encourage them to trust that that it can speak to them if they stay with it. The theme of suffering is also part of everyone's experience and can lead us into a deeper understanding of God and ourselves if we are prepared to look it squarely in the eye. The third theme that relates directly to our experience is that of doubt and despair. All of us have to be able to deal with the doubt that comes inevitably at certain times to us. The final theme, that of experiencing the kingdom of God now, is not so much an issue we have to deal with as an inspiration that can be of great motivation to us. Knowing that the kingdom is right here now in our midst can give us the strength to face all the spiritual challenges that come our way.*

Chapter Eleven

Sharing Our Sinfulness with God

WE DEVELOP OUR RELATIONSHIP WITH GOD by spending time with God. One of the main ways is to talk to God and to share with God what is happening in our lives. We normally think of asking God for what we want, but when our relationship grows, this element is not the most important. We can share with God our successes which may border on vanity. (God does not mind if we are vain because, in the exchange with God, the vanity will be challenged.) We can share with God the things we like doing and the people whom we like or in whom we have in some way become interested. We may be preoccupied with the job we are doing. (If this is the case, the pre-occupation will get in the way of our relationship because our job is coming before our relationship with God.) We can share our weaknesses with God, the questions we have, our anger.[118] We can even share our rage with God over something that has happened. We can share our pettiness with God and our sadness. In thinking of friendship, we normally think of sharing sadness and hopes

---

[118] See William Barry, *Praying the Truth*. Chicago: Loyola Press, 2012.

and needs but we do not think so quickly about sharing anger or pettiness. We can share things with God which we are embarrassed about.

When we talk in this way of what we share with God, talking about negative things becomes more possible. If we talk about embarrassments, then we can talk about sexuality and weaknesses and even sins. When we mention sins, however, we move into an area which causes problems. When we go on retreat, we think of the good aspects: we will have time to do nothing, time to relax, time to sit in the sun, all the things we have not had time to do in our ordinary working lives. Our directors will encourage us in this thinking because they do not want to move us into the area of sinfulness too quickly. If we think that we will have to face our sinfulness, we are more likely to run away from the retreat either physically or psychologically.

Negative Images of God

Much of the problem comes from the image of God we have developed. We have a conscious image of God as being someone loving and approachable but an unconscious image which is of someone fearful and frightening. We develop this image partly from our partial understanding of God as portrayed in scripture and from the way adults talked to us of God when we were children. But even if our childhood experiences were perfect, and if our understandings of God in scripture were well balanced, we would still have a fear of getting too close to God simply because God is other than us.

When we think of sharing with God our weaknesses, this may not seem so bad. There are some weaknesses that we are not afraid of talking about but others which we want to keep to ourselves. One way that can help us look at our sinfulness is to realise that as human beings we are all caught up in sin. We are like insects caught in a spider's web. We just find ourselves there. We may have heard of the expression, to act is to sin. This is true. To think that sin is part of our humanness can help. In one of the monologues of a play by Samuel Beckett, the narrator reflects on how he was earlier in his life. He says that he can hardly believe what a 'bastard' he had been.[119] Anne La Mott prays, 'Lord, help me not be such an arsehole'.[120] She says, 'Prayer is talking to something or anything with which we seek union, even if you are bitter or insane or broken. (In fact, these are probably the best conditions under which to pray)'. Becket and La Mott have come some way along the road to seeing their own sinfulness and their honesty can help us.

Recognising our Sinfulness

When we too look back on our lives we may become aware of things we did or said that embarrass us now. But if we just stay with them, we may find that they are easier to admit than we think. Beckett admits that he was a 'bastard.' Some things may be 'revealed' to us when we do this looking back. In fact, William Barry reminds us that being able to

---

[119] See Samuel Beckett, *Krapp's Last Tape*.
[120] Anne La Mott, *Help, Thanks, Wow*.

recognise our sinfulness is a grace. It is also a grace to accept the sin publicly.[121] I remembered, on reflecting back on my life in this way, how I had got up from bed one night and complained how some community members who had come in late were making a noise and disturbing me. I made a big show of this and was later embarrassed because when I looked back I realised what a 'bastard' I had been. I also remembered how in my first years as a formator I had not allowed the young Brothers responsibility to make their own decisions. I was able to reveal these two embarrassing memories to a class I was teaching. I told these experiences to the class and to further classes because I wanted to show the students that they did not have to be forever silent about their own mistakes. Some of these students were preparing to be formators themselves and I saw that they appreciated my trust of them.

Perhaps the major component of this theme of sharing our sinfulness with God is this one of recognising and admitting our sin. William Barry claims that secrecy poisons friendship.[122] I believe that my relationship with the class became considerably stronger when I told them of my faults of an earlier day. Barry gives examples from Alcoholics Anonymous groups. Alcoholics hide their problem. It is very difficult for an alcoholic to admit that he/she has a problem. Then at the end of an ordinary meeting, it is difficult for someone, when asked, to admit that at that moment he would like a drink. Alcoholics have a saying that we are only

---

[121] William Barry, *Praying the Truth*.
[122] William Barry, *Praying the Truth*.

as sick as our secrets. This applies not just to alcoholics but to everyone.

The Experience of Shame

The major reason for keeping something secret is shame. We are ashamed of not being able to give others responsibility, of coming from a certain family, of being too intelligent or not intelligent enough. We are ashamed of the size or shape of our bodies. We are ashamed that we are not better educated; we are ashamed of failure. When we hide our shame, we feel guilty or shaky or vulnerable. Women have almost invariably not revealed being sexually abused or harassed because of the shame attached to it. Physical abuse in families is also something shameful. It is a good exercise to go through some areas of our lives like family, childhood, adolescence, family home, education, friendships, intelligence, and see in what areas we feel shame. That would be the first step to publicly admitting it and, in this way, becoming free of its hold over us.

Psychologists speak of appearance anxiety among women and performance anxiety among men. These difficulties can be better dealt with if they are brought to the surface and looked at calmly. In this way, they lose their iron hold over us. An important current area concerning embarrassment and shame is gender. I recently attended a seminar on sexual orientation. Rather than a presentation by one person there was a panel each of whom spoke briefly. This was followed by questions asked of each by the facilitator. The panel consisted of three men, one gay, one transgender and one bi-sexual. Each spoke about the confusion and embarrassment he/she faced before 'coming out'. This was an enormous struggle which each experienced alone. They spoke of the breakthrough when they eventually revealed their orientation. The facilitator asked each of the panel if he had a difficulty about God accepting them as they were. Each said he had no problem talking to God about their sexual orientation and God did not have any problem with them. The next question was whether they had trouble talking about their sexual orientation in a church setting and here they said they experienced great difficulty.

I was particularly taken by Christina, the transgender person, wearing a dress but having the features of a man. At first, I found it difficult to hear someone who looked and sounded like a man having feminine mannerisms and speaking about how she felt she was a woman. Gradually as I listened, my attitude changed. By the end, I could understand why Christina wanted to have an operation which would change her physically from a male to female. I was convinced also that the struggle each of these people had to come to terms with their sexual orientation had been a key point in their growth as people. Each of them was articulate and confident. Later, I heard an interview with a man who was inter-sex. The gentleman spoke very openly about the enormous struggle he had to accept this physical reality about himself. His sexuality had not been totally resolved, but from what he said he had grown enormously in accepting and publicly professing his own sexual situation.

These examples so far have been about accepting who we are but not directly about accepting our sinfulness. We will now look at what is involved in someone coming to recognise their sinfulness before God. In the gospels we have the parable of the Prodigal Son which gives us a powerful presentation of sharing our sinfulness before God. In his treatment of this parable,[123] Henri Nouwen gives one way in which we leave our Father's house. In his father's house, the son knows he is beloved. He is safe and secure. But there is something in him which wants to leave the place where he is loved. And in doing this, he falls prey to false voices of need which torment him. He then searches for love outside the father's house and becomes dead to the voice of the Beloved Father who loves him unconditionally. We too fall under the spell of the false voices which promise us love. They say, 'You don't have it in you to live community'; 'You had better be successful; you will have to look good and do a good job'. Then the voices become more demanding: 'You have to be perfect'; 'You have to be better than others'; 'Everybody has to love you'.

God as the Hound of Heaven

In Francis Thompson's poem, The Hound of Heaven, another version of the parable of the prodigal son, the son is afraid of what the father will ask. The son (or daughter) has heard, or experienced, that there is a parent who is relentlessly faithful and who loves us with an unwavering love and never gives up on broken people.[124] But this daughter,[125] like the son in

---

[123] Henri Nouwen, *The Return of the Prodigal Son*.
[124] I am using some of the words here from *The Adaptation of The Hound of Heaven*. https://vimeo.com/89705938
[125] In Thompson's poem, the person fleeing is male but in *The Adaptation* it is a

Nouwen's version, still wants to move away. In fact, she starts fleeing from this loving presence because, if she lets him come in, she is afraid of what she will have to give up. Thompson's poem begins in this way:

> I fled Him down the nights and down the days
> I fled Him down the arches of the years
> I fled Him down the labyrinthine ways
> Of my own mind, and in the midst of tears
> I hid from him, and under running laughter.
> Up vistaed hopes I sped and shot precipitated
> Adown titanic glooms of chasmed fears
> From those strong feet that followed, followed after
> But with unhurrying chase and unperturbed pace,
> Deliberate speed, majestic instancy,
> They beat, and a Voice beat,
> More instant than the feet:
> All things betray thee who betrayest me.[126]

In this first stanza of the poem, many of the poem's major themes appear. First, the narrator is running away from Someone not just on one occasion but habitually. It is not one single action but it has become a permanent way of relating to the One who is pursuing. The narrator has left the Other's house and has stopped contact with him. He does not really intend to do this but he did it once, then again, and then again, and it has become habitual. It feels sad to

---

female.

[126] Francis Thompson, 'The Hound of Heaven,' *The Oxford Book of English Mystical Verse*, London 1917.

him even to the point of tears but the tears do not lead to any change. The person knows he is running away and even hiding but gives good reasons why this should be so. He still knows he is loved by the Pursuer and is unhappy and knows he is running and hiding. At the same time, he knows that the Loving Presence is following him calmly, majestically and deliberately. He knows that this Presence loves him and he feels guilty but his fear stops him from allowing the Other to catch up. It is an unhappy situation. The narrator also hears the voice of the Other say somewhere in his mind: 'All things betray thee who betray me', that is, 'All the attractions that you are looking for will not bring you happiness but will betray you because you are betraying me'.

The one who is fleeing gets some little glimpses of the One who is pursuing but these are simply glimpses and unsatisfying. They actually increase his guilt. The person knows that the Pursuer loves him but still feels resistance. We too fear that if we let God in, God will take everything else away from us. We may not know what God will take but we have the suspicion that God wants the whole of us and we are not prepared to give God everything.

The following lines reveal more of the relationship between the two parties, the pursued and the pursuer:

> I said to Dawn - be sudden, to Eve - be soon,
> With thy young skiey blossoms heap me over
> From this tremendous Lover.

The person feels in some harmony with the mornings and the evenings which keep passing and asks them to shield him from 'this tremendous Lover'. We have seen how the one pursued knows that he is loved; here we are given a hint of the nature of this love. The Pursuer is a Lover who is wonderfully attractive but also paradoxically frightening. How can love be frightening? It is because we do not want to be completely swallowed by the love. We want to retain our identity. If the one being pursued stops and engages with the Lover, he will not in fact be swallowed up but only fears that he will. Here we notice that there is something at work that wants to keep the Pursuer and the one being pursued far from each other and is succeeding. *The Adaptation of the Hound of Heaven* says, 'I sensed his devotion to me was great but I feared his power'. It continues, 'Afraid that if I opened my heart, he would rush in and I would be allowed nothing'. This fear of opening our hearts happens not just to those who have fled the Pursuer 'down the nights and down the days (and)... down the arches of the years' but to all of us for as long as we live. We too turn from the urge to look the way of the Pursuer and we hide our faces.

With the use of the term 'tremendous Lover', we move further into the area of affection that exists between the two parties. Both Thompson's poem and *The Adaptation* deal with this aspect to some degree. In *The Adaptation*, the person had pursued another soft and seductive voice but found that it was a fake with no love to give. She had then sought to find relief by throwing herself into helping others. This helped for a while but it was only a temporary escape and the ache for a deeper love returned. Then one night the footsteps came again, and it dawned on her that the Pursuer had always loved her. Then she says, 'I felt the tenderness of his presence' and she realised that it was this Pursuing Presence alone that would satisfy her:

> All which I took from thee, I did'st but take,
> Not for thy harms,
> But just that thou might'st seek it in my arms.

Here the relationship between the two parties is described in terms of romantic love. The one pursued now finds himself in the arms of his beloved. This line is followed by a gentler touching that is none the less tender:

> Rise, clasp my hand, and come.

Finally, in the last lines of the poem, the Pursuer, the 'tremendous Lover' stops beside the person. The pursuit has ended. The one pursued then realises that the sadness that he has been feeling was not from hostility of the Pursuer but caused by the shade of his loving hand:

> Halts by me that Footfall.
> Is my gloom, after all,
> Shade of His hand, outstretched caressingly?

And then we hear the words of the Pursuer who is now seen to be the Beloved One who has nothing but love in mind. The Beloved one tells him that it is sheer love unmixed with any fear that he has been fleeing all his life. This is the ending of the poem:

> Ah, Fondest, Blindest, Weakest,
> I am He whom thou seekest.
> Thou dravest Love from thee who dravest Me.

The poem deals directly with the relationship of us with God and the problem we have in admitting our sinfulness with God. The example in the poem is of a person who has kept away from God for a life time and it is understandable that this person will feel very uncomfortable in speaking to God about his sinfulness. But everyone finds it difficult. The first thing to do is to find out with some accuracy, if we can, where we stand with God. Have we been ignoring God in our lives? Are we trying to live in tune with what God wants? A person may not have been paying much attention to God and then they have an experience of God. They read a book which speaks to them of a loving God; they are attracted to someone who is a friend of God; they touch in some way into God's love for them and for the world. It can be difficult at this point for the person to look at her sinfulness. It is easy for her to argue that there is no need to look at the sinful areas of her life. At this point the resistance to getting closer to God shows itself. What will God think of her if she speaks to God about things she has done which she does not want to face? This is where the idea that being aware of our sinfulness as a grace comes in.

God will help us in this regard. If we are moving with God, God's Spirit will encourage us to keep moving this way. If we read the poem *The Hound of Heaven*, and have a strong sense of the love of God for us even though we have sometimes turned away from him or ignored him, it is a sign that God's Spirit is working and will continue to lead us calmly along. If we feel disturbed and guilty about things that might have happened at some time in our lives and feel upset or confused by this, it is probable that the evil spirit has come into the picture trying to set us on the path of giving God a wide berth as did the narrator of *The Hound of Heaven*.

The Problem of the 'Inner Policeman'

Another approach that we can take when the person becomes aware of her sinfulness is to see it in terms of what Andre Louf calls 'the inner policeman' of the person.[127] The inner policeman wants to be in control. He wants certainty in regard to doing the right thing. He is a perfectionist and will not allow any deviations. The inner policeman is something akin to the false self. In Freudian terms, it is the superego of the person. The crucial thing at this time in our relationship with God is to move out of the power of the false self and to let God take the initiative. If we see the situation in terms of good and bad spirits, the bad spirit makes us think that when we fail to keep all the rules we are a fake. The bad spirit sends us down to the depths of discouragement and makes us think that we might as well give up trying because to keep the rules is beyond us.

But as well as the voice of the bad spirit, there begins to emerge in us the voice of God's Spirit. This voice encourages us. This is the voice of God deep inside us telling us that God loves us in spite of our sinfulness. It tells us of God's deep and unconditional love and fills us with joy. We think, yes, we have failed, but we sense that this is the very place where God loves us the most. This is the moment of grace. Now we no longer need defend ourselves nor try to claim that we did not offend God. We can accept our weakness and our sin. We feel sorry for doing something that God does not want, but

---

[127] Louf, Andre, *Grace Can Do More: Spiritual Accompaniment and Spiritual Growth*, Kalamazoo, Cistercian Publications, 2002.

also deeply joyful because we feel God's forgiveness.

When we are really sure of God's love for us, we can then look at our sinfulness without panic. We then do not have to look for short cuts or evasions. We now go beyond the general sense of being enmeshed in sin to realising that we ourselves are sinful and that our actions matter in our relationship with God. Words that can help us see the reality of sin are contrition, repentance, metanoia and compunction. Contrition means literally to be crushed. Our thinking about ourselves and our sense of ourselves are crushed. We come up against the reality of who we are. I gave the example of myself realising I could not allow the young brothers in my charge to take responsibility for themselves. When someone pointed this out to me, I was very defensive. I denied that this was the case. I did let them be responsible for themselves! Was it not my job as formator to guide them and to be with them all the time? Gradually my defences fell and to my alarm I had to admit that I was possessive and judgmental. In this process of our coming to awareness, God's grace is at work. Ezekiel gives this oracle from God: 'I will remove their hearts of stone and give them hearts of flesh instead' (Ezekiel 36:26). Our stony hearts are broken down and we are faced with this negative or sinful aspect of ourselves.

An idea close to contrition is compunction. Compunction comes from the same root as the word puncture. It happens when something is punctured within us. It is like a nail entering a bicycle tyre. Our sense of self is punctured and for a time we do not know who we are. Our confidence is taken from us as we come to terms with this reality. In the parable of the prodigal son we are told how the younger son, 'came to his senses' (Luke 15:17). We see here another aspect of how God deals with us. When we are moving in the wrong direction as the son was, the action of God is strong. God has to shake us out of our self-complacency. This action reminds us that love involves not just showing tenderness, but also honesty and firmness.

A catechetics film that came out in the seventies on the sacrament of reconciliation shows very well this action of God. The film concerns a young man who, while driving under the influence of alcohol, hits a young girl aged about 10 years. The young girl is taken to hospital and he resumes his life, telling himself that it was not his fault. He avoids going to see the girl, saying that a visit would not do any good. But beneath this rationalisation he feels very uneasy about meeting her. There is a scene where the man is talking to his girlfriend. He tells her that he was not drinking much and that it was not his fault. He asks her what she thinks and she challenges him to keep thinking about it and advises him to visit the girl in hospital. He buys a bunch of flowers and is in great fear before he enters the room, terrified of the reaction he will receive. He goes in and gives her the flowers. She is full of joy that he has come and she says, 'I've been waiting for you to come all these days!' At this point, the man's defences crumble and he is now able to look honestly at what he has done. This is an excellent comparison with the way God receives us when we share with him our sins.

The two other words that can help us understand reconciliation are repentance and metanoia. These words are similar in meaning. The first message of Jesus in his preaching is, 'Repent and believe the good news' (Mark 1). To repent means to turn our lives around, to turn towards God and to move in tune with what God wants for us.

Changing Attitudes to Sinfulness

The attitude to sinfulness before Vatican II was, on the whole, one of great fear. There was great emphasis on making reparation for our sins. We were then still under the influence of Jansenism starting in France but coming to us through Irish spirituality. Jansenism presented us with the image of God as harsh, severe and demanding. The image was based not on love but on fear. Scrupulosity was common. St Thérèse of Lisieux was influenced by Jansenism but came to understand the vicious nature of the movement's image of God.[128] At one point, Thérèse did not want to go on retreat out of fear of what God would have to say to her. One turning point for her was to discover the image of God in Isaiah 49 as a mother; even if the unimaginable happened and a mother forgot her children, God would never forget his people. The discovery of the image of God as a mother was wonderfully healing for her. She describes how she cried when she saw some tiny chicks with their mother and how the mother hen reminded her of God's love for her. Thérèse came to realise slowly and against the general opinion of the day, that God is loving and compassionate. Here she speaks about her feelings towards God:

---

[128] I am indebted here to Guy Gaucher, *John and Thérèse: Flames of Love*, trans. Alexandra Plettenberg-Serban, Society of St Paul: New York, 1999.

Ah, the Lord is so good to me that it is quite impossible for me to fear him. He has always given me what I desire or rather he has made me desire what he wants to give me.

She eventually offered herself to God 'as a holocaust victim of Merciful Love'. This sounds off-putting but in fact, for Thérèse, it was the opposite. She offered herself as a victim of Merciful Love. She did this deliberately to go against the popular practice of the time where 'great and generous souls' would offer themselves as Victims of *God's Justice*. She saw God in terms of mercy and love, not of justice!

Thérèse's writings helped the church to see sinfulness with less anguish and fear. Before Vatican II, the issue of sinfulness was dominated by guilt. On the other hand, today there is often no sense of guilt at all. This is a reaction to the one-sidedness of the past. But in fact, we need to be aware of the damage that sin does to our relationship with God and with others.

Another ruse of the evil spirit is to have us think that contrition and sorrow for sin are only for *real* sinners. We tell ourselves: we are not real sinners who have done terrible things; our sins are not so bad. Haven't we got a relationship with God and are moving along the paths God points out to us? Have we not gone beyond the initial stages of our spiritual lives? Surely, we do not have to feel permanently guilty! These sound very plausible ideas for not being concerned very much with sinfulness. It is true that we do not want to go back to the Jansenist past. At the same time, we really are all sinners before God. The definition of a monk in the Benedictine tradition, according to Andre Louf, is the one who grieves for his sins.[129] Similarly, a Christian is one who knows she is a sinner before God, a sinner whom God loves.

The Prayer of the Publican

Jesus' parable of the Pharisee and the publican is sobering. The Pharisee puts himself in the position of someone who does not have to be concerned with his sin. He has gone beyond worrying about his sinfulness. He does not think of himself as sinful, but the opposite, full of virtue. Jesus says that this person is not 'at rights with God'. He is living in illusion. On the other hand, the publican stands at a distance, 'Not daring even to raise his eyes to heaven; but he beats his breast and says, "God, be merciful to me, a sinner"'. This man knows that he owes everything to God and can do nothing from just his own resources. He does not think of all the wonderful things he has done and he asks God to be merciful to him because he is a sinner. It is a big challenge to us when we read this parable. Is our attitude like that of the publican?

When we are like the publican, we please God. In Matthew's Gospel, Jesus sees a man called Matthew sitting by his office and tells him to follow him. He is not put off by the injustices that Matthew may have done while a sinner. While Jesus is eating in the house, a number of tax collectors and sinners come in to sit at table with Jesus. The episode shows that Jesus is comfortable in the company of sinners. God values our honesty when we accept the bad things we have done. God does not value our efforts to justify ourselves

---

[129] Andre Louf, *Grace Can Do More*.

and excuse ourselves. God is pleased when we go through the difficulties of accepting ourselves as we are. When Jesus hears the Pharisees ask his disciples why he eats with sinners, he says, 'It is not the healthy who need the doctor but the sick. Go and learn the meaning of the words: What I want is mercy, not sacrifice. And indeed, I did not come to call the virtuous but sinners' (Matthew 9:12, 13). These words tell us a lot about what interests God. They tell us that God is not concerned about good reputations, prestige and appearances but about honesty and humility.

A little later in Matthew, Jesus tells his disciples that whoever is like a little child is greatest in the kingdom of God. When we humbly enter into the process of reconciliation for our sins, we are great in God's eyes. Jesus identifies with little children. When we welcome them, we welcome him. If we want to eat with the rich and the powerful, we are not very great in Jesus' eyes. When we take an interest in the little ones who include children and the poor and the oppressed, God is delighted with us. He says:

> See that you never despise any of these little ones, for I tell you that their angels in heaven are continually in the presence of my Father in heaven (Matthew 18:10).

These statements tell us a lot about how God looks at our sinfulness. Understanding these sayings can take a great burden from our shoulders. We do not have to be obey all the rules. We do not have to be successful or be thought of well by everyone. What Jesus values is our readiness to look at our faults and moral blunders and admit that we did something that built a barrier between ourselves and others or ourselves and God. These values of Jesus come out clearly in the story in Luke of the woman who was a sinner (Luke 7:36-50). The Pharisee who invited Jesus to the meal complains when Jesus allows a woman who was known as a sinner to anoint his feet with oil. Jesus somehow knew this and entered into a conversation with the man and praises the woman for the great love she showed. What is important to Jesus is the love the woman showed and the attention she gave to him. Jesus does not speak about the sin she committed but of the love she showed.

What is important when we do wrong is for us to admit that we have done it (We have already seen the importance of this.) I have just read an interview with the tennis star, Serena Williams. This interview was conducted a few weeks after Williams went into a tirade during the women's final to the referee about how she had been badly treated. She called the referee a thief and a cheat not just after one game but several times. She said that she was showing her anger because she was being treated this way because she was a woman. I strongly felt that she was in the wrong over this but could understand that she had expressed strong anger. What I did not like was that, during the presentation, she persisted that she was in the right when she was evidently in the wrong. Then in the interview that I read she did not say she was in any way sorry. Her fault was not the persistent tirade but that she did not acknowledge that the way she expressed herself was wrong.

I also recently listened to an interview with two people about child sexual abuse. One of the people being interviewed was a psychiatrist who worked with sexual abuse victims and perpetrators. The interviewer asked the psychiatrist how he found interviewing priests or other perpetrators of abuse who were referred to him. He said that he always sought to be totally accepting of the person in order to gain their trust and also hear sympathetically their views. Sometimes, it was a priest who had committed the act or acts twenty or thirty years earlier and was very sorry and had worked though the factors that had caused him to offend. But there were others who totally denied that they had done anything wrong or even defended what they had done. He described this second group as narcissistic and out of touch with reality. He found it difficult to be sympathetic and open to these people and found it very hard to help them.

When we deny our guilt, we make it impossible for others to help us. We also keep God at a distance. What happens when we admit our wrongdoing? We are like the woman who anointed the feet of Jesus. This woman opened herself to the forgiving love of Jesus and found her own heart overflowing with love for him. She is a great example to us of humility. Her relationship with God contains both the sense of God's love for her on the one hand, and, on the other, a good sense that what she had done was wrong and that she needed to tell God.

Conclusion

In this chapter, we have gone through the major elements involved in becoming aware of our sinfulness. These elements are being aware that all human beings are enmeshed in what we have usually called sin. Sin is not so much individual acts as a tendency or tendencies in us to move away from others and from God. When we look back at our lives, we can get in touch with specific acts for which we are responsible and for which we now feel ashamed. There are aspects of ourselves which cause shame in us, and part of the move to growth in us is to acknowledge these aspects and to disclose them appropriately to others. We then looked at what is involved in coming to terms with the truth of ourselves and of sharing this truth with God. The poem The Hound of Heaven helped us look at the steps involved in coming back to God when this is necessary. We then saw that this process of opening ourselves to God in our sinfulness greatly deepens the relationship between God and ourselves.

References

Barry, William, *A Friendship Like No Other*, Chicago: Loyola Press, 2008.

_____, *Praying the Truth*, Chicago: Loyola Press, 2012.

Casey, Michael, *Grace: On the Journey to God*, Strathfield: St Paul's Publications, 2018.

St Teresa of Avila, *Life,* in *The Collected Works of Teresa of Avila,* trans. Kieran Kavanaugh and Otilio Rodriguez, Vol.1, Washington, D.C.: Institute of Carmelite Studies, 1976.

Louf, Andre, *Grace Can Do More: Spiritual Accompaniment and Spiritual Growth,* Kalamazoo, Cistercian Publications, 2002.

Nicholson & Lee, eds. *The Oxford Book of English Mystical Verse,* London, 1917.

The Adaptation of The Hound of Heaven. https://vimeo.com/89705938

Chapter Twelve

Coming to Terms with Suffering

AT CHRISTMAS, we read the infancy stories in the Gospel of Luke. If we are able to put aside the hustle and bustle of the preparations for Christmas, the Advent season is a time of joy and peace. We read of the angel Gabriel appearing to Mary and the message of joy which he has for her: The Holy Spirit is to come upon her and she is to conceive. The child, a boy, will be called Son of the Most-High. The joy which we experience in reading Luke's infancy narrative is focused mainly on the Annunciation, then the visitation of Mary to Elizabeth which ends in the prayer of the *Magnificat* (Luke 1:47-59). After some problems which have to be faced, we then have the canticle of Zechariah. The church takes these two canticles of Mary and Zechariah and gives them to us to say every day in the Prayer of the church. In doing this the church surely wants us to take the joy contained in these two prayers so that we can experience them not just at Christmas but on a daily basis.

The *Magnificat* tells us that those who have found life difficult and have suffered a lot, failed, been insulted by others or treated unjustly in some way, will be raised up by God. We are told that these suffering ones are the precious ones of God, the ones that God loves and whom God will raise up. The cause of our joy is that God will come and take us out of our misery (since we are certainly among the suffering ones).[130] God will turn things around for us. We are thrilled that God has been faithful to his people through the whole of their history and will be faithful also to us. God has in fact come in this child whom Mary is carrying to set things right for us. God has not forgotten us after all; God is faithful to his promise and we are about to experience this great generosity of God. In fact, we are experiencing God's generosity now in our lives.

The second canticle, that of Zechariah (Luke 1:68-79), spells out even more exuberantly this generosity of God. This canticle proclaims that God has raised up a Saviour as he promised, that he has visited his people and brought salvation.[131] It is very fitting for us as Christians to recite this canticle each day since, in doing so, we are proclaiming the great gift of God to us, namely, salvation, our liberation from death, from our enemies and from suffering of every kind. We celebrate 'the loving-kindness of the heart of our God, who visits us like the dawn from on high'. The canticle reminds us that every day is a day to rejoice and delight in what God has done for us.

---

[130] The 'anawim' of whom Luke speaks are underprivileged but all who read this canticle apply it also to themselves since we all are in equal need of 'salvation'.

[131] We are in desperate need of a better word than salvation since the word cannot touch people as it has done in the past.

Reasons for Suffering

If this is indeed the case, then where is the place for suffering? Does God intend our lives to be lives of unalloyed joy? I think this is a question that we do actually ask ourselves. We are surprised when we find suffering come our way. At community prayer on one occasion a Brother shared how he was feeling at the end of the day. He had been negotiating the purchase of a property next to the centre for disabled children which he managed. He thought that the negotiation was just about finalised when the owner of the property told him that he did not want to sell after all. As a result, the Brother felt frustrated and defeated. In his sharing he said, 'Why is this happening to me? Why do I have to go through these troubles? Others don't go through these difficulties!' We may smile when we think of the credulity of these questions. But I think we often find ourselves asking these very questions when we are in a similar situation. It is good in such a situation to think of reasons why there is suffering in our lives. I am thinking of reasons which can help us accept the suffering we are going through, that is, in some way influence our feelings so that we do not feel so engulfed in the suffering. Here are a few reasons that may helpful.

One reason that can be particularly helpful to us is that Jesus encountered suffering in his life. We will come back to this reason since the gospels have much valuable material on the ways Jesus suffered and the way he dealt with it. If Jesus encountered suffering, it means that we are in good company and that the reason for our suffering is not because God is not pleased with us.

The suffering may be in the form of anxiety. Anxiety can be a cause of mild discomfort or of very strong suffering which can lead people into depression or into contemplating suicide. Instead of agonising over our anxiety and thinking that we are the only ones who get anxious, we can look at it more realistically and tell ourselves that everyone gets anxious. We are not abnormal or incompetent or inferior if we feel anxious. We can even remind ourselves that some anxiety is good and will help us perform the task before us better than if we were perfectly relaxed.[132]

A powerful reason that can help us see that there is a purpose in suffering exists in the teaching of Dietrich Bonhoeffer on grace in his book, *The Cost of Discipleship*.[133] Bonhoeffer spoke of costly grace in contrast to cheap grace. He was speaking at the time when most of the leaders of the church in Germany at the time of Hitler failed to oppose Hitler's policies. Instead of courageously standing up to Hitler, they rationalised that it was not necessary to oppose him. They took the view that continuing to conduct church services and go on with their ordinary duties was enough. Bonhoeffer called this cheap grace. The leaders hid behind formalism, that is, simply continuing to do things as they had always been done, and legalism, that is, doing good works. They did not see that that they had to sacrifice their safety and perhaps their lives to stand up to Hitler. Bonhoeffer himself

---

[132] Positive psychology speaks of the benefits of anxiety. See, for example, books by Peter Seligman.

[133] See Eric Metaxis, *Bonhoeffer: Pastor, Martyr, Prophet, Spy*, Nashville: Thomas Nelson, 2010, xv-xvi.

publicly opposed many of the policies of the state. As a result, he was executed. This teaching of Bonhoeffer can tell us that at times we will have to suffer when we set out to follow the gospel. It seems to me that this is a powerful teaching which can help us be strong when faced with suffering.

We can give other reasons to explain the existence of suffering. Life is a mixture of light and darkness and we cannot get rid of the darkness without also destroying the light; Jesus himself told the parable of the weeds among the wheat to explain why God allows evil to exist alongside good; if we want to achieve something worthwhile then we will often have to put in a great effort and put up with opposition from those who see things differently or who may be envious of us for doing what they fail to do. We have only scratched the surface of reasons we can give for the purpose of suffering. We will continue to use reasons to help us cope with suffering, but reasons on their own are not enough. What we need is passionate inner conviction.[134] If we use reasons, they have to be reasons that fill our hearts with hope and give us a sense of invincibility. The reason why the canticles in Luke's infancy gospel are so significant is because they touch our hearts and give us a sense that God is faithful to us and loves us. We will look here at a story that fills us with this sort of conviction.

---

[134] Kierkegaard speaks about the need for faith even when we do not understand or when our reason tells us something opposite. See, Terry Eagleton, *Culture and the Death of God*, New Haven: Yale University Press, 2014, 37.

Engaging our Imagination

In a Bible study group, the women puzzled over this statement from the prophet Malachi: 'He will sit as a refiner and purifier of silver' (Malachi 3:1).[135] One of the women offered to find out the process of refining silver and to get back to the group with the reason. She called a silversmith and made an appointment to be present when he was working. As she watched, the silversmith held a piece of silver over the fire and let it heat up. He explained that one needed to hold the silver in the middle of the fire where the flames were hottest. The woman thought about this in connection with how God refines us. She asked the silversmith if he had to sit in front of the fire the whole time the silver was being refined. The man said yes he had to sit there the whole time and he had to keep his eyes on the silver the whole time it was in the fire. If he left it there a moment too long, it could be destroyed. She then asked him how he knew when the silver was fully refined. He smiled and answered her, 'That's easy, when I see my image in it'.

Suffering and Joy in Luke's Gospel

This story employs imagery rather than reasoning to move our hearts. It tells us that when we are suffering and are not sure if God cares about us or is with us; story pulls us into a great intimacy with God, an intimacy of identification. Not

---

[135] This story was given to me by Sr. Maire O'Nolan, IBVM. I do not know its origin.

only does God care but God closes the distance between the two of us. As a result, we feel not just close to God but one with God. We now feel that our suffering is nothing and that we would go through it a thousand times if necessary and not mind.

We began this chapter with the apparently unadulterated joy that pervades the infancy narrative of Luke. But even amidst this joy there is an undercurrent of sorrow. In the Temple, after blessing Mary, Joseph and the child, Simeon says to Mary:

> Look! This child is destined to cause the rise and fall of many in Israel. He will be a sign that will be spoken against, so that the secret thoughts of many hearts will be revealed. As for you, a sword shall pierce your heart too (Luke 2:34-35).

The child will be a sign which will bring about opposition to many and Mary herself will experience sorrow. The passage reminds us of another where Jesus says that he has come not to bring peace but the sword (Luke 12:49-50). In fact, we know that we cannot escape the theme of suffering in the gospels. Suffering is an integral part of the story and we must find a way of coming to terms with it. At this point we will look at a particular section of Luke's gospel where Jesus is faced with the prospect of his death. The section actually starts with his first prediction of his passion (cf. Luke 9:22-27). The prediction follows the section where Peter makes his confession of faith that Jesus is the Messiah. This confession is a great breakthrough for Peter but this statement cannot stand alone. It is only half the story. The other half is that

Jesus is destined to suffer and die and, only in this way, to enter into his glory (cf. Luke 9:21). Peter thinks he has the glorious answer to who Jesus is, namely the Messiah. He is happy in this knowledge but, like us, does not want to hear the part about suffering.

Immediately after this prediction of his passion, we have the transfiguration of Jesus on the mountain. The Transfiguration is a wonderful affirmation for Jesus that the Father is with him at this point and will accompany him in the suffering which will follow. We see here how suffering and joy exist together. We are dealing here with the central doctrine about Jesus and about our following of Jesus, namely, the Paschal Mystery, death and resurrection. When they hear the voice from heaven saying, 'My Son, my Chosen One', they hear also the words, 'Listen to him'. The disciples are being told to listen to what Jesus has been saying – that he will suffer and die. Instead of holding on to the vision on the mountain they are to go down the mountain and accompany Jesus in his suffering.

Soon after this, we have the section in Luke where Jesus begins the journey to Jerusalem, that is, the journey to his suffering and death. Many of the passages in this section deal with Jesus' suffering together with themes related to suffering. There is a moment of intense joy which encourages Jesus in his journey (Luke 10:21-24). Jesus tells us also in this section how we are to act in these times and how the Holy Spirit will be with us. The Holy Spirit during persecution will give us the sense of being enfolded in God's love. He tells us how to pray in times of need and especially the attitude we are to have when we pray. He tells others that if they wish to follow him, they will have to leave everything. We will now look at some of these passages in greater detail.

A Tougher Jesus?

Brendan Byrne says that, in this section of Luke's Gospel, we encounter a tougher, more determined Jesus and one who will spell out in greater detail how suffering will be part of the life of his followers.[136] The main message that we will focus on, however, is the way Jesus himself faces his suffering. Here we have a Jesus who goes through the suffering we go through. Luke announces this section solemnly and movingly, 'When the days drew near for him to be taken up, he set his face to go to Jerusalem. And he sent messengers ahead of him' (Luke 9:51-52). To set his face means that Jesus steels himself for something very difficult which he fears. He and his disciples immediately encounter a Samaritan village which will not receive them. With calmness Jesus simply tells his disciples to move to another village. Jesus is then approached by three different people who want to follow him (Luke 9:57-62). To each, Jesus points out the hardships they will have to suffer if they decide to follow him. These two incidents of the inhospitable village and the would-be followers indicate that difficulties will be there at every step as he goes on this journey.

When he sends out the missionaries (Luke 10:1-16) to preach, he warns them that they are going out like lambs

---

[136] For some of the insights in the following section, I am indebted to Brendan Byrne, *The Hospitality of God*

among wolves, that is, they will often feel very inadequate to carry out the mission. Many people will reject them. In all of this, they are to rely on God. After this, Jesus utters woes against the cities who do not receive the message he has to give them. Jesus here is forlorn that they reject the offering of peace he is giving them. We also sense that he is deeply sad and probably angry that they are rejecting him. In all of this section Jesus has to cope with a lot of rejection. Then the tone changes. The missionaries return telling Jesus of the marvels that happened when they preached in his name. Jesus himself rejoices. He is filled with exultation that in his own cosmic mission with Satan, that evil is being overcome. He says triumphantly: 'I watched Satan fall from heaven like a flash of lightning' (Luke 10:18). We see here that Jesus himself needs the encouragement of these victories amidst the experiences when he felt he was getting nowhere. We now have a passage where Jesus experiences a profound joy. He rejoices in the Holy Spirit, 'I thank you, Father, Lord of heaven and earth because you have hidden these things from the wise and intelligent and revealed them to infants'. His joy comes from the intense experience of his Father which he has at this moment. He realises that amidst all the suffering, the Father is with him and that what the Father wants is coming into being. He then says to his disciples,

> Blessed are the eyes that see what you see! For I tell you many prophets and kings desired to see what you see, and to hear what you hear, but did not hear it (Luke 12:23-24).

Jesus has the sense that, in spite of the present struggles and failures, that his mission will be ultimately successful. He is lifted for a moment out of the difficulties and is filled with joy because of the intense intimacy he is experiencing with the Father. The moment gives us a little glimpse of what is happening in the heart of Jesus. It is a moment like that of the Transfiguration.

We then move to the parable of the Good Samaritan (Luke 10:29-37) which Jesus tells in an exchange with a lawyer. We may wonder why this parable is placed in this point in the gospel. We can see it in the following way. The man who has been stripped, robbed and beaten stands for all of us who go through all sorts of sufferings in our lives. We often feel like this man and we have a desperate need to be healed and comforted. Jesus is telling the parable to show us the compassion that God has for us in our sufferings. The parable tells us that experiencing misfortune is not a punishment from God or a sign that God has left us. Rather, it is at these times that God comes in to show his tremendous compassion for us.

The visit of Jesus to the house of Martha and Mary follows (Luke 10:38-42). In the context of the journey to Jerusalem and the experience of suffering, the passage can tell us that suffering will come, but that our ordinary lives will also continue. We are not to get totally immersed in jobs but to pay attention to people. We are to strive to have the peace that Mary has in the midst of all the difficulties and responsibilities and to put the feelings of people ahead of whatever work we are doing.

In the next scene, the disciples see Jesus praying and ask him to teach them to pray Luke 11:1). He tells them they are to be concerned that the Father's will be done in their lives. This and the other things they are to ask for involve challenge and struggle. In these struggles, they are to look to their Father to provide all that they need while doing their part as well. But more than what they are to pray for, Jesus tells them the attitude they are to bring to prayer. They are to be totally confident that the Father will give them everything they ask for. They are to remember that God is not like them or their friends. If they themselves provide hospitality when a friend arrives in the middle of the night, then God who is their Father will all the more give them what they need. Would we give someone a snake if they asked us for bread? If this is ridiculous, then it is all the more ridiculous that God will not give us what we ask for from him. Jesus concludes his teaching with these words:

> If you then, who are evil, know how to give good gifts to your children, how much more will the heavenly Father give the Holy Spirit to those who ask him (Luke 11:13).

The mention of the Holy Spirit reminds us that love is the way that God relates to us since the Holy Spirit enfolds us and keeps us in the love of God.

The remainder of chapter 11 and then chapter 12 continue dealing with this struggle of Jesus himself against opposition and the struggle that we as Christians have continually in our lives. Jesus is accused of casting out devils by the power of Beelzebul (Luke 11:14-26). This passage shows the constant struggle in the world and the cosmos between good and evil in which we are all involved. Then someone comes to Jesus to praise his mother who bore him. Jesus, however, wants to keep the focus on the effort that is needed in life and says that they are blessed who hear the word of God and keep it (cf. Luke 11:27-28). The crowds then ask for a sign, that is, something that will remove all problems, but Jesus tells them there will be only one sign, that of Jonah who was in the whale. Jonah stands for Jesus himself who will overcome evil only by going through death. Jesus then says that his disciples are to be the light of the world, that is, they are to work continually to bring about God's kingdom. This little teaching is followed by a denunciation on the part of Jesus of the Pharisees who refuse to make the effort to live good lives themselves. They are hypocrites who refuse to enter into the struggle and are interested only in doing good actions that others will see.

Jesus then tells his disciples directly that they will experience persecution (12:4-12). He repeats his teaching that they are to remember that God loves them with great affection and they are to rely on this continual love being with them in the midst of the accusations against them. They are to look ahead to these times when they will be accused. They are not to worry because the Holy Spirit will take over. They will not have to worry about what to say because the Holy Spirit will give them the words to say. After this passage, Luke puts the teaching on divine providence found in the Sermon on the Mount in Matthew. It is very probable that Jesus is also encouraging himself to trust his Father. He can assure them about God's loving protection since he has experienced it himself. A passage on being vigilant follows (12:35-48). Along with our reliance on God we need to be continually aware and on guard. Reliance on God requires our attentiveness and effort as well. We are not to be like the slave who gives up, gets drunk and beats the other slaves.

We then have a key passage about Jesus' own suffering (12:49-50). In this passage Luke again gets into the mind of Jesus to see what is happening. Jesus tells his disciples that he is dreading what is to come. He speaks of a baptism with which he is to be baptised and he cannot wait until it is over. Again, we notice that Jesus does not run away from the suffering but looks at it and allows the accompanying feelings of fear to be in his heart. We sense that he is heavy at heart. We then hear that he has the burden of giving a very unpopular message to people. He has come to bring 'not peace but the sword'. He knows that no one wants to hear news like this.

We will stop here looking at this section of Luke's Gospel. We have seen that Jesus had suffering on his mind, starting with the first prediction of the passion. Unlike the disciples, he fearlessly looked at the suffering that is ahead. He told the disciples that they were to be wide awake to face all the challenges and suffering that were to come. They were also to be completely confident in God's continual help. As a result, they could be calm and at peace. Not just this, but in the midst of the suffering they would experience great joy. This was what Jesus experienced. Similarly, in the very midst of the suffering they would have the love of the Holy Spirit enfolding them.

Facing Suffering

Jesus was faced with a baptism, as he put it, which he did not want to face. He wished that he had already gone through this ordeal. But he faces it and goes ahead. Etty Hillesum

Coming to Terms with Suffering

(1914–1943),[137] a young Jewish woman who died at Auschwitz, gives a wonderful example of the strength we get when we face the suffering that is before us. Jews were being arrested and detained before being sent off to prison camps. She knew this was to befall her. Then she herself was arrested. In the detention centre where she was held with others, she saw people losing hope and all will to live. She wondered how she herself could continue. But at this point in her life she had developed a deep relationship with Jesus through her friendship with a Christian man who had been her mentor. She had deep faith in Jesus and she felt prompted to look at her prospective suffering head on. She looked it straight in the face. When she did this she felt a power and a strength coming into her from she knew not where. The prospect was still dreadful but there was that strength beneath the dread that she knew she could rely on. As a result, she was able to comfort the other Jews detained in the centre. When she was finally herself transported to the concentration camp, a note was found which said that she went off singing.

The disciples, we remember, after the death of Jesus and before he appeared to them, were filled with fear and huddled in the upper room. In the Acts of the Apostles, there was that time of fear before the Holy Spirit came on them at Pentecost. We must ask ourselves what happened in the hearts of the disciples. There was a profound change of attitude in them. From being terrified, they became fearless and wanted to proclaim the good news regardless of what might happen to

---

[137] See Etty Hillesum, *The Letters and Diaries of Etty Hillesum 1941-1943*, Grand Rapids: William B. Eerdmans, 2002.

them. They went out and preached openly. We know that it was the Holy Spirit who transformed them. We can say that the work of the Holy Spirit helped them look at the reality. They looked the fear that was paralysing them directly in the eye and found themselves changed. The Holy Spirit also has to transform us in this same way. We can be like Etty and look our suffering in the eye. We can be like the disciples and see that the fear does not have to paralyse us because we have God with us.

We are constantly faced with some sort of fear. The fear often seems to be bigger than the previous one. We think that if we get through this we will no longer be afraid. But this is not the case. We need to realise that we will always be faced with fear. It will not end when this particular fear ends. But when we realise that we do not have to continue like this, then we will not have to be continually terrified. As well as facing the fear, we need to remember the words of Jesus that we saw above. Some of them are below:

- I tell you not to worry about your life, what you are to eat, nor about your body, what you are to wear.

- Father, holy be your name, your kingdom come; give us each day our daily bread, and forgive us our sins as we also forgive all those who are indebted to us.

- Do not be afraid, little flock, for it has pleased your Father to give you the kingdom.

When you are brought before the synagogues, governors and rulers, do not worry about how you will defend yourself or what to say. For the Holy Spirit will teach you at that time all that you have to say.

The Promptings of Love[138]

The above quotations that have closed our reflection on the part of Luke's gospel that covers the beginning of the journey to Jerusalem all come from that particular section. They all speak of a deep relationship between the person and Jesus which Jesus recommends when we are confronted with suffering in our lives, and that can include our whole life. I want here to emphasise this element: that an intimate relationship with God coming from a deep awareness of God's personal love for us is the basis of bearing our sufferings with joy. We find this intimacy throughout the psalms:

> To you I call for you will surely heed me, O God;
> Turn your ear to me; hear my words.
> Guard me as the apple of your eye;
> In the shadow of your wings protect me (Psalm 16:6-8).

The psalmist is here calling out to God and knows that God will certainly hear her. She expects God to hear her because she believes that she is not just precious to God but that she is the apple of God's eye. There is a mixture here of need and of confidence which is the way we can face suffering in a healthy and joyful way. We are joyful because we know God will be with us in the trouble.

---

[138] This phrase comes from Charles Taylor, *A Secular Age*.

I am taking here almost at random antiphons and readings from the liturgy to show that, as Christians, we are called to accept our suffering with joy. The following psalm verse used as an antiphon shows us exalting in God's victory in our lives and boasting in God because of what he has done for us:

> We will rejoice at the victory of God and make our boast in God's great name (Psalm 19:6).[139]

The next passage from the prophet Baruch combines joy and suffering in the same way:

> Jerusalem, take off your dress of sorrow and distress, And put on the beauty of God's glory for evermore... for God means to show your splendour to every nation under heaven, and the name God gives you for evermore will be: Peace through justice and honour through piety (Baruch 5:1-4).

This passage tells us that we do not have to be sad. The time of sadness has gone and it is time to be aware of the glory of God in our lives. God's glory is blazing out in every created thing around us if we have eyes to see it. The passage is urging us to take our eyes off the sadness and lift our hearts to the joy that comes from being aware of the constant presence of God in our lives.

At the same time as these antiphons were occurring in the liturgy[140] the first readings were from the letter to the Ephesians. Chapter one of Ephesians lists the gifts that God

---

[139] This translation is the one used in the liturgy for this verse.
[140] The twenty-ninth and thirtieth weeks of Ordinary Time Year 2.

has given us: blessing us with all the gifts of heaven; choosing us in Christ before the world was made; he has made us his adopted sons and daughters. God has chosen us to put our hopes in Christ; we have not had to do anything! After the initial canticle the writer of Ephesians then makes a prayer for us, the readers. He prays that we will have 'a spirit of wisdom and perception of what is revealed'. The prayer continues: 'May (God) enlighten the eyes of (our) mind so that we can see what hope his call holds for (us)'. Unfortunately, we can read these passages with little response, even while the writer is praying and, as it were, pleading with us to be open to the reality of what God is giving us. If we only could see the love that God has for us! If we only had the wisdom to realise the extent of the gifts that God has given us! I was glad that when I read these pages, I felt tuned in to their meaning. I was able to take in to some extent that God was speaking to me in these lines. This is what God is constantly trying to do to us. If we were aware of these gifts of God, we would have a different perspective on the sufferings that come to us.

I have titled this short section The Promptings of Love because promptings do come to us constantly. They come to us from the scripture readings that are constantly available to us. They come to us through little kindnesses that people do. God gives us enough of these promptings to help us through our worst sufferings.

Going through the Suffering

Let us look specifically at what we might do when we are actually going through the suffering. We began this chapter with Jesus going up to Jerusalem. At this point 'he set his face to go to Jerusalem' (Luke 9:51). This is the attitude we need to have when we are going through the suffering. I am taking as an example the difficulties the Christian Brothers faced when they made the decision to send Brothers to East Africa.

It began when Brother Mark in 1986 visited one of the brothers, Bert, who went to East Africa without the approval of the congregation.[141] In visiting Bert, Mark made contact with Bishop Lebulu, the bishop of Same in Tanzania. When Mark returned to Australia Mark and Frank, the provincial, and the others on the leadership team thought of the idea of sending Brothers to the bishop's diocese. They sent a letter to the Brothers of the province proposing the idea. From there, two meetings were held to which all the brothers were invited. At the first meeting, the idea of opening a mission in Africa was raised. In this first meeting there was prayer and reflection. A second meeting began with prayer before it was put to the Brothers whether they were in favour of the idea. The Brothers then were invited to send their written responses to the leadership. The result was that a strong majority were in favour of going to Tanzania.

The Provincial Council then authorised Mark to write to Bishop Lebulu to see if he still wanted brothers to come since, by then, it was twelve months since Mark had actually visited. The bishop wrote back a very encouraging affirmative response. Mark in the meantime approached three Brothers about preparation to go to East Africa.

---

[141] This material of the founding of the Christian Brothers in East Africa comes from the writings of Br Frank Chappell which is not yet published.

The three Brothers to go to East Africa made different preparations, but by the beginning of 1988 it was decided that they would go to Tanzania and spend time at Musoma Language School. It was good not to have to rush into the responsibility of setting up a community immediately. It was also decided that Frank, as the provincial, should go and visit Bishop Lebulu in Same. He travelled from Australia to Addis Ababa, then to Entebbe, and then to Kilimanjaro International Airport where Fr Mansuetus, the director of Chanjale college, met him. Chanjale was the school where the bishop had invited the brothers to teach. Fr Mansuetus took him immediately to Chanjale, a journey of about an hour.

At Chjanjale, Frank met the bishop, an energetic man of forty-five. He was very welcoming and very positive about Brothers coming to his diocese. Frank said that the Brothers were interested in being involved informally with youth and with the poor. The bishop said that the diocese would provide accommodation for the brothers. They worked out a tentative agreement about the Brothers' stay when they arrived.

After a couple of days with the bishop which very much encouraged him, Frank left for Arusha on his way to Namanga and then to Nairobi to get his flight. While in Arusha Frank heard that the diocese was thinking of building a new secondary school. He put this into the back of his mind and remembered that Mark had written that it would be good, at a later stage, to have a second community of brothers in Arusha.

Frank was greatly encouraged by this visit to Tanzania. He also felt that his meetings with different people were somehow planned by the divine Mystery which we felt was guiding the Brothers. He thought of the words: Risking; Trusting. He felt that this was always the case when we move to do something for God.

Everything up to this that has been described is positive. When, however, the Brothers began to work in the diocese of Same, things changed. The bishop who had been very positive with the leaders, Mark and Frank, had a different attitude to the three Brothers who were sent to work in his diocese. The bishop expected that the three Brothers would do what he wanted in spite of what had been agreed in earlier conversations. Two of the Brothers who began to teach in the school in Chanjale found quickly that the male students were very negative towards them. The three Brothers started full of hope but at least two found themselves rejected and not supported by either the bishop or the staff of the school.

The venture of the Brothers from Australia going to East Africa which had begun so promisingly, at times seemed impossible. In time, the Brothers withdrew from Chanjale and began to build a school in Arusha. Again, there were many conflicts with the same bishop who was now the bishop of Arusha. Young men who joined the Brothers were told by the bishop that they were instead to study for the priesthood. In the building of the school and the beginning of classes the two Brothers involved, Frank and then another Frank, met opposition from the bishop at every turn.

This is probably a typical experience of religious congregations and even any missionaries going to foreign lands. In the account above I have not fully captured the struggles and suffering of the Brothers who were on the ground. Remember that two of them were rejected in the ministry which they had chosen. Neither of these Brothers flourished for a long time. Many missionaries return thinking they have accomplished nothing. As we listen to the stories of the founding Brothers in East Africa, especially of the two who had a particularly difficult time, we may think of the two disciples who met Jesus on the road to Emmaus. Jesus comes and walks along with them and they tell him of their bitter disappointment at what had happened to Jesus in contrast to what they had hoped. Jesus listens patiently and gradually gets them to see that the suffering was actually leading them somewhere. He tells them that in fact it was necessary for Jesus to die before he could enter into his glory. Eventually Jesus reveals himself to them in the breaking of bread so that in the end their hearts were burning within them at the knowledge of Jesus being with them.

John of the Cross imagines that the negative experiences we go through are like a dark night. John sees God present at these times. He sees all the struggles and difficulties of life as 'coming from the hand of God for the person's good'. The remedy is not to run away from the suffering because it is healing for us and brings a great blessing.[142] He says, 'When you are burdened you are joined to God. He is your strength, and he is with people who suffer. When there is no burden, you are just with yourself, your own weakness. It is in the difficulties which test our patience that the virtue and strength of the soul is increased and affirmed'.[143] It is difficult to look back after twenty-five years of the Brothers in

---

[142] St John of the Cross, *Collected Works*, 'Living Flame', 2:30.
[143] St John of the Cross, *Collected Works*, 'Sayings'.

East Africa without believing that the struggles and sufferings were an integral part of the experience. If the struggles had not been there, what would be left of the experience?

John of the Cross saw suffering as the privileged place of God's inflow into our lives. Iain Matthew in commenting on John says that pain has the power to unlock us at the point we cannot unlock ourselves.[144] Healing comes in situations that take us out of our own control and where we are bewildered.

Two Examples

In this time of suffering, the important thing is to acknowledge it, as we have seen with the examples of Jesus and Etty. In listening to Radio National (Australia) over two consecutive days, I heard an example of one person who looked back on his life when he was young and was very bitter about what happened to him. I picked up the story when he had reached the age of twelve. Until then, he had lived in a foster home. He did not say how his foster parents had treated him but said that for no reason he was taken from them and put into an assessment centre. At hearing this term, the interviewer showed that he completely agreed with the man's interpretation by saying that the word 'centre' was itself horrible. The man said he had been treated horribly and unfairly at every stage of his growing up. At no point of the story did he acknowledge that anyone had treated him well. I soon turned off the radio because I felt myself being swamped by negativity which was depressing me.

---

[144] Iain Matthew, *The Impact of God*.

The next night, I again turned on the same station and again heard someone else telling a story of his life. I thought that this story would be similar to the one the previous night and almost turned it off but did not. This man said that he had been very rebellious as a teenager, but he did not blame everyone at every point. He spoke generally about the ups and downs during his secondary school years until he came to Year Eleven. At that point, the chaplain of the school whom he described as a 'really good bloke' invited him to go to India. He was doing badly at school and felt he had no hope of passing so he accepted the offer. He found in India that people were in desperate circumstances and he felt that he himself might not have had such a good life but he was much better off than many Indians he saw, including those of his own age. He met Mother Teresa and was deeply impressed at the positive way that she spoke and the love that she showed. He spoke of nursing a boy his own age who was dying whose leg was rotting and almost falling off and of the courage that the boy showed. The boy, now a young man, went back to Australia and got a job on a farm and found that he loved riding horses and doing the jobs needed on the land. He became a successful farmer who loved what he did.

In contrast to my reaction to the story the previous night, I was rejuvenated in listening to this second story. I noticed the difference in the way the two men faced their struggles and setbacks. One blamed others and saw no good in what had happened. The second accepted the things that had happened and did not excuse himself from the outcomes. I also noticed in the first case that the interviewer listening to the story colluded in the version that he was being told by failing to challenge it in any helpful way.

Let us return to how, according to Iain Matthew,[145] John of the Cross advises that we should accept the dark night experiences which come to us. It is right to seek a remedy, grieve or take a stand, but we also need to remember that God is at work in the darkness. We need to trust that God is there and is filling the space that has been created. When we go up the mountain which John speaks about, we can seek a secure grip or take the hand of someone higher up. In other words, we can seek help from others. We can paraphrase what John says, 'God will not delay, if I do not fail to hope. I will not struggle for something I once had and have now gone beyond. Instead, I will take heart, persevere patiently, without pain, and I will trust in God in loving attentiveness'.

In summary, first, persevere, don't run away. Matthew says that the very fact of not running away is for John of the Cross an exciting event. Second, don't say yes to the self-pity but let the past go and say yes to the future. Let yourself be carried by God. The alternative brings unnecessary sadness. Third, do not suffer unduly or unnecessarily but only if the pain is unavoidable. Finally, and most important, trust in God's loving attentiveness. Let yourself be carried by God. This may seem easy but it will probably require huge effort. It may mean risking the loss of everything else.

In this chapter, we have emphasised the interplay between suffering and joy, darkness and light. We have seen that the first prediction of Jesus' passion in Luke's gospel was followed immediately by the Transfiguration. In terms of the Ignatian

---

[145] See chapters 9-15 of Iain Matthew, *The Impact of God*, London: Hodder and Stoughton, 1995.

rules of discernment, consolation does not follow far behind desolation. In all these ways, we are talking of the paschal mystery where new life follows death. We cannot get to the resurrection without going through death just as Jesus did. Suffering, that is, the cross, is a necessary part of life. Even if Jesus said nothing about the cross, we would still have to experience suffering. It is part of the pattern of dying in order to gain new life. There is no other way to new life than through death.

Not Consecutive but Simultaneous

One more point is important, namely, that death and resurrection do not just follow each other but we actually experience them simultaneously. This came home to me recently when I led a prayer for the community on death and resurrection. We read through some statements about the finality of death and how the prospect of death puts every other aspect of life into the background. We also had the following quotation from Malcolm Muggeridge:

> I am like a man on a sea voyage nearing his destination. When I embarked, I worried about having a cabin with a porthole, whether I would be asked to sit at the captain's table, who were the more attractive and important passengers. All such considerations became pointless when I shall soon be disembarking.[146]

This statement certainly drives home the finality of death. But following this quotation was another from *Lord of the* Rings:

---
[146] Quoted in Dale C. Allison, *Death Comes*, 45.

After Gollum and the great ring of power fall into the fires of Mount Doom, Frodo and Sam sit on a little ashen hill. As lava rises around them, Frodo speaks the obvious: 'An end comes. We have only a little time to wait now. We're lost in ruins and downfall, and there is not escape'. The two friends then slip into unconsciousness. But that's not the end. The eagles come, and the hobbits are borne away to safety. Later, when Sam awakens and sees Gandalf, he gasps, 'I thought you were dead! But then I thought I was dead myself. Is everything sad going to come untrue?'[147]

We also had a hymn from Kevin Bates, *Easter Expressions*, about how the raising up of Jesus totally reverses the suffering of death. In reflecting on this theme, it became clear to all those who shared a reflection that in our experiences of suffering, there is joy lingering somewhere. Joy exists alongside the most difficult and painful experiences. The events of Holy Week follow the sequence of Holy Thursday, Good Friday, Holy Saturday and Easter Sunday. But our experience is somewhat different. Life and hope and even joy were not lacking when Jesus was arrested and experienced his sufferings and death. Jesus did not promise that we would not suffer. More than once, William Barry quotes from John McMurray the following difference between false and true religion. False religion says, 'Fear not, trust in God and God will see that none of the things you fear will happen to you'. In contrast, true religion says, 'Fear not, the things that you are afraid of are quite likely to happen, but they are nothing to be afraid of'. Barry in his own words says:

---

[147] Quoted in Allison, *Death Comes*, 17,18.

Darkness and light, pain and joy, death and resurrection are fused, they are one experience, and darkness and death do not triumph.

Conclusion

In this chapter on suffering, we have seen the importance of being aware that God is with us in the suffering offering us courage and inner peace. Most of the suffering we experience is accompanied by joy and it is often difficult to separate the two. They are part of the paschal mystery of moving through death to new life. For several pages we examined two or three chapters of Luke's gospel to see how Jesus himself faced his coming suffering and the teaching he gave his disciples as they accompanied him on his journey. We saw the need to face suffering head on and went through an example of a group facing suffering. Besides being aware of the reasons for suffering, we need a deep experience of being loved during the suffering.

References

Allison Jr. Dale, C., *Death Comes: Death, Imagination, and the Last Things*, Grand Rapids: William B. Eerdmans, 2016.

Byrne, Brendan, *The Hospitality of God: A Reading of Luke's Gospel*, Collegeville: Liturgical Press, 2000.

Hillesum, Etty, *An Interrupted Life: The Diaries, 1941–1943 and Letters from Westerbork*, trans. Arnold J. Pomerans, New York: Henry Holt and Company: 1996.

Eagleton, Terry, *Culture and the Death of God*, New Haven: Yale University Press, 2014.

Matthew, Iain, *The Impact of God*, London: Hodder and Stoughton, 1995.

Metaxis, Eric, *Bonhoeffer: Pastor, Martyr, Prophet, Spy*, Nashville: Thomas Nelson, 2010.

St John of the Cross, *The Collected Works of St John of the Cross*, Trans. Kieran Kavanaugh, O.C.D. and Otilio Rodriguez, O.C.D., Washington, D.C.: ICS Publications 1991.

Chapter Thirteen

Experiencing the Kingdom Now

IN OUR CONTEMPORARY SITUATION, we think of the kingdom of God, which Jesus spoke about, as being already present among us rather than something that is to come in the future. In fact, if we start with Jesus as he was seen in the gospels and especially in the Pauline letters, there is no question that we are already experiencing the kingdom among us but not exactly in the way most people expect.[148] We will begin this discussion of the coming of the kingdom not with the life of Jesus or his teaching but with how Paul and the writers of the New Testament saw Jesus who was by then seen as the Christ. Raimon Panikkar tells us in his reflections on *Christ in Christophany*[149] that we can relate to another person in three ways. The first is to treat that person impersonally. We may even interact with the person but it

---

[148] Today there is emphasis on rectifying the injustices that exist in the world especially since the movement of liberation theology by writers such as Gustavo Guttierez. One scripture scholar, when asked what he expected the next life to be, responded that he did not care.

[149] Raimondo Panikkar, *Christophany: The Fullness of Man*, New York: Orbis Books 2004.

will have no effect on us. The second way is when we get into the consciousness of the other person and see the world in a similar way to the way of that person. In the case of Christ, we can think of how he chased the money lenders and merchants from the Temple or how, after dining at the table of a Pharisee, he told those present not to take the places of honour at table but to take the lower places so that the host would invite them to go higher. The Temple scene shows the passion Jesus had for the things of his Father. The parable of the places at table shows how Jesus saw the danger in seeking honour and prestige for ourselves. We can reflect on the gospel stories in this way and learn much about Christ and about the things he valued and how he felt about the world.

A third way of relating to a person (and to Christ) is at the level of being. At this level we strive to penetrate to the deepest levels of the person's being. We can do this with Christ and in so doing have an experience of Christ or what Panikkar terms a Christophany. In this experience, we are totally involved as in a mystical experience and afterwards we will not be the same. What follows are three passages from the Pauline writings which invite us into such an experience. In Romans we have the following:

> Neither height nor depth nor anything else in all creation, will be able to separate us from the love of God that is in Christ Jesus our Lord (Romans 8:39).

This sentence which comes at a climactic point in the letter to the Romans speaks of a union which is real and which is stronger than any other force in the universe. How will this union feel? We may not be able to describe this feeling but it will be one of the deepest experiences we have ever had. If we really believe Paul, we will be transformed.

The second passage is from the letter to the Ephesians:

> May you have the power, together with all the Lord's people, to grasp how wide and long and high and deep is the love of Christ, and to know this love that surpasses knowledge – that you may be filled to the measure of all the fullness of God (Ephesians 3:18).

Here, the writer speaks with a similar intensity about this same reality, namely, the love of Christ for us which he relates to the fullness of the love of God for us. The writer almost pleads with us, or with God, that we will experience this love and be convinced of it. Again, the challenge is for us to believe it. The passage assumes that believing in this love and also of having this belief can be a permanent reality. The third passage is from the first letter to the Corinthians:

> And so it was with me, brothers and sisters. When I came to you, I did not come with eloquence or human wisdom as I proclaimed to you the testimony about God. For I resolved to know nothing while I was with you except Jesus Christ and him crucified. I came to you in weakness with great fear and trembling. My message and my preaching were not with wise and persuasive words, but with a demonstration of the Spirit's power, so that your faith might not rest on human wisdom, but on God's power (1 Corinthians 2:1-5).

In this final passage, Paul speaks paradoxically of an experience which made him free of any expectations he had of himself of being a good orator or thinker. He knew from the experience that the message he was preaching contained the power of the Spirit of God and had nothing to do with his own gifts. He speaks here without any concern for what his hearers think.

I have quoted these three passages to show the extraordinary effect the coming of Christ, that is, the coming of the kingdom, has had on those proclaiming the message and what effect it can have on us. The passages assume that the kingdom has certainly come and is present and active among us.

The Letter to the Romans[150]

We now want to see how Paul in his letter to the Romans saw the event of Christ coming into the world. Paul, a Jew, had considered that it was the Law, a gift from God to the Israelite people, which was the key to overcoming the barrier created by sin. In the second and third chapters of Romans, Paul sketches the depths of misery and depravity into which humans had sunk. Paul paints a grim picture:

> ... they knew God and yet refused to honour him as God or to thank him; instead, they made nonsense out of logic and their empty minds were darkened. The more they called themselves philosophers, the more stupid they

---

[150] The treatment of the letter to the Romans which follows is based on Brendan Byrne, *Romans*, Collegeville: Liturgical Press, 1996. But see also Karl Barth, *The Epistle to the Romans*, Trans. E.C. Hoskyns, London: Oxford University Press, 1968.

grew, until they exchanged the glory of the immortal God for a worthless imitation, for the image of mortal man, of birds, of quadrupeds and reptiles. That is why God left them to their filthy enjoyments and the practices with which they dishonour their own bodies, since they have given up the divine truth for a lie and have worshipped and served creatures instead of the creator, who is blessed forever. Amen. (Romans 1:21-25).

It was not just pagans, Paul believed, who had put themselves at such a distance from God. In spite of their claim to be different from the pagans, the Jews also were in the same situation. The Law could not rescue them because, no matter how much they tried, they could not stop being unfaithful to the true God in their worship and in their behaviour. This was because as Paul explains later in the letter, they were under the power of a Master too powerful for them, namely, Sin. The Law had failed to rescue them. Therefore, God had to intervene. Paul refers to this intervention a number of times, each time with renewed enthusiasm. In Christ, God has revealed something marvellous:

> But now, apart from the law, the righteousness of God has been disclosed, and is attested by the law and the prophets, the righteousness of God through faith in Jesus Christ for all who believe (Romans 3:21-23).

God has proved more incredibly loving than anyone could have imagined. He goes on: 'They are now justified by his grace as a free gift, through the redemption that is in Christ Jesus...' (Romans 3:24). Paul is simply overwhelmed by this gift of God and wants to reveal it to the world since it involves everyone.

In sending his son, Jesus Christ, God justifies us, that is, he saves us from the predicament we were in from which there was no escape. Justification means that we are made right with God. Another word Paul uses is righteousness. Righteousness happens when someone does what he/she agreed to do in a contract. In sending his son, God acts righteously since God keeps his promises. The particular promise involved here is the one he made to Abraham. God promised that Abraham would have a son and thus his descendants would continue. God did this in sending Isaac. God also promised that he would give the people a land and he did this. Paul now brings up the question of why God, on his part, acts so righteously to Abraham. It is because God is faithful. God fulfils his promises in the past and now he is fulfilling them in sending his son, Jesus Christ. What of Abraham? Is Abraham made righteous by being faithful to the Law? Is Abraham someone who has managed to be faithful and thus been justified? The answer is no. Abraham has not been justified by keeping the Law but by putting his faith in God. Paul quotes Genesis 15 showing that Abraham was justified even before he was circumcised. Paul then asks what is going to justify us. He answers that we are to put our faith in the same God as Abraham, the God 'who brings the dead to life and calls into being what does not exist' (Romans 4:17).

In chapter 5 of Romans, Paul says we cannot boast about keeping all the observances of the Law, but we can boast about what God has done for us in Jesus Christ in making us righteous. And there is something else we can boast about, namely, our sufferings. Paul introduces here a new element: that because we have been made right with God, our own struggles are not over. Even though the outcome is assured, that is, we are close to God, we will still have to go on with our lives with its struggles and setbacks. The kingdom has come and the enemy, Sin, has been defeated, but there is still more to come, namely the living out of our lives as faithfully as we can. In this present struggle, we are to hope. Faith, hope and love are still the virtues we have to practise. Paul wants to encourage us by using all his oratorical skills:

> These sufferings bring patience, as we know, and patience brings perseverance, and perseverance brings hope, and this hope is not deceptive, because the love of God has been poured into our hearts by the Holy Spirit which has been given to us (Romans 5:3-5).

In chapter 5, Paul presses home his point that we are already saved. He contrasts the effects on us of Adam's sin and the grace given to us in Jesus Christ. Paul here is not emphasising sin but grace. He simply uses Adam as a foil for Christ so that we can appreciate all the more what Christ has done for us. Paul says,

> ... but the gift itself considerably outweighed the fall... Again, as one man's fall brought condemnation on everyone, so the good act of one man brings life and make them justified (Romans 5:15, 18).

Paul wants, in all the ways he can, to convince us of the immeasurable gift we have in Christ. We are to forget about the slavery we were in and enjoy to the full the grace we have been given. Paul drives home his point:

... but however great the number of sins committed, grace was even greater; and so, just as sin reigned wherever there was death, so grace will reign to bring eternal life thanks to the righteousness that come through Jesus Christ our Lord (Romans 5:20-21).

In chapter 6, Paul deals with the question of how we are to live knowing that we have been already saved. Does it mean that we can live as we like without paying attention to the Law? Should we go back to the situation all human beings were in what Paul has already described? The answer is certainly not. Surely now we are to imitate Christ. We are to live in a way appropriate to being in union with Christ. Do we want to live lives of 'rottenness, greed and malice, and addicted to envy, murder, wrangling, treachery and spite' (Romans 1:29-30)? The answer is no. The things we value now have changed; our lives and loves have changed. We can now see (at least to some extent) that this way of living will not lead us to happiness and fulfillment.

In chapter 7 and the beginning of chapter 8, Paul presents two scenarios, one that described our lives before grace came to us and the one we live now. The former type of life was one where we were dominated by Sin who was our master. We no longer have to live under that Master any more. Now our lives are guided by the Spirit. Paul declares: '...the law of the spirit of life in Christ Jesus has set you free from the law of sin and death' (Romans 8:1). Then further, Paul describes something as though it has certainly happened:

> Your interests, however, are not in the unspiritual but in the spiritual, since the Spirit of God has made his home in you. In fact, unless you possessed the Spirit of Christ you

would not belong to him... But if Christ is in you then your spirit is life itself because you have been justified; and if the Spirit of him who raised Jesus from the dead is living in you, then he who raised Jesus from the dead will give life to your own mortal bodies through his Spirit living in you (Romans 8:9-11).

We can see in this section how Paul moves between talking as though the Spirit has definitively conquered Sin in this battle, to admitting that Sin can still get the better of us. However, in the next short section, Paul speaks confidently of the victory of the Spirit:

The spirit you received is not the spirit of slaves bringing fear into your lives again; it is the spirit of adoption, and it makes us cry out, 'Abba, Father!' The Spirit himself and our spirit bear united witness that we are children of God. And if we are children we are heirs as well: heirs of God and co-heirs with Christ, sharing his suffering so as to share his glory (Romans: 8:15-17).

Paul wants to assure us that the outcome of the conflict between Sin and the Spirit has been won, but he knows that in fact it can still feel that we are being dominated by Sin. He does not want us to become complacent but neither does he want us to be discouraged. Hence he walks a tightrope between the two for a while. But here in this passage and for the rest of chapter 8, Paul speaks with certainty of the victory of the Spirit. In fact, he now invites us to celebrate the victory. He says,

Nothing therefore can come between us and the love of Christ, even if we are troubled or worried, or being persecuted, or lacking food or clothes, or being threatened or even attacked... These are the trials through which we triumph, by the power of him who loved us (Romans 8:35-37).

Even here we see the tension: we are going through trials and are even troubled and worried. We are not to be disturbed by these feelings because the victory has been won. And then we have the final lines we have already quoted that nothing can come between us and the love of God made visible in Christ Jesus (cf. Romans 8:38-39).

The Proclamation of the Good News[151]

In the above section, we used Paul's teaching in the letter to the Romans to present what an unprecedented gift God has given us in the death and resurrection of Christ. Paul wants to convince us in every conceivable way of the enormity of this gift: our salvation has been won; we are already justified. Yet even after this gift which, Paul tells us, had been kept hidden from the foundation of the world, our experience tells us that we still need to use all our efforts to live lives worthy of the gift. We have covered the theology of the gospel in what we have done. It remains now to look at how the kingdom has come into the world from another angle, namely, that of Jesus' life, his teaching and his understanding of himself. Our aim again is to help us appreciate the amazing reality of the gift God has given us.

---

[151] Byrne in *Romans* sets out the notion of the gospel which I draw on in this section as well.

The notion of gospel was a popular one at the time of Jesus. The Roman Empire had conquered Palestine and the people were living under the occupation of a foreign force which imposed taxes on them. There was great inequality between the upper levels, the governing class, the retainers and merchants and the priestly class on the one hand and the unskilled labourers of different kinds on the other. The upper level groups held all the power and the rest, the majority, eked out a living as best they could. We see several gospel scenes of poverty that existed such as the labourers who lined up for a day's work. The people were looking for a liberator. They felt that they were still in exile as they had been four hundred years earlier in Babylon. They were crying out for liberation. Jesus comes into this scene with powers of healing, casting out demons, and the teaching that the kingdom of God was at hand.

Each of the four gospels received inspiration from the book of Second Isaiah which announces freedom to the people during the Exile. Chapter 40:9 proclaims:

> Go up to a high mountain,
> Joyful messenger to Zion,
> Shout with a loud voice,
> Joyful messenger to Jerusalem.
> Shout without fear,
> Say to the towns of Judah,
> 'Here is your God'.

Here is another announcement that complements the above:

> How beautiful on the mountains
> Are the feet of one who brings good news,
> Who heralds peace, brings happiness,
> Proclaims salvation,
> And tells Zion,
> 'Your God is king!' (Isaiah 52:7).

When Jesus appeared with powers of healing and exorcising, there were great hopes that he would be the Messiah who would come and make the people prosperous again. Jesus announced that the kingdom had arrived and that people should repent and believe in this good news. The Messiah would free the people from their captivity under the Romans. Second Isaiah said that when the Messiah came, the deaf would hear and the dumb would speak. The gospel of Mark begins with John the Baptist coming on the scene. He is the announcer, the one who comes before the Messiah. Then Jesus comes and is baptised by John. Mark tells us:

> After John had been arrested, Jesus went into Galilee. There, he proclaimed the Good News from God. 'The time has come', he said 'and the kingdom of God is close at hand. Repent and believe the Good News' (Mark 1:14-15).

God is now fulfilling his promises. Jesus shows the generosity of God and the heart of God. God is to be trusted after all; their hopes have not been misplaced. All the hopes of the people seemed to have been false. But now the people know that God keeps his promises and that God is as powerful as they believed. Mark has Second Isaiah in mind in many passages of his gospel. After he heals the daughter of the Canaanite woman, Jesus is brought a deaf man who also has an impediment in his speech (Mark 7:31-37). Jesus takes the man aside, puts his fingers into the man's ears and touches his tongue with spittle, then looks up to heaven and sighs and said, 'Ephphatha' that is, 'Be opened'. And the man could hear and began to speak. The passage ends with the following: 'He has done all things well', they said, 'he makes the deaf hear and the dumb speak'. This healing fulfils the prophecy of Isaiah of what would happen when the Messiah came:

> Then the eyes of the blind shall be opened,
> The ears of the deaf unsealed (Isaiah 35:5).

In Luke's Gospel, Jesus begins his public ministry with the following announcement which is almost a direct quotation from Isaiah 61:1:

> The spirit of the Lord has been given to me,
> For he has anointed me.
> He has sent me to bring the good news to the poor,
> To proclaim liberty to captives
> And to the blind new sight,
> To set the downtrodden free,
> To proclaim the Lord's year of favour (Luke 4:18).

We can see in these quotations how the gospel writers were inspired by the vision of the writer of Second Isaiah to interpret what God was doing in the life and ministry of Jesus. Reading the whole of Second Isaiah can help us pick up some of the enthusiasm and spirit of the evangelists in the gospels they wrote. In Mark's Gospel, we see that God's power in Jesus is unlimited. Jesus begins to heal immediately and to cast out devils. It is said that the people bring all the sick and he heals them all.

In chapter 5 of Mark we have two miracles which show this unlimited power.[152] The first story, the cure of the Gerasene demoniac, shows that, because Jesus is with us, we do not have to fear outside forces like the terrible Roman army or any psychological forces like madness or even the spiritual forces of Satan. Jesus gets off the boat to be confronted by a man from the tombs whom no one can restrain. The man cries out continually and bruises himself. He comes to Jesus and falls at his feet and shouts at the top of his voice, 'What do you want from me, Jesus, son of the Most High God?' Jesus, talking to the evil spirit within the man simply says, 'Come out of the man, unclean spirit'. Then Jesus allows the devils, since there are many in the man, to go into the herd of pigs that are there on the mountain. The pigs immediately charge down the cliff and into the sea.

In this passage, Mark colourfully builds up the forces of evil, the tombs, the pagan territory, the many devils in the man, the huge heard of pigs which represent the Roman army. The brutality of the presence of the Roman army is symbolised by the man in chains and his self-mutilation. Jesus comes into this hopeless situation of slavery and degradation.

---

[152] See Megan McKenna, *On Your Mark: Reading Mark in the Shadow of the Cross*, New York: Orbis Books, 2006. McKenna presents these two passages from Mark with great vitality and originality.

The passage tells us that there is no situation into which Jesus cannot come and create something new. Jesus comes and gives new hope not just to the people who were present in this scene but to the whole nation. He gives them new heart and spirit.

What I called the second miracle in chapter 5 of Mark is actually two miracles in one, the hemorrhaging woman and the cure of Jairus' daughter. It begins with large crowds pressing around Jesus which tells us the hopes the people have for Jesus. The two miracles merge in many ways: they establish that Jesus has power over both sickness (the woman who has had the hemorrhage for twelve years) and death (the girl who is twelve years old); Jesus banishes the categories of clean and unclean (woman is unclean and girl is not); both the woman and the girl are unnamed.

Jairus, a synagogue official, approaches Jesus with faith and asks Jesus to come and lay his hands on his daughter to cure her. Jesus accompanies Jairus to the house where the girl is. As the crowds press around him, a woman touches him and he notices it. The unclean condition of the woman is described in detail: 'after a long and painful treatment under various doctors she had spent all she had without being any the better for it, in fact, she was getting worse' (Mark 5:26). This information simply emphasises the effectiveness of the power of Jesus in contrast to these doctors. Jesus touches her and she becomes instantly healed. Jesus' clothing has power showing that he is in the tradition of Elisha (cf. 2 Kings 4) but he is even greater than Elisha. Her sickness (and our sicknesses) do not repel God but attract God to us. Jesus knows that power has gone out of him and he asks,

'Who touched me?' The woman approaches him in fear and trembling. We notice that her fear in the face of divinity does not prevent her from revealing herself to the huge crowd. Jesus speaks tenderly to her, 'Go, my daughter your faith has saved you'. She is a model of faith. We too have to overcome our shame as she did.

The report comes to Jesus and Jairus: 'Your daughter is dead'. Jesus says to him, 'Do not be afraid, just believe'. We are about to see that Jesus has power over death as well as illness. Peter, James and John accompany him inside the house. People are wailing and weeping loudly. The story emphasises how the crowd mock Jesus when he says that the girl is not dead but asleep all the more to show the power of Jesus. We are told, 'So he turned them all out, and taking with him the child's father and mother, and his own companions (Peter, James and John) he went into the place where the child lay. And taking the child by the hand he said to her, 'Talitha, kum' which means, 'Little girl, I tell you to get up'. Mark wants to emphasise the enormity of the miracle Jesus has just performed. Other wonder workers may have been able to perform cures but who is this who can raise the dead to life! Megan McKenna says here that when Jesus enters the house it becomes a church.[153] The solemnity indicates to us, Mark's readers, that this is the equivalent of a sacrament. When baptism is performed, the person becomes a new-born since she shares in Jesus' resurrection.

Here are some other elements we can glean from this story. One is the age of the two persons. The woman's illness

---

[153] Megan McKenna, *On Your Mark: Reading Mark in the Shadow of the Cross.*

for 12 years and the girl's age of 12 years symbolise the 12 tribes of Israel. This detail shows the story has a social meaning, that is, a meaning for us. The ages also show the breaking down of age and of social background and of rich and poor. A second point is that Jesus in his healing journey with Jairus takes a detour to listen to the pain of the crowd. Only when the outcast has been cured can he go on. Third, we see that Jairus and the woman would do anything to be healed. Will we do anything? And finally, in the new family of Jesus, resurrection occurs and society's fear of contagion and of social difference is put aside.

The Language of the Kingdom

These initial chapters in Mark want to build in us a picture of what it means that the Messiah has come. Mark is as dramatic as possible in showing us this reality. After these chapters, the story becomes more complex in keeping with what actually happens: Jesus is rejected in his home town; his disciples do not understand him and then have great trouble in understanding what sort of a Messiah he is going to be. They constantly expect him to be a miraculous conqueror of the Romans whereas Jesus is going to have to suffer and die. But very gradually, people show faith in him. It takes the rest of the gospel for Mark to show that Jesus certainly is the Messiah but a Messiah who will suffer and die before being triumphantly raised from the dead.

In speaking of the gospel and of what happens to Jesus, we are also speaking of the kingdom of God. We have seen that the gospel writers, particularly Mark, tell us that the kingdom of God certainly comes into the world with Jesus. Until now, we have not used the terminology of kingdom of God. But the term is used constantly in the gospels. Jesus spoke about the kingdom of God particularly in his parables. In this teaching by parables, Jesus challenges his hearers to get rid of their prejudiced ideas and wrong assumptions about the kingdom of God. In correcting our ideas of the kingdom of God, Jesus is also correcting our ideas about life and about God.

Let us take first the parable of the labourers in the vineyard in Matthew's gospel (20:1-16). The landowner makes an agreement with the workers for one denarius a day. Then later in the morning, he finds that more workers have turned up and he employs them as well. He goes out later and finds more workers and employs them. Then at almost the end of the day, he finds even more men wanting to be employed and he employs them as well. When the workers come to be paid, they all receive the same amount, one denarius. Those who came early complain to the landowner that they should receive more. The landowner says to one of them, 'My friend, I am not being unjust to you... Have I no right to do what I like with my own? Why be envious because I am generous?' The passage concludes, 'Thus the last will be first, and the first, last'.

With this parable, Jesus turns the attitude of his hearers upside down. The parable tells us much about the kingdom of God. In the kingdom, there will be a different understanding of justice. The human attitude to justice is to deal with everyone according to what they deserve. This will not be so in the kingdom. Everyone there will be treated with an inexplicable generosity. The parable tells us that we are no better than others when we have done more good deeds than they. The hearers of this parable are left asking themselves: will we be able to accept this sort of generosity or do we have to earn what we receive? It is difficult for us to accept this sort of generosity from God.

There is a similar theme in the parable of the Prodigal Son (Luke 15:16-32) when we see it from the viewpoint of the older brother. When the father comes out to talk to the older son when the young one has returned and been forgiven, the older son refers to his younger brother as 'This son of yours'. He does not want to be thought of as being like that brother. He does not consider that he has any sins to be forgiven. The parable brings out how we find it hard to accept God's forgiveness. The trouble is, first, that we have a false idea of ourselves. We see ourselves as special, better than others. Another parable is helpful here, that of the Pharisee and the publican. This parable tells us that we are all sinners; we are all like the publican, sinners and wretched. And so the publican goes home at rights with God but not the Pharisee. The Pharisee is still under the illusion of his own perfection. Hence he is still at a distance from God.

A further parable, that of the Good Samaritan (Luke 10:29-37), also deals with this theme of how we as humans see ourselves. The Levite and the Pharisee in the parable who see the man in the ditch and pass by, have no compassion for this man in the ditch. They see themselves as God-fearing while this man has been robbed and must be a ne'er-do-well. He must have done something to deserve what has happened to him. The Samaritan, however, who comes by, sees the man in the ditch as a brother. He does not see himself as better than this man in need of his help.

These parables tell us that in the kingdom of God, everyone is equal. When the kingdom of God is present, we do not see ourselves as better than anyone else. In the kingdom of God, God loves all equally regardless of who they are or what they have done. John Fuellenbach[154] sees a threefold pattern in all the parables: when we hear a parable, the values we presently hold are challenged. We have certain understandings, preconceptions, attitudes which we do not question. The parable challenges us to question these assumptions. If we take in the meaning of the parable, we will be changed. The parables speak about how the kingdom of God breaks into our lives through the new perspectives which they present. They invite us to a reversal of our values.

Fuellenbach takes the parable of the treasure in the field (Matthew 13:44-46) to illustrate this pattern. The landowner finds the treasure in the field and he is bowled over by this incredible gift which comes to him. Second, he holds everything else that he thought as valuable before the finding of the treasure as of no worth compared with the treasure. This reversal of values that he experiences leads him to action, that of buying the field.

What really drives the individual to action is the joy over the unexpected treasure, the great blessing of what we traditionally call salvation. These days, this word has lost its punch somewhat. We may speak now of the great intervention of God into our world in Jesus. Another way of saying it is that we have had the wonderful good fortune of having the kingdom of God breaking into our little world.

---

[154] John Fuellenbach, *The Kingdom of God: the Message of Jesus Today*, Eugene, Oregon: Wipf and Stock, 2006.

The battle with the kingdom of Satan

Jesus saw his mission not just in terms of this-worldly justice but in terms of forces of evil beyond this world. Apocalyptic ideas which were very popular in the time of Jesus saw the world as being ruled by the forces of evil. In this view, the present world is under the influence of Satan, the Prince of this world. From this perspective the world was not able to be saved. Apocalyptic spoke not just of the present age but of the age to come. Jesus was influenced by these views. Jesus had a sense of the all-pervasiveness of evil in the world. He knew there were life-denying forces that he was to confront. We find this struggle in several places in the gospels, e.g. in Mark 1:16 to 3:12. First, Jesus goes into the desert and is tempted by Satan. He emerges and begins to do battle with the forces of evil expressed through illness and possession. He cures many and drives out demons. The demons ask Jesus, 'What do you want of us, Jesus of Nazareth?' (Mark 1:22). In Luke 13:16, Jesus tells the synagogue official, 'And this woman, a daughter of Abraham whom Satan has held these 18 years – was it not right to untie her bonds on the sabbath day?' It is clear from this statement that Jesus saw human actions as coming from a deeper source than the merely human. From this viewpoint, the kingdom of God which Jesus preaches and brings into the world is the force of good coming to do battle with the forces of evil. In this conflict, the kingdom of God will be evident in many ways but no definitive victory will be won in this present life.[155]

---

[155] Byrne in *Romans* first alerted me to the importance of apocalyptic in the

We may see the Beatitudes in the Sermon on the Mount in terms of the kingdom of God breaking into the world. In the beatitudes, Jesus is saying that those who are held in little account in this world will eventually be the ones who will be happy. He is saying that the present order will be overturned, not immediately and forcefully but nonetheless inevitably. It will be the gentle and the meek, those who are pushed around now who will eventually be the ones who will be happy. Those who now mourn, those who fight for justice now who will experience be fulfilled. The world will find that those who are merciful and peaceful, those who are persecuted, will eventually be the victorious ones. The weak ones now will be seen to be in fact powerful when the kingdom comes fully.

The God of the Kingdom

A keynote passage, Exodus 34:6-9, presents how the people in the Old Testament saw God. God is 'a God of tenderness and compassion, slow to anger, rich in kindness and faithfulness' (34:6). God is faithful to his promises; God continues to love his people through their infidelities; he continues to forgive them no matter what they do. There were times when it seemed that God's promises would never be fulfilled, but the people still knew that it was faithful love that characterised God. There was also the God who challenged the people and who sent prophets who prophesied woe unless the people

---

gospels. See also, Tony Kelly, *Eschatology and Hope*, New York: Orbis Books, 2006, and Jurgen Moltmann, *The Coming of God: Christian Eschatology*, Augsburg Books, 2004.

turned back to him. In the gospels, we have a difference between John's image of God and that of Jesus. Jesus may have at first identified with John the Baptist in thinking that God's judgment would come upon those who did not change their ways, but if so, this belief did not last. John may have feared the future but Jesus believed that reality was gracious and not threatening. He told his disciples on several occasions not to be afraid. He said not to worry about where their food and clothing would come from. Reality was gracious because God was gracious and trustworthy. Jesus had an unbounded trust in his Father. Hence, he could love himself and others. His Father was the father in the parable who saw his wayward son a long way off and ran to meet him without thinking of his own status or importance. His Father was prodigiously forgiving and hence Jesus preached that we could forgive unconditionally those who did wrong to us. He poured out his love in his teaching and in his service to others through his healings and his personal care for them. This attitude which Jesus had towards life came from his boundless trust in his Father's love for himself and for the whole of creation.

Since this was the way Jesus saw God, he believed that the kingdom was present when these qualities of love, trust and forgiveness existed among people. This is what he came to bring about and what he strove for and preached. His passion was that this kingdom would become more strongly established in this world.

In the final section of this chapter, we will look at the part that the death of Jesus played in bringing about the kingdom.

Jesus Entering the Realm of the Dead

Let us remind ourselves what we mean by the kingdom of God. It is the reign of God over God's people. It is the kingdom that Jesus prayed for in the Our Father. It is the state of peace between God and the creation where love and trust prevail. The death of Jesus relates to all these elements of the kingdom. The death of Jesus was needed to bring about peace between God and God's people both living and dead. We wish to see here what was needed to bring about this peace and how Jesus' death in fact brought it about when nothing else could. We will examine also how the great enemy, death itself, is overcome in the death of Jesus.

We have seen in Romans how God intervened by sending his son Jesus to rescue humans from the miserable state they were in because of human depravity and the insufficiency of the law. Paul, however, does not deal with how Jesus' death brought life to those who had died before he came, especially those who had died and who had rejected God. We read in the Acts of the Apostles in the sermon of Peter on Pentecost Sunday:

> You that are Israelites, listen to this: Jesus of Nazareth was a man accredited by God to you by miracles and signs which God did among you through him, as you yourselves know. This man was handed over to you by God's set purpose and foreknowledge, and you – with the help of those outside the law – put him to death by nailing him to the cross. But God raised him from the dead, freeing him from the torments of Hades, because it was impossible for death to keep its hold on him... God has raised this Jesus to life, and we are all witnesses to the fact (Acts 2:22-24).

It is God who is doing the actions and Jesus is passive. The passage tells us that when he died, Jesus entered into the realm of the dead and had to be freed from this realm. He was set free 'because it was impossible for death to keep its hold on him'. We do not read much in contemporary literature about Jesus' descent into this realm of the dead, but it was not so in other historical eras. Balthasar draws upon the literature from the Fathers and elsewhere to shed light on this journey of Jesus into the realm of the dead. Balthasar says, 'The Redeemer showed himself... as the only one who, going beyond the general experience of death, was able to measure the depths of that abyss'.[156] No one before or since had been able to do this. In going into this realm, Jesus experienced death a second time, this time in its aspect of separation from God. Here Jesus showed the dead compassion in their death which was different from the compassion shown to Jesus on Good Friday. Jesus who was dead, experienced Hell, that is, separation from God, which these dead souls themselves experienced. In fact, Jesus took this pain upon himself or rather he allowed the Father to have him experience this pain since he himself was dead, lifeless and powerless, like the other dead in this place. Balthasar quotes this very vivid passage from Nicholas of Cusa about Jesus' descent into the underworld:

---

[156] Balthasar, *Mysterium Paschale*, Edinburgh: T & T Clark, 1990, 169.

And since the death of Christ was complete, since through his own experience he saw the death which he had freely chosen to undergo, the soul of Christ went down into the underworld, ad inferna, where the vision of death is... The lower or deeper underworld is where one sees death. When God raised Christ, he drew him, as we read in the Acts of the Apostles, from out of the lower underworld, after delivering him from the torture of that underworld. Christ's suffering, the greatest one could conceive, was like that of the damned who cannot be damned anymore. That is, his suffering went to the length of eternal punishment... He alone through such a death entered into glory.[157]

The letter to the Hebrews takes the view that those who have fallen away from the faith cannot be rescued:

... it is impossible for them to be renewed a second time. They cannot be repentant if they have willfully crucified the Son of God and openly mocked him. A field that has been well-watered by frequent rain, and gives the crops that are wanted by the owners who grew them, is given God's blessing; but one that grows brambles and thistles is abandoned, and practically cursed. It will end up by being burnt (Hebrews 6:6-8).

But Hebrews does not take into account that Christ has gone into this very state of being finally abandoned and rejected which is the state of these souls. Christ experienced just this state and, by taking it upon himself, nullified it so that it no longer had any power. Christ experienced what it

---

[157] *Mysterium Pascale*, 171.

was like to be eternally separated from God. And from this worst of all situations, God brought him forth as we have already seen from the sermon of Peter at Pentecost, 'But God raised him from the dead, freeing him from the torments of Hades, because it was impossible for death to keep its hold on him...' (Acts 2:24). It was impossible because God is stronger than death. Balthasar considers this consequence of everyone coming forth with Christ from the realm of death as inevitable since Christ definitively overcame death, the final enemy. Balthasar also describes how Christ took on all the horror and evil of death in order to break its hold. Only a dead Christ could have done this since if he had not been dead he would not have been able to take their sin upon himself as one of them.

In this final section, we have focused on what happened after Christ's death on the cross. It has been necessary to do this to show how death itself was conquered. Once death had been conquered, the kingdom could come into all the realms of humanity. The victory had now been fully won until the time comes for Christ to usher in the end of death and all suffering.

Conclusion

God intervened in Christ to save us from a hopeless situation and brought us grace (the letter to the Romans); Jesus came to announce that the kingdom had come into the world; Jesus spoke about the kingdom especially in the parables he told; he proclaimed a reversal of values in the eschatological time; Jesus also revealed to us who God is whose kingdom had come and will still come. Finally, we saw how Christ's descent into the world of the dead completed the victory over death until now. The final coming of the kingdom will be when Christ comes a second time at the end of the world. These are the areas we have discussed in this theme of the coming of the kingdom of God.

References

Balthasar, Hans Urs von, *Mysterium Paschale*, Edinburgh: T & T Clark, 1990.

Byrne, Brendan, *The Hospitality of God: A Reading of Luke's Gospel*, Collegeville: Liturgical Press, 2000.

_____, (1996) *Romans*, Sacra Pagina 6, Collegeville: Liturgical Press, 1996.

Dowd, Sharon, *Reading Mark: A Literary and Theological Commentary on the Second Gospel*, Macon: Smyth & Helwys 2000.

Fuellenbach, John, *The Kingdom of God: the Message of Jesus Today*, Eugene, Oregon: Wipf and Stock, 2006.

McKenna, Megan, *On Your Mark: Reading Mark in the Shadow of the Cross*, New York: Orbis Books, 2006.

Oakes, Edward T. *The Theology of Hans Urs von Balthasar: Pattern of Redemption*, New York: Continuum Publishing, 1997.

Panikkar, Raimon, *Christophany: The Fullness of Man*, Orbis, 2004.

Chapter Fourteen

Overcoming Doubt and Despair

Overcoming Doubt and Despair

I RECENTLY SAW A MOVIE titled *Silence,* directed by the famous American director, Martin Scorsese. The film is based on the novel *Silence* by the Japanese Catholic novelist, Shusaku Endo, who was interested in probing the paradoxes and contradictions of faith. The film raised questions for me which I had not pondered before, of the tension between our election by God and our human freedom as well as the extent to which we are actually free. In this chapter, I wish to reflect on this theme.

The film *Silence*[158] begins with a conversation between two young Jesuit priests and their superior over whether they will go to Japan to continue the mission there. The historical period is 17th century Japan in a time of continued persecution of Catholic missionaries. The Christian faith had been introduced into Japan by the Jesuit, St Francis Xavier, a

---

[158] Some details here are from Sr Rose Pacatte. https://www.ncronline.org/blogs/ncr-today/how-film-silence-art

century earlier. The two young priests are full of fervour and determined to go to the mission no matter what the dangers. The superior refuses them many times but at last gives in when he finds that they are determined. The two set out and somewhere off the coast of Japan, they find a Japanese man, Kichijiro, who is persuaded to escort them to the Japanese mainland. As soon as they arrive on Japanese soil, we see how grim the situation is. They make contact with a group of Christians and at first they hide, but soon make contact with other Christian groups.

From the beginning, we hear that there are reports that one Jesuit priest, a leader of the missions, Fr Ferreira, had renounced the Christian faith. The two young priests cannot believe this along with many others. It is unheard of and unthinkable that committed missionaries would renounce their faith. The Japanese party of the Inquisitor, the authority with the duty to find and punish Christians, comes to the village and three of the dedicated Christians are executed in a slow, painful way. Christians are asked to renounce their faith and each time, Kichijiro does so and moves away but just as regularly comes back to ask for forgiveness from Fr Rodrigues. The two priests, Rodrigues and Garrupe, decide to separate. Rodrigues' faith remains strong. He still cannot understand the behaviour of Kichijiro whom he sees as a Judas figure nor of the possibility that Ferreira may have apostasised. But, at last, Rodrigues is captured along with a small group of Christians.

The Inquisitor, Inoue, continually works on Rodrigues saying that Christianity is a Western idea and cannot adapt to Japan. Eventually when they meet, Ferreira also gives these same arguments. He learns here that it is true that Ferreira has renounced the faith. This is a very difficult time for Rodrigues whose faith is challenged on all sides. His former companion, Garrupe, turns up and dies while trying to rescue the Christians with him who are being wrapped in straw blankets and thrown into the sea. At the sight of the death of his fellow missionary, Rodrigues becomes desperate. At this time, he sees a picture of Jesus which he revered from his seminary days appearing to him in water from his basin. We think that in seeing these reflections, Rodrigues' faith may be strengthened. But it is not so. Separated from the other Christians, he hears cries of anguish and he is told that these companions are being tortured and threatened with death while he has to listen. This is too much for him and he renounces his faith by stepping on an image of Christ.

The review by Sr Rose Pacatte speaks of the director Martin Scorsese's answers to questions about the film. He had previously made *The Last Temptation of Christ* where he wrestled with the idea of the humanity of Christ. He said that this last movie *Silence* was much more challenging for him. He made the film to answer questions about faith and doubt and how much faith humans can actually have apart from saints, who are in a category of their own. Scorsese saw himself 'as a believer, unbeliever, doubter'. He claims that there can be faith underneath the renunciations of those who have apostasised. He sees it this way: 'Because when (Rodrigues) does apostasise, he gives up everything he's proud of, and he has nothing left except service and compassion. So, he gives up his faith in order to gain his faith. Wow! How do you do that?' We may not see Scorsese's logic here fully, but this act of renunciation of someone until then committed to Christ is not simple. Frs Rodrigues and Garrupe had been full of zeal, generosity and faith at the beginning. It seemed that their faith was unshakeable. The film certainly raises the question: what can happen to our faith when it is put to the test?

We have examples in the gospels of reversal of roles, those who are last will be first and those first last. We may be challenged in the story of Zaccheus, that Zaccheus, the tax collector and 'outsider', is the one whom Jesus chooses to dine with. Are we at home with the inclusiveness of Jesus in allowing into the community outsiders like tax collectors or are we like the Pharisees who see people like Zaccheus as sinners and who are therefore not welcome? In the case of Rodrigues in *Silence*, the dedicated priest who finally, under intense pressure, gives into the pressure on him to renounce his faith, he is the one we tend to exclude. The challenge of the community that Jesus sets up is that it excludes nobody.

The Dark Night of the Spirit

St John of the Cross in Book 2 of *The Dark Night* speaks of the dark night of the spirit which is much more searing than the dark night of the senses which he deals with earlier.[159] Many of the points John makes can be applied usefully to the crisis of faith of Rodrigues which leads to his renunciation of the faith. John says that when the person is in the dark night,

---

[159] St John of the Cross, *The Collected Works of St John of the Cross*, Trans. Kieran Kavanaugh, O.C.D. and Otilio Rodriguez, O.C.D., Washington, D.C.: ICS Publications 1991.

there is an inflow of God into the person which purges the soul of its 'habitual ignorances and imperfections, natural and spiritual'. The inflow of God also illumines the person:

> This dark contemplation is painful to the soul in these beginnings... The soul must necessarily undergo affliction and suffering. Because of the purgation of its imperfections caused by this contemplation, the soul becomes a battlefield in which these two contraries combat each other (5.4).

We can see how Rodrigues felt that he was in a dark night as the pressure was placed on him to renounce his Christianity. He could not hear God answering his prayer or giving him any guidance at all. John, however, says that this is 'an inflow of God' into the soul. God's purpose is to deny the soul the feeling of glorying in itself for all its virtues. The following effects described by John also apply to Rodrigues:

> Because it seems that God has rejected it, the soul suffers such pain and grief that when God tried Job in this way it proved one of the worst of Job's trials, as he says: 'Why have you set me against you, and I am heavy and burdensome to myself?' (Job 7:20) (5.5).
>
> ... the soul thinks it will never be worthy, and there are no more blessings for it. This divine and dark light causes deep immersion in its knowledge and feeling of one's own miseries and evils; it brings all these miseries into relief so the soul sees clearly that of itself it will never possess anything else (5.5).
>
> Both the sense and the spirit, as though under an immense and dark load, undergo such agony and pain that the soul would consider death a relief (5.6).

Rodrigues does indeed feel that God has rejected him; he suffers continual pain because of the relentless pressure put upon him by the Inquisitor who is determined to wear him down and to use all the tricks he knows to give up his stand for the Christian faith. He certainly experiences physical deprivation but his spiritual deprivation is far worse: he no longer has the good feelings he had when embarking on the venture to go to Japan, and God is giving him no sense that God loves him or cares what is happening to him. The pain strips him of all sense that he is better than the little band of Christians he is leading. It strips him of feelings that he is special, that he is a priest belonging to the elite order of the Society of Jesus.

In chapter 6 of Book 2 of *The Dark Night*, John lists four kinds of pain that the soul endures:

- There is a stripping of the habitual affections and properties of the old self. The soul feels it is melting away and being undone by a cruel spiteful death.

- What it feels most is the conviction that God has rejected it, and with abhorrence cast it into darkness (6.2).

- The soul feels very vividly indeed the shadow of death, the sighs of death, and the sorrows of hell, all of which reflect the feeling of God's absence, of being chastised and rejected by him and of being unworthy of him, as well. As well as the object of his anger.

- Such persons also feel forsaken and despised by creatures, particularly by their friends (6.2).

- The soul feels also its own intimate poverty and misery. Such awareness is one of the chief afflictions it suffers in the purgation (6.4).

John continues:

... the (dark) contemplation annihilates, empties, and consumes all the affections and imperfect habits the soul contracted throughout its life. Since these imperfections are deeply rooted in the substance of the soul, in addition to this poverty, this natural and spiritual emptiness, it usually suffers an oppressive undoing and an inner torment (6.4).

John quotes Psalm 69:1-3: 'Save me, Lord, for the waters have come even unto my soul; I am stuck in the mire of the deep, and there is nowhere to stand...' John also quotes Job 16:22: 'I who was wont to be wealthy and rich am suddenly undone and broken; he has taken me by the neck, he has broken me and set me up as his mark so as to wound me'.

These references to the psalms and Job remind us that we all go through this purification in our lives. We apply these lines from the psalms to ourselves and pour out our own feelings to God. John, however, is talking specifically of 'souls' who are well advanced and who have gone through the night of the senses. He is focusing particularly here on the spiritual suffering of these persons. I think we can see strong similarities between what John is describing and what Rodrigues experienced and Ferreira before him. These men who renounced their faith went through these terrible sufferings of spirit.

John says:

> One ought to have deep compassion for the soul God puts in this tempestuous and frightful night. Individuals in this state find neither consolation nor support in any doctrine or spiritual Master.
> ... until the Lord finishes urging them in the way he desires, no remedy is a help to them in their sorrow... They resemble one who is imprisoned in a dark dungeon, bound hands and feet... They remain in this state until their spirit is humbled, softened and purified, until it becomes so delicate, simple, and refined, that it can be one with the spirit of God (7.3).

I do not think it is being fanciful to say that Rodrigues and Ferreira received no consolation and could do nothing except allow themselves to be 'humbled, softened and purified'. Is it too fanciful to say that their spirit too became 'delicate, simple, and refined' and 'one with the spirit of God'?

For people in this situation, John has the following advice:

> Indeed this is not the time to speak with God, but the time to put one's mouth in the dust... that perhaps there might come some actual hope (8.1).

We see Rodrigues continually asking God to come to help him without hearing any response. There came a time when he stopped asking God for help and just hoped that God would help him. God did not seem to help him. When Rodrigues renounces the faith, however, he seems to gain peace. We might ask the question: at what depth in himself did he make this act and how free was he? Had God really deserted him when he apparently renounced his Christian faith?

Going into the Darkness

We see that John does not shy away from moving into the dark places where our journey to union with God takes us. In fact, he considers these dark places to be the very places where we meet God most deeply. He wants us to go into these places in our own lives because in the darkness we will meet God. In fact, he describes the journey in terms of a romantic encounter. We do not see it as a romantic encounter at the time but John assures us that the journey into the darkness leads us into a deep love affair with God which we can have in no other way. It is because of this conviction that John has that we can venture into looking for a positive side of the terrible experience of Fr Rodrigues and of his former mentor, Fr Ferreira.

John Philip Newell has written the following prayer:

> Whichever way we turn, O God, there is your face
> In the light of the moon and patterns of stars
> In scarred mountain rifts and ancient groves
> In mighty seas and creatures of the deep.
> Whichever way we turn, O God, there is your face.[160]

In using this prayer, I thought of a visit I had made that afternoon. I had had lunch with my friend, a religious sister, and had returned to the house to chat further. The other member of the community came back just then and joined us. My friend had told me that this second sister had been

---

[160] John Philip Newell, *Praying with the Earth*, Norwich: Canterbury Press, 2011, 31.

going through a hard time. She had health problems and did not have a definite ministry to give her a sense of purpose in her life at that time. It seemed that, as a result, she had been moody and, to a great extent, only half-interested in things that were happening. I thought, when I read the prayer, that God was asking me to see his face in this sister. I thought also of a fellow Brother whom I visited in prison a few weeks earlier who had been convicted of child sexual abuse. I wondered what sort of journey he was going through. There was another member of the community who was highly qualified but was angry because he seemed to be suffering from the beginnings of dementia and who could not hold down his job. The next day, I read of a nine-month-old baby girl who was found washed up on the beach. She had been apparently thrown into the sea by a man, her father, who thought that she was possessed by an evil spirit.

The prayer quoted above speaks of places where we find the face of God. It is not easy to search for God's face in our own past experiences which we are embarrassed by. We do not like seeing people whom we have known for long and now seem to be foundering in their lives. We would rather put those scenarios aside and think of the times when we felt loved. Times of feeling loved are, of course, essential. But also essential is for us to go into the dark places of life exemplified by the experience of Fr Rodrigues who finally seemed to give up his faith.

Our Response to Apostasy

How are we to respond when we hear a story like that

of Rodrigues in *Silence*? What is the appropriate response to someone who has apostasised? Our first reaction is to be repulsed and even incredulous. We think: this could not happen if the person was really trying to be faithful to the beliefs they hold most precious! We have seen that Rodrigues and Ferriera did not renounce their faith easily. Their story does not seem to be of people whose faith was not deep as is the case in the gospel story of the wheat being planted in different types of soil. These two men had a very strong faith and did everything they could to nurture it.

After this type of reflection, our defences against being touched by the story in *Silence* may gradually break down. We may get to the point of not blaming these two men. If this change in us occurs, I believe we move to being like the publican in the parable of the Pharisee and the publican. We begin to see that we really are sinners and capable of anything without God's love and mercy. The story can help us get insight into the defences we build up around ourselves to protect us from seeing our own weakness.

The apocalyptic discourse in Mark, as in the other synoptic gospels, invites us to let into our minds the most terrifying scenarios we can imagine. Jesus says to his disciples:

> In those days after that time of distress, the sun will be darkened, the moon will lose its brightness, the stars will come falling from heaven and the powers in the heavens will be shaken. And then they will see the Son of Man coming in the clouds with great power and glory; then too he will send the angels to gather his chosen from the four winds, from the ends of the world to the ends of heaven (Mark 13:24-26).

The purpose of texts like this is to help us see that there are powers in the world that we cannot cope with on our own. They help us be realistic about our situation. Our only way of acting is to remember that God is present with us and that when we are with him we are safe. The first reading which accompanies this gospel on the 33rd Sunday of Ordinary Time is from the prophecy of Daniel. This reading speaks of Michael who will fight against the powers of darkness. The dead will arise and those among them who have been faithful will experience life and the wicked will be punished. The emphasis, however, will be on those who have been faithful. The purpose of such a reading is seen in the response and responsorial psalm. The response says:

Keep me safe, O God; you are my hope.

The reading is meant primarily to encourage us to be faithful to God and to do what God wants of us. We know there are consequences to our actions if we are unfaithful. This warning, however, is not meant to frighten us but to encourage us to be faithful and to choose life and love over death and despair. We can be greatly encouraged by the response above. These apocalyptic readings are intended to help us take our lives seriously rather than being presumptuous. Presumption means that we take for granted God's love rather than appreciating it as a priceless gift. When we read a story like that of the two priests in *Silence*, we may experience the salutary fear that we are capable of doing what they did. Hence, we cry out to God to keep us safe. The story shakes us up and stops us from just presuming that we are okay and that we do not have to exert ourselves much in our spiritual lives.

How Free Are We?

Let us look now in more detail at the degree of freedom involved on the part of Rodrigues and Ferreira in their act of abandoning their faith. We will do this by taking as an example of lack of faith the resistance of the Jews to Jesus in chapter 6 of the gospel of John.[161] The crowds are happy to be fed in the wilderness by the bread that Jesus miraculously provided. Jesus challenges them that they are following him just because they had bread to eat. He then speaks about the bread which comes down from heaven. Are they able to follow him in believing in this bread? The dialogue makes it clear that belief in Jesus himself or rejection of him is at stake. The Jews ask each other how he can be the bread from heaven since they know his father and mother. Jesus then says,

> Stop complaining to each other. No one can come to me
> Unless he is drawn by the Father who sent me (John 6:44).

In commenting on this verse, Brendan Byrne points out the tension between the Father's gift and free human response. When we make a decision, we are not making it by ourselves alone. We are already held 'within the gracious will of the Father whose only desire is to give us a share in the divine, eternal life'.[162] When weighing up the importance of God's gift and our free response, we have to say that God's gift to us of drawing us to himself far outweighs the importance

---

[161] Byrne's commentary on John's gospel, *Life Abounding*, has been helpful to me in reflecting on this chapter of John's gospel.

[162] Brendan Byrne, *Life Abounding: A Reading of John's Gospel*, Collegeville: Liturgical Press, 2014.

of our response. In the case of the priests in *Silence*, it is what God does that is more important than what they do. We must keep this reality in mind when evaluating the extent of their guilt or lack of it.

In the case of the Jews and Jesus, we are seeing not a weakening of faith as may have been the case with the priests, but a more deliberate hardening against Jesus. Here the Jews have the advantage of dialoguing with Jesus and of having answers from him while the priests, as far as we know, encountered only silence. Jesus challenges the Jews to believe that he is not just the bread come down from heaven, but also that he is going to give his life for the life of the world and that they are to eat his flesh. It is difficult for the Jews to accept this additional reality about Jesus. It is too much for them.

In verse 59, Jesus speaks not now to the Jews but to his followers. It is his followers now who complain against what he is teaching. They complain that no one could be expected to believe what Jesus is saying. We then have this comment from the evangelist:

> For Jesus knew from the outset those who did not believe,
> and who it was that would betray him (John 6:64).

This statement is saying that God already knew that they would desert Jesus and in fact that this desertion would fit into God's plan. We have this foreknowledge of God as well as knowing that no one can come to Jesus unless he is drawn by the Father. On the other hand, we have the freedom of these followers to abandon Jesus. How do we square these two apparently contradictory statements? In the Bible, this is not seen as a problem since God's sovereignty overrides all human freedom, but this issue is a problem for us. We can say, however, that just as here the non-belief of the Jews does not prevent the divine plan from proceeding, so the action of the two priests abandoning their faith is ultimately taken up and made good by God.

Jesus himself had the temptation to abandon the mission the Father had for him. In the temptations in the desert at the beginning of his ministry, the devil offered him the whole world if he would kneel down and adore him thereby renouncing the mission of his Father. Jesus chose discomfort and constant effort over effortless accomplishment and success. Throughout his life, the temptation to shrug off his call to go to Jerusalem was in Jesus' mind. He forcefully rebuked Peter when the latter told him that he would not have to suffer. He resolutely undertook the journey to Jerusalem and met every difficulty on the way. In the garden of Gethsemane, he asked the Father to take the chalice from him. Then on the cross many, including von Balthasar,[163] interpret his cry, 'My God, my God, why have you forsaken me' as a genuine indication of how Jesus felt, namely, that the Father had abandoned him. But it was in the plan of God that Jesus would be faithful to the end and die on the cross. Balthasar's teaching of Christ's descent into hell indicates that he tasted the depths even of hell in order to fulfil the mission of his Father. In the light of John 6:64, we can say that Jesus knew from the outset that he would be faithful to his Father to the end even though, on the cross, he went through the

---

[163] Von Balthasar, *Mysterium Pascale*, Edinburgh: T & T Clark, 1990.

agony of feeling abandoned by the Father. Similarly, we can say with the two priests in Japan who renounced the faith, that God knew all along that this would happen. But God also knew the faithfulness they had shown right up until the end, under enormous pressure.

God Beyond Our Respectable Concepts

We saw earlier how we could easily see Zaccheus as not being a man who would be included by Jesus because of his occupation as a tax collector and because of his marginality in the society. Zaccheus was an outsider and one excluded from many social settings including those we ourselves would tend to go to. He would have been someone who was not often seen in the parish or at Mass. But Jesus looks up into the sycamore tree and bids Zaccheus come down. He then calls him a true son of Abraham and arranges to dine at his house that evening.

The famous Australian novelist, Patrick White, had an intense sense of the numinous and the divine in human life, yet did not feel comfortable in churches. The following passage from Mireille Juchau shows the genuineness of his sense of the divine while also finding himself uncomfortable with organised religion:

> White began attending St Paul's Church after a visionary experience during a summer of fires and storms in 1951. One rainy afternoon, writes David Marr in *Patrick White, a Life*, White slipped in mud 'somewhere between the jacaranda and the old piggery' at Dogwoods. 'I stood in the rain, the water up to my ankles, and pouring off me,

as I proceeded to curse God', White recalled. Though he was not a believer, he suddenly sensed a divine presence and this revelation flowed into his books with their preoccupation with secular faith and mysticism.[164]

It is easy to see how White would not fit well into a parish setting. For one thing, he was in a permanent gay relationship with his partner, Manoly Lascaris, something frowned upon by the church at the time. He saw too many things he did not like in the church many of which he puts into his characters, Mrs Flack and Mrs Jolley, in his novel *Riders in the Chariot*. He saw them as hypocrites and busybodies casting judgmental eyes at everyone who was a little eccentric. In that novel, we have four characters, Miss Haire, Alf Dubbo, Mordecai Himmelfarb and Mrs Godbold, the riders in the chariot, who are varied in personality but all marginalised and excluded. They are the people whom White identifies with the divine.

These four visionaries were outcasts or exiled in some way from their formative environments: Mrs Godbold, mother of 6 from England; Alf Dubbo from his home on an outback reserve after he is forcibly removed from his mother; Miss Hare a child recluse within her dysfunctional family; Mordecai Himmelfarb, a Holocaust survivor from Germany. The chariot referred to is that of the Old Testament prophet, Ezekiel. Mrs Godbold washes clothes for a living and lives with an abusive husband. She is constantly caring for others including Miss Mary Hare, a tiny lady who inherited a mansion but who is hounded and persecuted by the busybodies, Mrs Jolley and

---

[164] Mireille Juchau https://sydneyreviewofbooks.com/patrick-white-riders-in-the-chariot/

Flack, who spread rumours about her. Mrs Godbold witnesses a vision that Mary had while nursing her through pneumonia. Alf Dubbo is an Aboriginal artist and addict who roams the streets of the town. Finally, Mordecai Himmelfarb has been through the horrors of the holocaust and a devout Jew. These four people are described as visionaries by White and are clearly people close to the divine. Juchau speaks of the tone of the novel in the following lines:

> From the very beginning, with its epigraph on the prophet Ezekiel, *Riders* alerts us to its interest in 'the infinite in everything'; in the metaphysical. This is intensified by White's use of elevated language to describe events that are firmly rooted in the everyday – we see the Jew in 'mineral splendour'; 'consecrated' on his journey; Alf Dubbo's hands 'gilded with his own gold'; 'benedictions of light and water'; 'light smote the ragged bushes' – we're continuously reminded of an ineffable dimension beyond the familiar, solid shapes of suburbia.[165]

It is clear from this description that White is an intensely religious person. Yet he does not conform to what the official church might see as a holy person. He is clearly prophetic. With him we might include others like Simone Weil, the French Jew, who became a great believer in Christ yet felt that it was not her vocation to be baptised, and Samuel Beckett who, in his plays and other writings, probed deeply into the mystery and meaning of life.

The lives of Patrick White and many others we could include, as well as people like Zaccheus from the gospels,

---

[165] Ibid.

show us that we cannot pin God down. We often do not know where God is acting and in whom he is acting. The characters in *Riders in the Chariot* as well as Patrick White himself are clearly people in whom God was acting but not in ways we would expect.

Within the Wider Plan of God

Balthasar discusses Christ's descent into hell or the nether regions, not something often discussed at the present day. He says that Christ died, and while dead, was taken into these nether regions by the Father. Being like the souls already there, he could experience what they experienced, namely, separation from God. Let us repeat this: Christ, according to Balthasar, experienced what it was like to be eternally separated from God. Nicholas Healy says that the central question of Balthasar's eschatology is: what is the meaning of the world to God? He goes on:

> What would God who wills the salvation of all 'lose' if a portion of his creation were to suffer eternal damnation?[166]

If we accept that this is a legitimate question, the answer is that God would lose much. It would mean that God's plan in creating the world and of bringing the world into final union with himself would be partially thwarted. Balthasar concludes from this that we can reasonably conclude,

---

[166] Nicholas J. Healy, *The Eschatology of Hans Urs von Balthasar: Being As Communion*, London: Oxford University Press, 2006, 19.

though not prove absolutely, that Christ in experiencing the abandonment from God of those who were in the nether world before he died, brought all these souls out of abandonment and into union with God. In returning to our central example of the two priests who renounced their faith in seventeenth century Japan, it seems that Balthasar's teaching is particularly relevant. It is a concrete example of how salvation emerges from the depths of doubt and despair in this poignant example.

Conclusion

We began with the story of the two young Jesuits from the film *Silence*, who courageously went to Japan to spread the gospel of Christ and found that they could not carry out their deepest hopes. But our purpose in this chapter was more extensive than examining just this one case. The purpose was to see how we can be consoled and encouraged when we are faced with the possibility that we may fail in our intentions of following Christ. We can read again the words of Paul in Romans:

> For I am certain of this: neither death nor life, no angel, no prince, nothing that exists, nothing still to come, not any power, or height or depth, nor any created thing, can ever come between us and the love of God made visible in Christ Jesus our Lord (Romans 8:38-39).

References

Balthasar, Hans Urs von, *Mysterium Paschale*, Edinburgh: T & T Clark, 1990.

Byrne, Brendan, *Life Abounding: A Reading of John's Gospel*, Collegeville: Liturgical Press, 2014.

St John of the Cross, *The Collected Works of St John of the Cross*, Trans. Kieran Kavanaugh, O.C.D. and Otilio Rodriguez, O.C.D., Washington, D.C.: ICS Publications 1991.

Mireille Juchau, 'Riders in the Chariot by Patrick White', https://sydneyreviewofbooks.com/patrick-white-riders-in-the-chariot/

White, Patrick, *Riders in the Chariot*, Melbourne: Penguin, 1974.

Index

a
Aboriginal people 164, 207, 341
Abraham 29, 31, 96, 179, 211, 300, 339
Adam 301
Age, The 12, 223
Alison, James xiv, 2
Allen, Woody 11, 224
Anawim 160, 165
Annunciation 265
Apocalyptic 5, 315, 334, 335
Apostasy 333

b
Bagavad Gita 122
Balthasar, Hans Urs von 319, 321
Barry, William viii, xii, 11, 60, 62, 211, 244, 245, 292
Bates, Kevin 292
Ba, Mariama 73

Beatitudes 159, 316
Beckett, Samuel 244, 341
Beelzebul 276
Benedict XVI 198, 202
Bernanos, George 200
Berry, Thomas 233
Bonhoeffer, Dietrich 213, 268
Buddhism 158
Buechner, Frederick 124, 126
Byrne, Brendan 232, 273, 336

c
Cassian, John 145, 149, 151
Christophany 296
Clement, Jane Tyson 143
Compunction 255
Consolation 54, 57, 87, 96, 104, 109, 151, 153, 155, 162, 186, 187, 188, 193, 205, 211, 213, 291, 331
Contrition 255, 258

Culture of death 9, 13, 15, 20
church leaders 48, 117, 204, 205, 212

d

Dark night 87, 88, 90, 92, 97, 108, 109, 113, 287, 327, 329
Day, Dorothy 55
Delaney, Sue 75
Despair iii, 35, 55, 78, 241, 324, 335
Deuteronomy 22, 24, 25, 30
Diakrisis 151
Discernment, Ignatian, rules of 38, 186, 290
Disenchantment 70
Doubt iii, vii, 66, 71, 109, 149, 172, 241, 324, 325, 327, 329, 331, 333, 335, 337, 339, 341, 343
Dream 74, 76, 183
Dynamics of Spiritual Self Direction 217
de La Salle, Jean-Baptiste 141

e

Earth, caring for 157
Earth, economy 233
Earth, Summits 234
Ecclesiasticus 28

Elijah 40, 165
Elizabeth, Mary's cousin 111, 160
Endo, Shusaku 324
Eschatological imagination 5
Exile 305, 340
Exodus 35, 42, 211

f

Faithfulness 24, 31, 36, 221, 316, 339
Fears ix, xiv, 18, 104, 173, 180, 184
First Spiritual Exercises 167
Fuellenbach, John 314
Funk, Margaret Mary 146

g

Gaillardetz, Richard 203, 214
Gerasene demoniac 308
Gethsemane 338
Good News 3, 306
Good Samaritan 275, 313
Grace 58, 90, 109, 111, 178, 245, 255
Grace, cheap 268
Grant, James 156
Grenville, Kate 207
Griffiths, Bede 121, 130

Grumbling 42, 104, 134, 219

h
Hafiz 152
Hansen, Michael 167
Healy, Nicholas 342
Hebrews, Letter to 320
Hillesum, Etty 278
Hispanic church 201, 206
Hopkins, Gerard Manly 55
Horn, John 17
Hound of Heaven 241, 248
Humility, degrees of – Rule of Benedict 236, 238

i
Immanent frame 206, 210, 213
Inner Policeman 254
Into Deep Silence 163
Isaiah 27, 45, 171, 188, 257, 305, 307

j
Japan 198, 324, 339, 343
Jeremiah x, 27, 31, 63, 64, 65, 191
Job 28, 31, 32, 328
John of the Cross iv, x, xii, 59, 69, 87, 287

John Paul II 198, 202
Johnson, Elizabeth 201

k
Keating, Thomas 108, 113, 163
Kibera 34, 222
Kierkegaard, Søren 102
Kingdom of God 241, 305, 311, 314, 315
  Language of 318
Kirtana 142

l
La Mott, Anne 244
Laudato Si' 157
Lawrence of the Resurrection 125
Lebulu, Bishop 284
Letting go of control 108, 125, 132, 194
Leunig 166
Levandoski, Alana 162
LGBTIQ 156
Lieutenant, The 207
Life directives 178, 217
Life situation 178, 180, 190, 217, 219, 223, 236
Louf, Andre 163
Love, make your way 162

Luke
  Infancy narrative 265
  Suffering and joy in 270

m
Manning Clark 151
Mark, Gospel of 306, 307, 308, 311, 334
Marr, David 339
Mary 160, 161, 165, 265
Matthew, Gospel of 5, 15, 56, 66, 127, 133, 192, 259
Matthew, Iain 87, 288, 290
May, Gerald 125
McDonald, Julian 221
McKenna, Megan 308, 310
Mentor 139, 207
Merciful 36, 259, 316
Merciful love 258
Messiah 271, 272, 306, 311
Metanoia 255, 256
Micah 216
Midlife 74, 75
Mill Hill Fathers 134
Mindfulness 117
Moods 147, 152, 168, 193
Musoma 285

n
Nagging spirit ix, 173, 178, 182, 185
Nebreda, Alphonso 197
Newel, John Philip 332
Nigerian proverb 158
Nouwen, Henri 248

p
Panikkar, Raimon 295
Paralents 192
Pope Francis 202, 203, 214, 230
Pre-adolescent 72
Prodigal Son 221, 248, 313
Promptings of Love 198, 283
Proverbs 227
Providence iii, 95, 133, 277
Psalm 14 227
Psalm 62 101, 103
Psalm 95 222
Psalms 28, 31, 56, 99, 281, 330

q
Qoheleth 28, 31

r
Rahner, Karl 213
Realm of the dead 319
Reconciliation, sacrament of 256
Resistance to change 203

Riders in the Chariot 340
Righteousness 221, 299
Rodrigues 325
Rohr, Richard xiv, 18, 27, 39, 47, 76, 119, 122, 137, 158
Rolheiser, Ronald 38, 52
Roman Empire 305
Romans, Letter to xv, 189, 296, 298, 318, 321, 343
Rumi 44, 46

s
Sadness 62, 177, 242, 282
Santa Teresa 164
Satan, kingdom of 315
Scorsese, Martin 324, 326
Self, large and small 120
Sensus fidelium 203
Sexuality 243
  Sexual orientation 246
Shame 71, 237, 310
Silence 19, 96, 102, 163, 324, 334
Sirach 28
Sirleaf, Ellen Johnson 187
Social movements 146, 168
Song of Songs 125
Spiritual canticle 97
Spiritual direction ii, 17, 63, 152, 155, 182

Suffering
  going through 267
  reasons for 267
Sufism 158
Suite Française 53
Superego 254

t
Tagaran 208
Take this Waltz 41
Tanzania 284
Taylor, Charles 198, 206
Teresa of Avila iv, xii, 59
Testimony and counter-testimony 29
Thérèse of Lisieux iv, 108, 199, 257
Thich Nhat Hanh 54
Touchstone moment 150
Transfiguration 13, 272, 290
Treasure in the field 6

v
Vatican II 157, 198, 203, 214
Virgin of Guadalupe 201
Visit, The 161
Vonnegut, Kurt 225
van Kaam, Adrian 178, 217, 221, 222

W

White, Patrick *339, 341*
Williams, Michelle *51*
Wisdom *28, 102*

Z

Zaccheus *327, 339*
Zechariah, canticle of *265*

www.ingramcontent.com/pod-product-compliance
Lightning Source LLC
Chambersburg PA
CBHW010244010526
44107CB00063B/2676